The Crisis of America's Cities

The Crisis of America's Cities

Randall Bartlett

M.E. Sharpe
Armonk, New York
London, England

Library of Congress Cataloging-in-Publication Data

Bartlett, Randall, 1945–
The crisis of America's cities / Randall Bartlett.
    p.   cm.
Includes bibliographical references (p.   ) and index.
ISBN 0-7656-0301-2 (hardcover : alk. paper).
ISBN 0-7656-0302-0 (paperback : alk. paper)
1. Cities and towns—United States.   2. Cities and towns—United States—History.
    3. Urban policy—United States.   I. Title.
HT123.B324   1998
307.76′0973—dc21   98-23185
CIP

Printed in the United States of America

The paper used in this publication meets the minimum requirements of
American National Standard for Information Sciences—
Permanence of Paper for Printed Library Materials,
ANSI Z 39.48-1984.

                              ∞

EB (c)   10   9   8   7   6   5   4   3   2   1
EB (p)   10   9   8   7   6   5   4   3   2   1

To Catherine,
Randall,
Ellika, and
David

Contents

Acknowledgments

Although my name appears as the sole author on the cover of this book, in truth I have not written it alone. Javiera Sequeira served as an able research assistant during the drafting of this book. Although she was only in her first year of college, I turned her loose, time and time again, with only the vaguest guidance. Time and time again she came back with valuable sources and contributions. I also asked her to read the draft as it emerged. She thus saw what was happening to the material she found, yet she never once complained about either the process or the product. I owe her real thanks for her exceptional efforts. I am also grateful to Steve Dalphin who was executive editor at M.E. Sharpe when I first submitted the manuscript.

My explicit goal in writing this book has been to make the process of urban evolution come alive for intelligent readers who care about, and hopefully will affect, the future of America's cities. I wanted to reach people who are unencumbered by excessive professional specialization. Thus when it came time to ask colleagues to read drafts I turned not to my economist colleagues but to "real" people. Dennis Hudson, professor of world religions at Smith College, read several of the early chapters and offered a perspective unavailable from any economist. He made me see my subject through different eyes, as he often does. Some of his insights I was able to incorporate; others I was not. I appreciate his perceptive contributions as well as his friendship, here and always.

Marion Van Arsdell read it all and made useful comments without a penny of compensation. She had to. She is my sister. Jean Bartlett also read it all. In addition to her substantive suggestions she acted as unpaid copy editor. She also had to. She is my mother and has been doing both those jobs for many decades. For that, and for so very much more unrelated to this book, I am forever grateful. Both of them fit clearly into my target audience of intelligent people who care about what happens in this world, and I was much encouraged by their positive response.

And then, of course, there is my immediate family. My children continue to fill my days and nights with excitement. So much so that this project took longer to finish than I would have liked, but I would not have given up a moment of the time spent with them. When I last completed a book several years ago I included mention of my wife Catherine in the acknowledgments. I cleverly noted that unlike some authors, I could not give her credit as an unnamed coauthor. She had not read that book, did not really know what it was about, and maybe did not even care. Our children were young. She was building a medical practice, and musings about economic theory were, rightly, low on her priority list. There was much we all asked of her in those years and she always gave more than was asked. This time, somehow, even amidst the extraordinary demands of being a full-time physician, an exceptional mother, and the true joy of my life, she did find time to read it all and make valuable comments. She is not doing anything else less. I do not know how she found the time to do more. I am eternally grateful for her and all that she does. Reading this book was the very least of it, indeed.

Prologue

Today the vast majority of Americans live in large cities and their suburbs. Begun as a nation of widely dispersed rural farmers, generation after generation we have become more and more urbanized. We are now, and for the foreseeable future will continue to be, a nation of cities. Yet it is clear that all is not well there. The issue is not whether we will continue to live *in* cities, but rather how we are going to live *with* them. Pick up any newspaper, observe any political campaign, visit any major city and the theme of a growing "urban crisis" will be there. Too much poverty, too much decay, failing infrastructure, insolvent local government, the collapse of public education, fear of ever more violent crime, racial isolation, smothering traffic congestion, a growing loss of jobs—the list of urban problems is seemingly as endless as the political conflict over them is apparently irresolvable. For better or for worse, for now and for later, cities are where we live.

Everything that we do must be done *somewhere.* Indeed, it is where we decide to work, to play, to call "home," and how we move between these places that collectively and individually define our "space." I considered giving this book the title *Exploring Space,* but finally abandoned that idea for fear that confused booksellers would place it in the science fiction section. Although the title has been changed, the metaphor persists throughout. This book *is* an exploration of space, not in the outer reaches of the universe but here on the surface of the nation where we locate and relocate ourselves.

Cities are unique places where large numbers of people have chosen to live and work in proximity to each other, crowding into small spaces, straining natural resources, yet somehow surviving. Urban living as the norm is very recent. For most of human history, any society predominately organized into cities would have been unthinkable and certainly unsustainable. Majority urbanization would have quickly resulted in mass starvation. It is only advances in technology that have made urban nations like the United States possible. It is technology that first permits and then prescribes living in cities.

We Americans are not forced to live in these concentrations. We choose to do so. Businesses are not compelled by law to produce their products in urban settings. It is simply more economic for them to do so. But it has not always been so. There is always a *logic of location,* a rationale for being and doing in one place over another. People inevitably respond to that logic in their choices. As technology evolves, the logic of location is itself altered until the use of space that made sense in one era becomes "illogical" and is abandoned in another.

The challenge in this book is to explore this earthbound space, seeking answers to a few fundamental questions. What do we do where and why? Why have our cities grown first so large and then so troubled? What does the future hold for them? The fundamental premise is that the answers will come from understanding how changes in technology, policy, and our perceptions alter this logic of location over time and how our use of space inevitably changes in response. The crisis in our cities has been a long time in the making. It is the product of forces begun long ago and well beyond our conscious control. What will become of our cities is also a long-term issue and our ability to affect their future has real limits. We cannot do just anything with them. We cannot make future cities out of a past logic. We cannot dictate just *any* use of our space.

The questions asked about our cities are loaded questions. In the United States today it is common to express strong feelings about cities and their problems; it is uncommon to step back and seek objectively the roots of those problems. It is easy to accuse; it is difficult to understand. The specific problems listed in the opening paragraph are real, immediate, and important, but they are also, in the most literal sense, "superficial." They take place on the surface of larger, subsurface currents that shape the direction cities can and will take. To explore effectively means going beneath the immediate surface problems to seek out and understand the powerful currents behind cities' history and their future. It is those currents that will define the direction in which urban spaces will evolve and the pace at which they will change. We may be able to use public policies to move between channels on the fast-moving surface, but there are no viable policies powerful enough to reverse, to stop, or to redirect the main flow. We *are* going along for this ride, and thus it behooves us to explore and understand the territory to the best of our ability.

In the pages that follow, Part I presents an overview of the current urban situation and develops the tools and the perspective needed to explore changing space. Part II looks to the historical roots of the present. It examines how technology has reshaped the logic of location and ultimately the organization of cities in key periods of the nation's history. It explores how our definition of a "natural" city has changed over time as new technology has redefined what kinds of spatial arrangements "make sense." Part III focuses on the key policy choices made in modern times and the consequences they have had for where we are today. Finally, Part IV looks downstream toward the future, seeking to make out the outlines of what is yet to be, looking to clarify the options that are available and the paths that are possible. It may be a difficult journey at times, but this is an expedition worth taking.

I

Exploring Cities

1

Cities in America

A few years ago one of the Hollywood studios released an action feature titled "Escape from New York." Set in the not too distant future, life in America's urban centers had become so intolerable that the island of Manhattan in the center of New York City had been entirely abandoned. The only use left for a space so decayed and depressed was to serve as a dumping ground for the very worst criminals, a sort of Devil's-Island-on-the-Hudson. Indeed, it was even worse than the original Devil's Island for there were no wardens, guards, or officials to enforce any semblance of order. Convicts were simply dropped onto the island to fend for themselves in an anarchy composed of the most vicious felons that a violent society had to offer. The movie was fantasy, of course, but it was a fantasy that carried at least a degree of plausibility. If our cities continue down their current path, total destitution and abandonment of their cores are not inconceivable. We are a nation of cities, but our cities are in trouble.

America uses its space very unevenly. Eighty percent of the population lives on less than 2 percent of the land. Anyone who has driven across eastern Montana and then through the heart of Los Angeles or New York City knows that we use our space very unevenly. The vast majority of us now live and work in high-density areas. Eighty percent of Americans live in what the Census Bureau defines as "Metropolitan Statistical Areas." Many of us live, literally, on top of one another, clustered together in cities while vast tracts of land go largely unoccupied. In the United States today there are over *fifty* cities whose Metropolitan Areas contain a population of at least 1 million. They, collectively, account for approximately one half of the nation's total population. In over a dozen cases these cities have become so large that they have bumped into one another and merged into giant "megalopolises" with more than one center. The Census Bureau collects data on these in a category called "Consolidated Metropolitan Statistical Areas." The largest, the area surrounding New York City, covers portions of three states and contains a total population just under 20 million—approximately one out of every thirteen persons in the entire United States.

We were not forced into these cities by some national program of coerced urbanization. Something seemingly positive has drawn most of us together, yet the very word "urban" has become a code word for poverty, crime, violence, and decay. When Lyndon Johnson used seed money from federal housing programs in the 1960s to help create a policy institute to concentrate on finding solutions to poverty, the appropriate name seemed obvious. It was to be called The *Urban* Institute. As the first major migration of African Americans from the rural South to the cities of the North took place in the early years of this century, a variety of social problems demanded attention. What else to call one of the earliest and most significant civil rights and antipoverty organizations but the National *Urban* League?

Those urban spaces are themselves divided into distinct patterns. They are themselves unevenly developed. As cities grew in population they needed more space, but political boundaries have not always followed economic development. At the center of each metropolitan area there is at least one central city, divided from the rest by political boundaries but economically tied to it. Surrounding the central cities are rings of suburbs that are more recent in origin. Over the life of the nation cities have drawn more and more of us to them, but taken as a whole, today our urban centers seem to be in desperate straits.

Crime

Fear of crime is one of the most pervasive elements of social life in contemporary America. It is ironic that in communities where strangers seldom speak to each other one of the most common communications between strangers is the ubiquitous sign in automobile windows announcing that the vehicle has "No Radio." It is not just ready access to musical distraction that crime in cities denies us. There is a general loss of personal security as well.

American cities today are marked by violence of extraordinary proportions. In his troubling account of life in the projects of Chicago, Alex Kotlowitz shared in the lives of two young boys for over a year as they witnessed the violence endemic to their neighborhood.[1] In one of the most poignant moments of the book, he recounts the way in which the youngest

Table 1

Crime Rates by City Size (known offenses per 100,000 residents)

City Size	Total rate	Ratio: city/rural	Violent rate	Ratio: city/rural	Property rate	Ratio: city/rural
Rural	2,116	—	233	—	1,883	—
<10,000	4,798	2.27	429	1.84	4,369	2.32
10,000–24,900	4,788	2.26	448	1.92	4,339	2.30
25,000–49,999	5,590	2.64	582	2.50	5,007	2.66
50,000–99,999	6,390	3.02	773	3.32	5,617	2.98
100,000–249,000	8,034	3.80	1,093	4.69	6,940	3.69
>250,000	9,204	4.35	1,711	7.34	7,492	3.98

Source: Uniform Crime Reports, 1993. Federal Bureau of Investigation.

of the two, ten-year-old Pharaoh, spoke of his future. Kotlowitz noted that Pharaoh would always say "if I grow up" rather than "when I grow up." Pharaoh is not misperceiving his situation. The prevalence of violence in American cities is so severe that medical journals have begun devoting significant space to it as one of the major public health issues of our day. For the nation as a whole the homicide rate is approximately 10 per 100,000 annually. The homicide rate per 100,000 in our core cities is approaching 30 per year. For African-American males in central cities it is approaching 150 annually. For nonurban areas the corresponding homicide rates are 2.9 and 15.5, respectively.[2] The death rate from violence in the inner city today approaches that of a society at war. An African-American male has a one in thirteen chance of dying in a homicide—*one in thirteen*! Children living in the inner city, surrounded by extraordinary levels of violence, face an uncertain future at best. The issue of crime, and particularly violent crime, is a national tragedy with a distinct spatial dimension.

There is also a direct correlation between city size and crime rates in America. As cities increase in population, the number of known crimes per 100,000 increases as well. Table 1 clearly demonstrates this. In the largest class of cities the rate of *total* crime is more than four times higher than it is in rural areas. The increase in the rate of *violent* crime is even more severe—more than seven times higher in the largest cities. In the official statistics, the rate of known crimes actually reaches its peak in cities just below 1 million in population and then declines somewhat. Perhaps that is because crime itself starts to drop off, or perhaps it is because the residents of those cities are so inured to crime that they are less likely to bother filing reports with the police.

Poverty

The Bible notes that the "poor are always with" us and that has certainly been historically true. It is only periodically that we pay much attention to them. In 1890 Jacob Riis published *How The Other Half Lives,* an exposé of conditions in the poorest tenements of New York City. His stark photographs shocked the nation into an awareness of problems it preferred to ignore. Questions of poverty were placed on the national political agenda for the first time, but as the First World War intervened the nation's attention shifted. Concern diminished, but as always, the poor were still with us. Seventy years later Michael Harrington provided the intellectual impetus for Lyndon Johnson's War on Poverty when he published *The Other America.* That war on poverty was officially waged for many years, but a controlled withdrawal was begun during the Nixon administration. Today, nearly forty years after Harrington's book, poverty remains a persistent problem. The poor are still with us, though we are most comfortable when they are not too near. Diminished in scope over the years, poverty in America has not disappeared. It has, however, been relocated.

Today the poor are still with us, but now they are most likely to be found in our cities. When we say the word "city," and especially "inner city," most of us hear "poor." What exactly does that term mean? The federal government today has an official poverty line and collects statistics on the incidence and location of poverty. It measures money income and then draws a fairly arbitrary line. If a household's income falls below that line, it is officially poor. If its income is above the line, it is not. The line is established by calculating the cost of food sufficient to maintain health and then, assuming that food should constitute about one third of a budget, that number is tripled. In 1994, poverty for a family of four was defined as an annual income below $15,000. That works out to a maximum expense per person per meal of about $1.15. Under that definition, 38 million Americans, approximately 14.5 percent of the total population, still lived in poverty in 1994.

The American population as a whole has urbanized over the last two centuries. So also has poverty, though more recently. As recently as thirty-five years ago when the last round of concern with poverty was just beginning, the majority of the poor (56 percent) lived in rural areas. There was urban poverty, of course, but cities were still seen by many of the poor as their best hope for a better job, and thus a better life. Today nearly 75 percent of all the poor in America live in urban areas; indeed nearly 43 percent of the nation's poor live in central cities. Fully 60 percent of the urban poor live in the central city, while only 38 percent of the total urban population resides there.

There is significant regional variation. In the Northeast, 88 percent of the poor are urban and almost two thirds of those live in central cities. In the Midwest, 70 percent are urban and nearly two thirds of those also live in central cities. Poverty in the South is somewhat less urbanized; 66 percent of the southern poor live in cities and half of those live in central cities. Poverty in the West is the most highly urbanized; 85 percent of its poor live in urban areas, half of those in central cities.

For some groups the concentration is even more severe. For the nation as a whole, over 30 percent of the children who live in central cities live in households whose incomes fall below the poverty line. More than half of the African-American children who reside in central cities live in households with poverty-level incomes.[3]

There is thus ample reason for the term "inner city" to have come to connote a neighborhood where poverty is the norm. The Census Bureau has created new measures in response, defining a "Poverty Area" as a census tract with at least 20 percent of the population living below the poverty line and defining an "Extreme Poverty Area" as one with at least 40 percent below official poverty. Twenty percent of the nation's population lived in "Poverty Areas" at the time of the 1990 census. In fully 38 percent of the seventy-seven central cities with populations in excess of 200,000 the poverty rate for the *entire city* exceeded 20 percent. In the city of Detroit, nearly a third of all its residents fell below the poverty line. Four percent of the nation lived in "Extreme Poverty Areas." There are a dozen cities where over a quarter of the entire population lives in an Extreme Poverty Area.[4] These concentrations of poverty are primarily in central cities, and most of these concentrations are getting more severe. Those able to leave do so, leaving behind those who cannot. Poverty has a spatial component in our cities. "Urban" today has become a code word for "poor."

Employment

The incidence of poverty in a community is obviously related to the level and types of employment opportunities there. Most of us earn our income from participating in labor markets. We work for a living. To do so there needs to be someone willing and able to pay for that work. In recent decades there has been a clear shift in national labor markets away from the kinds of manufacturing and construction jobs that provide entry-level positions for workers with limited education and training. We are moving more deeply into an economy dominated by growth in "knowledge-based" jobs. That alone will create severe problems for the least educated among America's work force, but there is an added spatial dimension here as well.

At the same time that the poor are increasingly concentrated in central cities, the jobs that might offer them a path out of poverty, and that still exist, are no longer located in central cities.

The total number of jobs in New York City fell by some 30 percent between 1953 and 1989. The shift in the composition of those jobs was even more dramatic. Total manufacturing and construction jobs fell from over 1.1 million to 268,000 in the same period, a decline of 75 percent. Retail and wholesale jobs also declined, but not as markedly, falling from approximately 800,000 jobs in 1953 to 350,000 in 1989—a 56 percent decline. Only in the area of information processing has there been a significant increase in employment, doubling from 646,000 to 1.3 million over the same period.[5]

This pattern has been repeated all over the United States. Central-city jobs have declined absolutely in most of our older cities and have declined in relative terms even in the newest. New jobs are likely to be in the suburban ring rather than the city per se. In all cities, the composition of central-city employment has shifted dramatically away from manufacturing and handling goods in favor of processing information. Education and training are prerequisites for access to the growing portion of the urban labor market.

Consequently, unemployment rates in our central cities are generally higher than they are for either their Metropolitan Areas or the nation as a whole. In Poverty Areas and Extreme Poverty Areas, measured unemployment typically reaches levels the nation has not known since the depths of the Great Depression in the early 1930s. Even that understates the scope of the problem, for "unemployment" is defined as "actively seeking but unable to find work." There is a well-documented effect known as the "discouraged worker phenomenon," whereby individuals see so little hope for success in the job search that they simply stop looking, and hence stop qualifying as "unemployed." In our central cities today there is an abundance of poor people and a critical shortage of jobs that could lead them out of poverty. It is not surprising that our poor and our unemployed overlap significantly. That has perhaps always been true. What is more recent is that these problems and the people suffering their consequences are increasingly isolated in destitute communities located in older central cities.

Physical Decay

Cities grow from the inside out. New structures are primarily added on the edges. Only occasionally is the draw of the center strong enough to justify the added expense of removing old structures to make way for new. Because of this, the closer one gets to the center of a metropolitan area, the farther into the central city, the older the infrastructure one encounters. Older streets, buildings, water systems, and transportation networks are harder to maintain for two reasons: they embody older and less efficient technology and they are simply older and more worn.

When people leave the central city they leave behind aging residential structures. When jobs leave the central city they leave behind aging physical plants. Unable to maintain these structures, cities find their physical plants falling into disrepair and decay. When Jonathan Kozol describes the physical characteristics of some of the nation's inner-city schools in *Savage Inequalities*, he must use the vocabulary of deterioration. When the federal government surveys the condition of bridges and roadways it finds a frighteningly high proportion to be dangerously undermaintained.

Public Services

In the fall of 1975 New York City made headlines all over the nation when it was unable to raise the funds necessary to meet its bond obligations then falling due. With insufficient tax revenues coming in, unable to borrow in financial markets, and turned down in its requests for aid from the federal government and the state, its bank accounts simply ran dry. It had been trying to provide more services than its resources would support.

The situation in New York was extreme but certainly not unique. Since then the schools in Chicago have periodically run out of funds, the city of Cleveland, too, has teetered on the brink of bankruptcy, and Los Angeles County Hospital, the primary provider of health care for that region's poor, is on the verge of closing its doors. There is no major central city in the United States that has not been financially strained over the last few decades. What they need has grown. What is available to meet those needs has decreased. There are a number of reasons why.

The spatial organization of income within Metropolitan Areas is one clear factor. Incomes and tax base per capita rise consistently the further one gets from the central city. In virtually all cases the tax base per person in the central city is a fraction of the base in the suburban ring; in a few extreme cases it is barely over half. To raise equal revenues in the central city requires higher tax rates than prevail in the suburbs, but equal revenues per person are not even enough! The cost of providing services in central cities is systematically higher. This is partly because the concentrations of low-income families create a need for a broader range of services and partly because much of the infrastructure is more expensive to operate.

Central cities are losing population in all income groups except the poor. As more and more Poverty and Extreme Poverty Areas develop within cities, welfare, health, and police services are in ever greater demand. Schools are called upon to provide services unneeded in more affluent communities. Cities that fail to meet these demands deteriorate faster yet. Cities that attempt to respond create major drains on their financial resources.

Central-cities' structures are also older and often ill-maintained. They have been losing population for the last twenty-five years, but sections of sewer and water systems, miles of highways, and portions of school buildings have not followed people to the suburbs. We have discovered no way to close down sections of our cities when population falls, and so city governments must continue to operate systems with excess capacity and full costs but with fewer people to share those costs.

It is also true that most of the services that local governments provide also provide jobs that are crucial to urban labor markets. As other forms of employment leave, cities that lay off significant numbers of municipal workers may find that the savings are eroded by increased need for other services and accelerated decay of neighborhoods.

With rising need and diminishing resources central cities have found themselves in an ever tightening financial squeeze. One possible solution would be for higher levels of government to use some of their revenues to provide aid to local government. That approach, through targeted grants and general revenue sharing, has kept many a city afloat over the past thirty years, but with the ever-increasing pressures of the federal government's budget deficit problems and the "Republican Revolution" abandoning any federal response to urban problems, cities will be left alone to deal with the imbalance between their needs and their resources.

If tax rates are raised above the level of other jurisdictions there is an incentive for businesses, jobs, and population to leave in order to avoid the expense. If services are cut, there is a similar incentive to relocate where schools are better, streets are safer, and transportation is more readily available. Cities are not only the location of people living in poverty; they are also where the most financially pressured local governments are to be found.

"Where We Face Our Failures"

This is a frightening vision of the organization of space in the United States. Many of those who study these trends, or worse, bear responsibility for responding to them, see a distressing present and dismal prospects for the future. Joseph Ganim, the mayor of Bridgeport, Connecticut, recently told Congress that our "[c]ities are where we face our failures as a civilized nation."[6] *The place where we face our failures*—that is a strong statement. Senator Carol Moseley Braun (D-IL) sees ". . . a hopelessness in the inner cities of urban America. . . . Our cities have, for all intents and purposes, become cordoned off islands."[7] Carrie Saxon-Perry, mayor of Hartford, Connecticut, has ". . . witnessed a seething aura of despair and hopelessness that engulfs our inner cities." [8] Henry Cisneros, former Secretary of the Department of Housing and Urban Development, worries about ". . . the new face of poverty—geographically isolated, economically depressed, racially segregated. Cities have become the warehouses of our poorest."[9]

The Way We Were

It has not always been so. There has been a major reorganizaťion of American space over the life of the nation. There has been a major shift in what cities are and do, as well as a major change in how we see them. In the early days of the nation, cities were of a very different scale, they played a very different role, they were seen in very different terms. Unlike European cities that were central places within a settled hinterland, the earliest American cities were staging platforms for forays into, and protection from, what the European immigrants viewed as wilderness. The first American cities were merely central portions of plantations. To the extent that they offered safe harbors to ocean vessels they served to facilitate trade between the Old World and the New.

As John Winthrop crossed the Atlantic on his way to help found Boston in 1630, he envisioned a new Puritan society there that would "bee as a Citty upon a Hill." He was not, of course, expecting the Massachusetts Bay Colony to be an urban society. To him an ideal "city" was a community of wealth and virtue, visible to all around, "a Modell of Christian Charity," not the place where a society would "face its failures as a civilized nation." Had he viewed a city as the locus of crime, poverty, and inhumanity he would have chosen a different metaphor for his utopian vision.

The city that Winthrop helped found quickly flourished. Only twenty years later, a contemporary scribe would wonder at Boston's success at becoming a

> City-like towne whose continual enlargement presages some sumptuous city. The wonder of this Moderne Age that a few yeares should bring forth such great matters by so meane a handlfulle. But now behold, in these very places where at their first landing the hideous Thickets in the place were such that Wolfes and Beares nurst up their young . . . the streets are full of Girles and Boies sporting up and down.[10]

Strong cities to serve as connections to Europe were seen as essential to the process of colonization. When William Penn devised his initial plan for the development of Pennsylvania, he decreed that "so soon as it pleaseth God a certain quantity of land or ground plat shall be laid out for a large town or city," an instruction that led to the establishment of Philadelphia in 1681.[11] Philadelphia was not simply to be a place of commerce, however, though that figured prominently in the original choice of site and plans. A city could provide a better life in a better community. In towns "the children can be kept at school and much more conveniently brought up well. Neighbors also can better offer each other loving and helpful hands and with united mouth can in public assemblies praise and extol the greatness of God."[12]

American cities began, not as permanent sites for most of the population, but as temporary sanctuaries and as limited commercial and religious communities. New arrivals in the colonial era did not come seeking urban employment. They came primarily in search of land and used the cities as disembarkation points from which to move into the unsettled hinterland. There was little for them to do in the city and most quickly passed through.

It is hard for those of us who now see the United States as an urban society to understand how atypical it was to live in a city two centuries ago. Virtually the entire population of the nation (approximately 95 percent) was engaged in subsistence agriculture. At the time of the American Revolution barely 5 percent of the nation lived in cities or towns. There were no cities at all of a scale to appear large to the modern eye. There were only five cities in the entire nation that had a population in excess of 8,000 persons. None was large enough to qualify as a Metropolitan Statistical Area under the modern definition. New York City, the largest, had only 25,000 residents; the Big Apple was barely a seed. Wall Street, near the southern tip of Manhattan, got its name from a defensive wall built along the edge of the city in the 1600s. At the time of the Revolution, development had gone only slightly beyond that barrier.

Philadelphia was a close second to New York. William Penn's "great city" had about 24,000 residents and was still small enough to be, in principle at least, the kind of community of neighbors that its founders had envisioned. Boston, the site of much of the most vigorous opposition to British rule, would today be seen as a modest town at best. The Sons of Liberty were effectively a local lodge in a town of 16,000. Newport, Rhode Island, had 11,000 residents and Charleston, South Carolina, had 12,000. Beyond that there was no place in the colonies that even approached an urban setting. Small country towns and inland trading posts existed, but significant cities were unknown, except those five serving as outlets for European trade.

They were the "wasp's waist" between a network of European manufacturers and scattered American producers who would trade goods at local country stores. The store proprietors would accumulate stocks of trade items and would periodically transfer them to the larger merchants in the seaport cities. As major commercial centers through which all trade had to pass, the emerging cities were centers of wealth and power rather than poverty and hopelessness.

How Cities Were Seen

What did seventeenth- and eighteenth-century Americans think of these towns and cities in their midst? Many saw them as commercial necessities or as civilizing influences to be encouraged. In *History of Urban America* Charles Glaab and A. Theodore Brown cite several examples of the early view of cities. One belonged to a major investor in the Carolinas, more concerned with economic development than with morals, who attributed the South's inferior economic position to its failure to keep up in "the Planting of People in Townes . . . the Chiefe thing that hath given New England soe much the advantage over Virginia." Glaab and Brown cite a Virginia author who encouraged more towns because people ". . . ought to live together in visible united societies, in cities, towns, or villages." They note a New England preacher's scolding of those that leave the city for a rural life, for in so doing they "bid defiance, not only to Religion, but to Civility itself." Glaab and Brown conclude that "[t]here was little doubt among the colonists that the city was man's proper habitat."[13]

That is perhaps too strong a conclusion to draw. Certainly some contemporaries saw cities as corrupting influences. Thomas Jefferson envisioned a nation of yeoman farmers and feared the impact of city living on political stability. "The mobs of great cities add just so much to support of pure government as sores do to the strength of the human body." Indeed he took solace in the spread of disease in urban areas as a limit to their growth. "The yellow fever will discourage the growth of great cities in our nation, and I view great cities as pestilential to the morals, the health, and the liberties of man."[14] Still it was continued growth and economic success that virtually everyone foresaw for American cities. Some feared the impacts on morals or political stability. Few indeed were worried about their ultimate decay and destitution.

Poverty in Early Cities

As today, early American cities were organized according to income and wealth, but they were "inside out" from a modern perspective. They were characterized by wealth surrounded by poverty. The most advantaged citizens competed for the most central location, and for good reason. All trans-portation was by foot. There was no other means of commuting to the warehouse or counting house. Much business was conducted at home. Shops were centrally located and could only be reached by foot. Central-city streets were the best paved and lighted. There was great advantage in living close to the center of activity, and rents and housing costs rose steeply in those favored locations. The wealthy thus lived as close to the center as possible, and the few urban poor lived in the suburbs where rents were lower.

For the wealthy, then, the public policy "problem" was how to keep the poor out of the central city. For the poor, the problem was how to get in! Following English law and tradition, local communities were responsible for the poor in their midst and had to raise funds for poor relief through local taxation. Many cities early on thus enacted immigration restrictions, requiring potential new residents to prove their ability to support themselves and/or to be vouched for and sponsored by current residents.

In order to limit the burdens imposed by the urban poor, much of the aid was distributed in kind (i.e., in the form of food, clothing, or firewood), and the poor were expected to provide as much as possible for their own upkeep. Many communities established "work houses" with the expectation that the residents would underwrite much of the costs of their maintenance. The poor were sometimes bound over to private enterprises with their wages garnished to provide their support in one of the municipal poor houses.

There were no large-scale manufacturing establishments in colonial cit-ies. Goods were made almost exclusively by hand, under the supervision of independent craftsmen. Workshop and home were the same. Apprentices and employees generally lived with the employer. There were no large working-class neighborhoods and no central-city slums to speak of. Urban poverty was a distraction rather than a main concern for the leaders of the early American cities that were growing and accumulating wealth.

Achieving City Status

Urban areas are also structured politically. The drawing of jurisdictional boundaries defines who will have control over areas of wealth and responsi-bility for solving problems in areas of poverty. Today most suburbs are relieved to be politically separated from the economic conditions of the central cities. Any move to expand city jurisdiction to encompass outlying areas is seen by the suburbs as an attempt to capture and expropriate their wealth. In the nation's early days, as commerce and population increased in cities they became seen as important sources of wealth for states and counties. Incorporation, creating independent local governments, was seen as threatening a loss to the larger jurisdictions and a separation of wealth and privilege *within* the cities!

To be sure cities were looked upon by many with real suspicion, but precisely because they were so successful. Rural interests feared cities' growing wealth and power and often looked for ways to restrict them. In many cases there was serious political opposition to attempts to incorporate even major urban centers. Merchants in Boston tried to achieve municipal status as early as 1784 but did not finally succeed until 1822.[15] The largest cities were often purposefully bypassed when selecting state capitals so that their commercial power could be more effectively constrained. It is no accident that the state legislature in New York meets in Albany rather than New York City.

From Then Until Now

In the early days of the nation, cities grew and came to be seen as the locale of great wealth and of even greater potential. When magazines of the day looked at their cities they saw a great future, not a landscape replete with abandoned hulks. In the early 1800s *Hunt's Merchant News* in New York City wrote glowingly of cities' growing wealth, commerce, and population. The commercial interests saw the city as the hope of the future. Less than 150 years later the editors of *Fortune* magazine, one of the key commercial periodicals of our day, published a volume on the bleak conditions of the city.[16] How has a nation that began with few cities, small in scale but noted for their wealth and power, surrounded by a dispersed agricultural population, become one characterized by so many large cities, filled with so much poverty and despair? That is an inquiry worth undertaking. We and our children will live in these spaces, and it behooves us to explore them with care. How did we get from there to here? Where will we be a generation or two down the road?

There are distinct patterns to these changes in space, but just as it is hard for us to see the Milky Way galaxy when we are in the middle of it, it is hard, sometimes, to see our terrestrial space clearly when we are in its midst. The cities we have today are all that most of us have ever experienced. To us they are simply there, natural and inevitable. But that space is worthy of fresh exploration and not just "because it is there." How it will change over the future is not yet determined. Indeed it is within our power to affect the outcome. Will the vision of *Escape from New York* be prophecy or fantasy?

Great athletes are often distinguished by their extraordinary ability to see "where they are." In athletics an understanding of the placement of one's body in relation to other players and objects on the field is the essence of athletic grace. In other areas the metaphor is equally apt. Until we know where we are and how we and others are moving we can plot no effective direction for our future actions. That is true in policy and it is true of cities.

The transition of urban centers from being the site of "civility itself" to the "place where we face our failures as a nation" has not been abrupt. Elements that we see today as indicative of modern decline have, in many cases, been present for generations. Fearful of gang violence in American cities today, there is perhaps some solace in noting that gangs and juvenile crime were considered major problems in many American cities as early as the 1840s. The chief of police in New York City made it the single topic of his annual report in 1849.[17] The overrepresentation of African-American and Hispanic youth in those arrested for crime in our nation's cities is cause for real concern, but that type of disproportionality is not new. Over half of all the persons arrested in New York in 1859 were born in Ireland. In 1860, when about one half of the population of New York was foreign born, 80 percent of those convicted of crimes in the city were as well.[18]

Evolution of the forces that define how we use our space is the topic of this book. Evolution always occurs over time. The present we experience today arose from events in the past. The future we face will result from events experienced and policies chosen in the present. To influence where we are going, we must know where we are. To understand where we are, we need to see where we have been. This kind of exploration demands as much courage and clear-headedness as does the exploration of outer space. This book is a metaphorical expedition into America's cities and their structures. Shaped and reshaped by the interaction of technology, policy, and perception, those cities place us, our activities, and our interactions within space. They are where we live. They define "where we are." The first stage in that exploration must be a recognition that cities cannot exist at all until there is a fundamental ability to sustain large populations in close space.

2

Unnatural Aggregations and
Natural Perceptions

Cities are so much a part of the modern American experience that we take them for granted, a natural part of our social existence. We find it hard to see something so common as wholly extraordinary, indeed in a very funda-mental sense, as wholly *unnatural*. If nature can be said to abhor a vacuum because a local absence of matter violates physical laws, it can hardly be said to have any more regard for a city. A modern city is a mass of individ-uals permanently bunched together and spatially isolated from their sources of food and energy. No other organism on the face of the earth uses its space quite like that. It would seem a sure path to extinction, yet humans now predominately adopt that spatial organization and somehow survive. Some would even say thrive. We must, therefore, have found ways, un-available to other species, to stretch the limits of spatial concentration.

Population Biology

The subfield of ecology that tries to explain levels of, and fluctuations in, the populations of organisms is known as *population biology*. It seeks to determine in what parts of the world a given organism can be found, in what numbers and concentrations it exists, and how it is spread across its range. Given the explosive reproductive capacity of virtually all species, any one that reproduced to its full potential over any extended period would rather quickly engulf the earth. It is hard to grasp the scale of reproductive potential. The numbers quickly become too large to comprehend. Currently the human population of the entire world is estimated to be approximately 5.8 billion, or 5.8×10^9. If, in the year 0, the human population of the earth had been a mere 1,000 persons, and if each pairing of adults had produced but four children (far below maximum reproductive potential), each of whom lived to reproduce at the same rate, the total population would have doubled in each generation. At that rate it would by now exceed 1.2×10^{27} or more than 8 *trillion* people for every square meter of land area on the earth's surface.

Fortunately, neither humans nor any other animal species expands its population at their full potential rate for long. What is mathematically possible and what is environmentally sustainable are very different. Populations adjust and disperse in balance with the resources necessary for life. In that balance, ecologists examine three separate elements of spatial organization. The first is a species' *distribution,* a concern with the geographic range over which the organism can be found. Tropical plants do not appear in regions that experience harsh winters. Polar bears cannot be found in the Caribbean. Highly adaptable, humans have an almost unlimited distribution. We can be found in virtually all regions of the earth, adjusting to the most hostile of environments, or perhaps adapting the environment to our needs.

The second measure used is of the *dispersion* of individuals over the whole, or portions of, their range. In some cases a population will spread very evenly. For example, in the nesting colonies of many bird species each nest is located just outside the reach of its neighbors. The entire space is broken up into equal territories of a consistent size and shape. In other cases the dispersion of the population shows no systematic pattern at all and may be characterized as random. Still other species display "clumping" where localized aggregations of individuals gather in proximity, one to another, while unoccupied spaces still remain within the species' range. Cities are clearly clumps of humans.

Finally, population biologists measure the *density* of populations, the number of individuals per unit of space within various portions of the range. How many trout can a given river support? What is the density of breeding sea lions? How many red oak trees can be found per acre in New England forests? Thus if we ask how many individuals can live within the fixed space of a city we have entered the realm of population biologists, and the answer to that fundamental question will depend upon the resources that are, or can be made, available there. High concentrations of individuals are only possible in the presence of high concentrations of resources, and since most resources are limited, so also is the carrying capacity of a place. Many of the limits to local population growth are *density dependent.* "Of prime importance among these must be limitation by food supply and places to live."[1]

"Natural" Aggregations

In order to live in a high-density, clumped pattern some solution to the problems of limited food and space must be found. For most species they must be "selected." I use that word in its evolutionary sense. Individual organisms do not rationally "choose" survival strategies. Variants of behavior that are most successful are naturally selected for the species. Individuals who gather in high-density aggregations must experience some reproductive advantages over individuals who do not for that behavior to become selected and to become the norm for the species. Aggregative behavior must have advantages for many species for it recurs often in nature, but once any aggregation exceeds the food and space resources of its place, any further gathering can only confer disadvantage on the community.

Protection from predation is probably at the base of the herding behavior displayed by many herbivores. Indeed the larger the herd, the greater the protection for any individual. There are multiple examples of vast herds congregating in close quarters to breed and feed. Today wildebeest in East Africa, and in another era bison in North America, come together in the millions. Such a dense population in a fixed location would quickly consume all available food. The herd's "solution" to this density-dependent limitation is to continually move the entire aggregation, migrating over great distances to take advantage of the seasonal availability of food in different locales. Many "natural" aggregations survive by constantly moving from place to place.

Some permanent, high-density aggregations do not have to migrate to survive, but they are mostly limited to locales with exceptionally favorable conditions. Huge colonies of coral can remain in one place, but only because ocean currents continually replenish the local store of food. If nature should fail to deliver, the entire colony would soon die. Coral have no means to control or affect the replacement of the food supplies upon which they depend. The maximum sustainable size of the population depends on how much food is regularly delivered and how much space there is. Past some point, more simply cannot eat; more simply cannot fit.

Other "natural" aggregations survive only by being impermanent. They disperse into a low-density pattern for most of each year. Breeding colonies of birds or sea mammals concentrate in the same protected locales, year after year, either to give birth to vulnerable young of one generation or to find mates for the next. There is never enough food within the immediate borders of the colony to support such high density for long. Food must be imported in one of two forms: either via storage in the form of previously accumulated body fat or via forage from food gathering excursions away from the colony. In either case each adult is responsible for the importation of his or her own food. With the occasional exception of sharing among mates, it is literally do or die for each adult member of the group. Newly hatched (or born) young may be able to depend upon assistance from their parents, but from strangers they can expect nothing. Inevitably individual provisioning fails, and the whole colony must disperse as local food supplies are depleted and body stores used up.

Only among certain groups of insects are there permanent "natural" aggregations that remain in a fixed locale for long periods, depending on the continuous importation of resources by cooperating, specialized individuals. Known as "eusocial" insects, their colonies are distinguished from mere aggregations by the presence of three unusual traits:

> (1) cooperation in caring for the young; (2) overlap of at least two generations capable of contributing to colony labor; and (3) reproductive division of labor, with a mostly or wholly sterile worker caste working on behalf of individuals engaged in reproduction.[2]

On the surface these special aggregations seem to share many of the special characteristics of human cities. They display continuity and permanence over time, made possible by social mechanisms for transporting food and resources into a larger communal setting. But upon close examination it is clear that they achieve this spatial organization only through extraordinary evolutionary adaptation, wholly different from the processes leading to human urbanization.

Most "eusocial" colonies display "polymorphism" wherein individuals take on different physical forms, each best suited to performing particular functions. In some species of ants there are several classes of specialized workers. Some develop weaponry suited to a soldier caste; others develop physiques suited to a life of labor in service to the colony. Honeybees come in three distinct physical forms: female worker bees, male drones, and a single dominant queen. In the day-to-day functioning of the hive there are no males, only the two forms of females, and all of the worker bees are sterile sisters, offspring of the single productive queen. The differences in individuals' form is not the result of variations in the genetic composition of the individuals, but of differences in their developmental environments. The colony creates different forms to fulfill different collective functions.

For example, whether a honeybee egg becomes a new queen or a sterile worker depends on the type of chamber in which it hatches rather than on any characteristics of the egg itself. If hatched in a royal chamber a larva feeds on special chemicals placed there and develops the distinctive physical shape of a new queen. An egg laid in this special environment takes only two thirds of the time to produce a mature adult as does an identical egg laid in a standard chamber. If, in the very earliest days, an egg from a normal chamber is moved into a "royal" chamber, it will develop into a queen. If, instead, the royal chamber's egg is transferred to a "worker" cell, it will develop into a sterile worker. It is not a genetic difference in the eggs that results in the special form and development, but the exposure to special diet and conditions. Only when the *colony* needs a new queen is a royal chamber built (in response to biochemical signals from the current queen). Individuals are biochemically shaped to fulfill collective needs, and their lifetime roles are physically and irrevocably established at birth.[3]

All of the members of a eusocial colony are siblings. All but the queen are sterile. No individual can long survive outside the colony. No outsider can ever move in. All members of a specific aggregation are born into it. None can ever leave. These behaviors are in no sense "chosen" by the individuals. They are literally *selected* in an evolutionary sense. The move from nonsocial to social insect status requires the development of new species of organism. Aggregating is not a change in individual behavior but a selected change in species biochemistry.

No termite can choose to switch colonies in response to better opportunities elsewhere. Bees do not individually or collectively move into a colony. They must all be born into it, and are all literally physically shaped in order to contribute to it according to group needs. Each colony is self-sufficient. There is no commerce among them. Only what the members of an individual colony can produce or acquire is available to the aggregation. They are fascinating social structures, but in no sense are they cities.

"Unnatural" Aggregations

Standing alone among all of these are human cities, places where people choose to settle in permanent locales in very high numbers, far exceeding the resources naturally supplied. Cities are permanent. They do not move on as local supplies and resources are diminished. The very survival of urban populations depends upon the constant replenishment of resources, but no natural forces exist that accomplish that as ocean currents do for coral. Individuals not part of the community for some reason expend time, energy, and treasure to gather food and resources from far afield and deliver them to be consumed by urban residents. No biological altruism based on shared genes can explain this. There is no systematic process of altering the physical form of individuals in future generations to create worker castes in service to a queen. Human city dwellers display no polymorphism. No natural selection of social behaviors via genetic evolution explains the shift to high-density urban space. Cities exist because humans have created them. They have made individual and collective choices that have led to concentration as a rational act, rather than a programmed behavior. Urban humans are the same exact species as current and past rural ones. People can still choose not to concentrate. They can move in and out or between cities at will. What is unique about their aggregations is that they derive from the development of technology that makes possible so many of these specialized structures that seemingly violate the natural order of things.

To concentrate successfully in vulnerable places devoid of adequate food sources and to rely upon other individuals to undertake the effort to deliver adequate resources are both major acts of faith and major accomplishments of culture. Human cities are made possible by technological progress. They are made predominant by the operation of a logic of location that makes them superior locations for many human activities. As technology evolves and the logic of location changes the placement, the size and the shape of cities adapt. Cities are human creations. For better or worse, whatever they are, whatever they become, we make them.

The Population Structure of the United States

The history of the United States is, among other things, a tale of humans changing their distribution and dispersion in space. Over the span of only a very few generations the population has reorganized from a dispersed, low-density pattern into a connected system of "unnatural" aggregations. The human "range" has extended over the whole continent for millennia, but for almost all of that period population was widely dispersed and low in density. Aggregations were small in size and often impermanent in location. Different cultures ascended and faded over time, but the fundamental characteristics of the spatial organization remained much the same.

Before Europeans arrived on the North American continent the indigenous population was thinly distributed throughout the expanse. In 1607 the first European attempt at permanent settlement in what is now the United States was made in present-day Virginia. The British found there an already well established political system under the control of Chief Powhatan, later to be reincarnated in the Disney movie *Pocohontas*. The Powhatans had an empire that extended throughout the Chesapeake region, having virtually exterminated the Chesapeake tribe and suppressed all other local groups. They demanded significant payments of tribute, but even with that external support they were not able to live in large, permanent settlements. Early descriptions of Powhatan "towns" tell of groups of fifteen to twenty impermanent houses on a three- to four-acre site. The Powhatans expressed surprise at the attempts of the English to live in larger towns, expecting and observing recurring problems with hunger and starvation in such large groups. It is possible that the Indians clearly preferred unconcentrated living. It is certain that technologically they had no other choice.[4]

There were some long-lived groupings among the pueblo dwellers of the Southwest, but these too were relatively small in size. They were absolutely limited by the food production in the immediate region as well as the availability of water. When climatic changes altered the carrying capacity of a local area, their aggregations broke up or moved on. The region is filled with ruins left behind by people who depended on nature to support higher density organization. They lacked the means to bring food and water to the people. When local supplies failed, the people had to move to where there was adequate food and water.

There were exceptions, of course, notably the Aztec empire with its capital city of Tenochtitlán on the site now occupied by Mexico City. Here they built a large city by world standards of the day, but it was possible only because of an extended system of military conquest and the forced transfer of food and goods from the hinterland to the capital. Extraordinary military effort was necessary to sustain the population of the capital.

The Aztecs also had to find ways to make large numbers of people work to maintain the city despite nature's persistent pressure to disperse. In some ways they mimicked the colonies of eusocial insects by establishing special castes of service workers, but they did so culturally rather than biochemically. For example, in order to solve problems of transporting goods into the city, the Aztecs had their *tlamemes* who were a "hereditary group trained from childhood to engage in lifelong portage labor."[5]

For the vast majority of the indigenous population of North America, low-density, and often nomadic, living was the only possible option. Nature was self-regulating in regard to too-large gatherings. George Armstrong Custer and his command lost their lives, in part because of their experience with, and beliefs about, the size of sustainable Native American aggregations. Permanent large gatherings of Plains tribes were unknown. Temporary gatherings were rare and of necessity very short in duration. The presence of perhaps 2,000 Lakota in a single camp was beyond their experience. Unable to imagine such a gathering, they did not recognize it even when they encountered it. Had the Seventh Cavalry arrived a few days later, the concentration would have already begun scattering. It would not have been possible to sustain so large a grouping for so long.

So many people and animals consumed [such] immense quantities of game, forage, and firewood that they could not remain long in one place, or even together in one village. It had come together in this strength only in the few days preceding, and it could stay together for more than a few days or a week only through luck, frequent moves, and constant labor.[6]

As Europeans' immigration and reproduction increased, they pushed westward, replacing indigenous populations, but *not* materially affecting the spatial structure. The earliest European settlers were as dispersed in non-clumped, low-density patterns as had been the native population. By the time the nation was founded as an independent entity, the Euro-American population was spread fairly evenly across their portion of the human "range" in small farms. Few indeed lived in cities. Yet today the entire spatial structure has changed. Most of us live in urban "clumps" of very high density. We are the same species, but during the short life of the United States we have completely reorganized ourselves in space.

The earliest years were ones of increasing dispersion and *decreasing* density. New arrivals and newly formed households moved out of the towns into the open "space," believing that open land brought the best chance for economic improvement. People living in cities were definitely not "normal" in the formal sense of the word. As late as 1690 perhaps 10 percent of the European population was still clustered in the few "beachhead" communities along the Atlantic coast. Most were waiting for the opportunity to move outward to "tame the wilderness." They did just that over the next hundred years until the proportion of the population living in cities at the time of the American Revolution was only half as great.[7]

Yet something finally began to draw population, more and more, back into concentrated urban settings. After independence, new cities formed and old ones grew in size. By about 1820 the nation was again 10 percent urbanized. At first people gathered into relatively small aggregations, but by the end of the nineteenth century, the biggest cities had developed the strongest pull and were growing at a rate far beyond that of the smaller ones. Metropolises became a new category of space, both in number and in size.

The driving force behind this reorganization of space is of human origin. It was humans who created the conditions that allowed these cities to exist and to grow. It is we humans who have conceived cities and created them, sometimes consciously, sometimes not, but they are ours. They are not natural. Indeed, urban life is fundamentally "unnatural" in its essence. Its dramatic expansion over a very short space of time eliminates any physiological or evolutionary explanation for urbanization. We have not become termites. We have not changed as a species, but we now live differently in our space. The story of urbanization in the United States is a tale of evolving institutions rather than evolving species. It is a story of changes in technologies, policies, and perceptions.

Accelerating History

Could Americans somehow have accelerated history and economic development by adopting the current spatial organization 200 years ago? What would have happened if President Washington had "seen the future" and adopted a progressive policy of urbanization, relocating the majority of the population into cities? The answer is simple; in short order they would have all starved to death. We then lacked the technology to support so many unnatural aggregations. Cities of the modern scale were just not possible then. Successful urbanization requires solutions to a series of overlapping problems of technology and social organization. Until these solutions were available the aggregations were impossible.

First, of course, it must be possible for some persons to produce stores of food in excess of their own needs, that is to generate an "agricultural surplus," for others to be able to live separated from the land. That is a simple technical requirement. It cannot be ignored. In the closing weeks of the Civil War, as he pushed north toward Virginia, General Sherman distributed land parcels of forty acres each to freed slaves in coastal South Carolina, and promised aid in acquiring a mule. That policy gave rise to the political slogan of the day that defined a reasonable scale of farming for a family—forty acres and a mule. Times and technology have changed. I went to graduate school with a friend who grew up on a "family farm" in Oregon. When his father was preparing to retire, he had to decide whether to continue his career in academics or return home and farm his family's 6,000 acres—alone. He farms today with hundreds of thousands of dollars worth of machinery rather than a mule, and he thus is able to produce, by himself, enough food to support a multitude of city dwellers. The ability to produce an agricultural surplus is the first prerequisite to urbanization.

The second problem that must be overcome is that an agricultural surplus is of no value to city dwellers unless there is some means of overcoming the "friction of space," some way to move it to the cities. Bulk items of varying degrees of perishability require great effort to move. Without appropriate vessels and some form of energy to propel them, food surpluses will rot while city dwellers starve. What an individual can carry, walking significant distances over land, would scarcely feed him/herself on the journey. The survival of a city requires well-developed transportation technologies and systems. The greater the population of a city, the greater the need for imported food and the greater the distances over which it must transported.

Fly into a great city like Chicago and look carefully as you descend. You will see an enormous transportation network keeping it alive—vast numbers of tractor-trailer terminals, a network of rail lines and switching yards, extensive port facilities, and a web of highways all feeding the city. Cut off from the outside world, Chicago (or any other major city) would very quickly wither and die. It is connected to an extensive life-support system, transporting necessary food and resources to the aggregated population.

The military conquest of a city has always been achieved most easily simply by surrounding it and choking it to death. During the Second World War the Nazis imposed a near fatal stranglehold on Leningrad that resulted in massive deprivation and ultimately death by starvation of as many as 1 million of its residents. Only the onset of the subarctic winter saved the city from complete annihilation. As heavy ice formed on the surface of Lake Ladoga to the east of Leningrad, round-the-clock truck convoys had a new access route, safe from the German forces. The opening of new transport connections with the rest of Russia allowed the city to be resupplied and its remaining residents to survive.

The twin capabilities of producing an agricultural surplus and moving it efficiently from place to place are the technological *sine qua non* of urbanization, but they alone are not sufficient. There is a fundamental social problem to be solved as well. Before there can be cities, there also must be some mechanism to make potential producers of that surplus *willing* to put forth the necessary effort for the benefit of distant strangers. Sociobiologically induced altruism among bearers of shared genes will not suffice here. A social mechanism is needed. In all other species, the actual members of each aggregation supply the colony with its food and resources. Even the developed societies of the eusocial insects live entirely on resources brought into the colony by its own resident members. There is no example in nature of "foreigners" producing and delivering food and resources to aggregations—none. What humans do in their cities is unique.

Even when it is *possible* for outside persons to produce and transport food and necessities to the cities, it will not happen unless there are also reasons for them to be *willing* to do so. There needs to be a social incentive to support cities. Historically that has often been accomplish by the threat or use of violence. In modern cities, the cooperation of producers and transporters is more likely induced via rewards distributed through the market. Thus, cities have had to develop the ability to produce large quantities of trade goods. That is the third prerequisite to urbanization. The technology of how and where manufacturing can efficiently be done has had to evolve in conjunction and cooperation with the other two "solutions." Cities must import or they will die. They must export or they will be unable to import.

Large-scale urbanization would, therefore, have been technologically impossible in 1789 because there was no known way to produce sufficient food, no way to transport it to cities even if it were produced, and no way for cities to have paid for it if it arrived. It is only the development of technology in these three areas that has created sufficient "gravitational force" to draw the American population inward from its "natural" dispersion to its current "unnatural" aggregations.

Living in Cities—Technical Problems

In each period the technology available to solve these three fundamental problems of urbanization defines both how, and how many, people can *come together* in a city. There is another set of local problems that must be addressed—defining how they can *live together* once there. First there is the fundamental organic problem. Humans consume food, water, and energy. They use up resources. They create bodily wastes, trash, and garbage. The more dense their distribution, the more pressure they put on the carrying capacity of their environment. Without technological solutions to these problems, a given area can only support a limited population. Local water supplies run out. Accumulating garbage breeds disease. Excessive waste pollutes water supplies. Even if there is a global agricultural surplus and ample means for long-distance bulk transport, local density-dependent limitations will prevail. If local populations are to exceed that limit, they must create *socially consistent* solutions—investments in water systems, in waste disposal, in food distribution sufficient to permit large numbers to coexist in small spaces.

That, of course, leads to the second technical problem. Humans themselves occupy space. It defies the laws of physics to attempt to place a vast multitude at a single point, or even in a small area. They simply cannot be made to fit. Even if there is a single "best" place to be and all residents of a city agree on where that may be, they cannot all simultaneously be there. They must be spread out within the city, and yet in so doing, some are by necessity farther from the "best" places. There will thus always be a competition for the most valuable position, and there must be some means of resolving that competition. Humans have had to develop that technology as well.

Once located, people need to be housed. In all but the most favorable of climates some form of shelter must be built, but that of course also requires the use of materials and resources far beyond those likely to be found in a single location. Those too will have to be imported into the city from outside. What kinds of structures are technologically possible? What kinds are economically feasible? What kinds are socially permissible? Do they create privileges or problems for neighbors? Third, then, every city will have to have policies and possibilities regarding housing that will define how people will live in proximity with each other.

Finally, the more densely crowded they are around prime locations, the more difficult it is for people and things to move in that region. People occupying desirable spaces make it difficult for other people and things to move through. As there are more and more people in a city or neighborhood, crowding becomes an increasing problem. All of those people need to be able to move around within a close area, filled with ever more people also trying to move. Aggregation inevitably leads to congestion; congestion inevitably limits aggregation. To reduce congestion, more and more of the urban space has to be devoted to transportation channels and mechanisms. Scarce central space must be left open, yet by doing so prime areas are made unavailable for housing or production, leading to increased competition for the other spaces.

There is a systemic connection among the various elements of city space. Residential locations are desirable when they permit easy access to jobs, services, and amenities. They are accessible when they are close to other activities or to easy intracity transportation. But the more space is devoted to production and transportation, the less is available for living. The more space devoted to transportation, the more accessible distant locations become, the less central space can be used for other things. In each city, in each era, there is a balancing that must take place between the demands for housing, the need for space for producing, and the need to set aside transportation channels connecting the two. How and by whom this balancing is done is an important factor in urban development.

Living in Cities—Inventing Institutions

The technical problems of living in extreme proximity are inescapable. They are what make urban aggregations so thoroughly unnatural. Cities' existence and growth also depend upon the development of special cultural mechanisms to resolve the inevitable competition for space and to provide the infrastructure necessary to sustain communal life. Who will get what location? What can they do with it? Who can decide? Animals settle the competition for territory via the rule of tooth and claw. Each lion is ruler of "his" pride and "his" territory only until a stronger individual comes and takes them. Human cities cannot develop with violence as the force that settles these claims.

With their permanent and regularly interacting populations, and their need for fixed buildings and infrastructure, cities have historically developed only in the context of larger social and political institutions that peacefully resolve the competition for space and provide some surety in location. For most of human history, the competition has been resolved via central authority. In ancient Asian and medieval European cities space was allocated by custom and decree. Rulers would grant locations to particular persons and activities. Neighborhoods would reflect the administrative decisions about space made by princes and potentates. To be sure, continued occupation of a location was at the pleasure of the monarch, but at least it was not threatened by all at once. In modern socialist societies the process is much the same. Central authorities decide where housing is to be placed, who may live in it, where they may shop, and where factories may be located. Competition over location is resolved by shifting all decisions to a single authority who administratively allocates the scarce space within the community.

There is an alternative method of allocating space that is surely as ingenious a human invention as are railroads and rockets. Markets, especially in items as complex as real estate, are relatively recent in origin. They differ from centralized authority by leaving the decisions about the use of space to individuals who hold socially enforced property rights. Appropriate legal and political institutions thus have had to be invented in order to affix social title to land and all structures on it to some individual. The power of central authority is then used not to enforce *its* decisions about the use of space but to enforce those of the *owners* who can build on it, leave it vacant, live on it, transfer the use of it to another for a limited period (i.e., rent it), transfer all rights to it forever (i.e., sell it), give it away, or will it to their heirs.

What is done where is ever changing. When the logic of location changes, markets are a mechanism that allows the use of space to respond. The use of space within a city becomes very fluid under this invention. Should anyone else value a space more than the current owner or user, he or she can acquire it via a trade that transfers all of those rights to the buyer for a price. If the relative payoffs from different uses of a location shift, then the use to which it is put will also change. Each parcel of land in a city based on markets will thus be drawn, inexorably, to its "highest and best use," defined economically in terms of profitability rather than abstractly in terms of "aesthetics" or "justice."

When Adam Smith first published his 1776 treatise describing how this relatively new form of social organization could increase the *Wealth of Nations,* he was not speaking of city space but of market-based economies in general when he noted that these decentralized decisions solved social competition and coordination "as if by an invisible hand." The power of this "invisible hand" should not be underestimated. It is not a gentle beckoning hand but a powerful push with an iron grip. For better or worse, markets once invented, like other technological adaptations, have been a powerful force in shaping America's cities.

No unnatural aggregation can long exist without a central authority, or a market, or some combination of the two to allocate urban space among competing users and uses. These are forms of social "technology" as necessary for solving fundamental problems of urbanization as is the technology of transportation. If cities are to exist they must be regulated by markets or monarchs. Those are the only real choices.

The Past Set in Stone

No human city can long exist without solutions to these technical and social problems; they are too unnatural to survive otherwise. Each city is shaped and sized in accordance with the interplay of these elements during the period of its formation. Each city is today a reflection of past technology and prior policies, literally set in stone—or at least concrete. This chapter began with the questions of population biology. How large a population can a given locale support? When are its density dependent limits reached? What causes changes in local population density? For all other species the answers to these questions change only when something in the natural environment changes. Local populations respond to exogenous changes in nature. For human cities the answers depend upon the evolution of human culture itself. Change is endogenous. For better or worse *we,* and not nature, create our own cities, and it is *we* who make them what they are.

To understand cities today we have to explore the evolution of technologies aimed at solving the fundamental problems of unnatural aggregation and the kinds of spaces they have produced. Our cities clearly reflect the physiological needs of the humans who live there. There is, however, one more dimension of urban space that must be considered before that exploration begins. What we will see in cities depends not only on what is objectively there but on how we perceive it.

Perceiving Space

There is a challenging little puzzle that begins by presenting a space consisting of nine dots arranged in a square. The object of the puzzle is to connect all of the dots using four (or fewer) straight lines, following two simple rules. First, the lines must be connected, that is, you may not pick up

Figure 1.

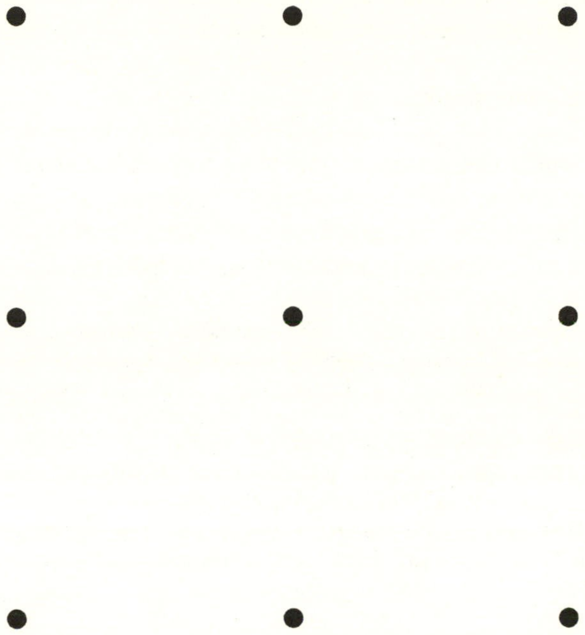

●   ●   ●

●   ●   ●

●   ●   ●

your pen and draw disconnected lines, and second, you may not retrace a line without counting that as a second line. You may want to try your hand at the puzzle (see Figure 1).

The puzzle stumps most people, not because it is objectively difficult, but because they inevitably *see* it as different than it really is. The *actual* puzzle consists of nine dots in unbounded space. What most people *see* is nine dots defining a *closed* space. When their lines reach any edge dot, they feel that they must end the line segment and turn a corner, though that is not at all a requirement of the puzzle. If line segments are extended beyond the dots, then the solution becomes fairly simple, as can be seen at the end of this chapter.

If we cannot see nine dots on a page without distorting the space they occupy, what chance do we have of seeing city spaces clearly? Certainly the spatial structures we are about to explore are far more complex than that of any puzzle. It is clear that human minds ultimately have created these cities. Are they capable of clearly understanding them? The greatest obstacle to a successful exploration of these unnatural aggregations may well be that we have to take *us* along. We already live in cities. We already "know" what is wrong with them. We have already "seen" what is there. We already "know" what the problems are and who or what is responsible for them. We "know" that space ends at the dots, or does it? It is often hardest to explore the places with which we are the most familiar.

Persistent Misconception

When Christopher Columbus set out to sail to Asia but ended up in North America instead, his expectations clearly shaped his perception of everything that he found there. When he explored a place he did not expect to be, he was unable to see it as anything other than his intended destination.

> For three months Columbus sailed about the Caribbean, dispensing new names to the islands and trinkets to the natives, reading references to the Great Khan or the land of Cipangu into every garbled native legend or ill-pronounced name that he heard, and always hoping that the next island in the offing might be Cipangu itself. On arriving in Cuba on 24 October he declared, "I believe this is the island of Cipangu, of which marvelous things are told. And in the globes and planispheres I have seen, it is located in this area." He seems to have realized very soon that this was an illusion, but he discarded it if favour of an even more adventurous assumption: that Cuba could be part of the mainland of Cathay.[8]

Columbus was not unique in the persistence of his misperceptions. Social psychologists find this phenomenon of *belief perseverance* to be a ubiquitous aspect of human perception. During the first two years of the American Civil War, General George McClellan commanded a Union Army that was exceptionally well organized and trained but was frustratingly ineffective. The enemy that McClellan faced in his mind was always much stronger, much closer, and much better equipped than the one he faced in the field. So persistent was he in his misperception that his intelligence network soon began providing him with only the kind of information he expected to hear. He was absolutely certain, even though he was certainly wrong, and no amount of new evidence could change his mind. "[F]acing odds existing only in his mind's eye, he would not dare to pursue decisive victory."[9]

Few of us indeed ever set out to challenge our own beliefs or expectations. We all tend to explore where we *think* we are, even when the evidence indicates that we are actually someplace else. Nor does cumulative exposure to more and more evidence inevitably lead to any increase in the accuracy of our perceptions. Sometimes increasing the amount of "hard" information about a topic just increases the degree of disagreement among people. Psychologists have found time and again that, when presented with conflicting hard evidence about beliefs, humans tend to accept uncritically any that supports the prior view and reject as flawed or biased any that is counter.[10]

Confirmation Bias

Not only do we tend to distort and discount any discomforting evidence to which we are exposed, we tend to bias which information we are likely even to encounter. We seek out the evidence that will confirm our beliefs and avoid exposure to any that might undermine them. Rush Limbaugh's audience is conservative *before* they tune in. They are confirmed, not converted. Charlie Rose's audience is liberal *before* they turn on their televisions. They watch to see why they are right, not to discover why they may be wrong. Psychologists have found both belief persistence in interpreting information and this phenomenon of *confirmation bias* in acquiring it to be virtually universal. Thus, as we set out to explore America's cities we risk failure from these natural responses. Apparently a simple commitment to keeping an "open mind" is not enough, for the psychological evidence is that "closed minds" are those that refuse even to consider any more evidence while "open minds" are those that are willing to look for new evidence that will support what is already "known." Rare indeed is the mind that is open to a true reexamination of beliefs held, rather than simply to a confirmation of them.

How, then, can we explore the cities where we already live if that is so? There is some evidence that people asked to build a case for why the opposite of their position *might be true* find it harder to discount or discard evidence that does not conform to their prior beliefs. They are thus forced to accept provisionally information *before* deciding to reject or discount it. It reduces their confidence in the surety of their positions and perceptions. It begins to open their minds in abnormal ways.[11] Can we impose this condition on ourselves? It is clear that we seldom do, but in undertaking an examination of a phenomenon as complex and contentious as the nature of American cities, with consequences so significant for the future of American society, it would be dangerous to begin the exploration with answers already well established. In the chapters that follow we may well encounter a number of propositions that are counter to what we "know" to be true about cities, as well as evidence that seems clearly "wrong." The challenge of genuine exploration is to break from the norm of only seeking confirmation and to make an abnormal commitment to reconsider explicitly what might make "untrue" propositions true. If we accept that challenge and then, at the end, choose to reject what we find, fair enough. However, if we are unwilling to do that, we will not be truly able to explore urban space. We will be like McClellan, seeing what is not really there.

This is not simply a matter of intellectual honesty. Our urban policies arise from our shared visions of urban reality. How we see our cities shapes what we are collectively willing, and likely, to do about them. If our visions are wrong, or inaccurate, or misconceived, will we be able to tell? If someone presents evidence that conflicts with our shared beliefs, will we respond by rejecting that person's ideas rather than confronting them? Must we wait for generations to change before any new perceptions about our cities can be accepted? Those are crucial questions for the fate of urban America. Without a commitment to fresh exploration the answers are not encouraging.

Moral Space

There is one last obstacle to be overcome. People naturally tend to see social phenomena in the simple terms of a Hollywood film, to imagine that all ills are the consequences of bad actions undertaken by evil people and all solutions involve the last minute arrival of superheroes to thwart the villains' plans. When Joel Garreau wrote his book about the changing shape of cities he admitted that he initially approached his topic as an investigative journalist of the true modern style. "In the back of my mind was the notion that if I could find out who was 'doing this to us,' it might be possible to get the SOBs indicted."[12] He was not unique in having that view. It is ubiquitous in American politics. What was unusual was that as he probed more and more deeply into the processes of urban evolution, he came to recognize that they were more complex than that. Impersonal forces and innocent actions can combine into systems that result in outcomes unplanned by anyone, unwanted by anyone, perhaps even unpreventable by anyone.

It is popular and easy, but far too simplistic, to look for all collective answers in individual moral failings. It is not hard to find assertions that urban poverty persists because of the actions of "bad" welfare mothers who neither work nor teach their children to do so, or that it is caused by "bad" bureaucrats who corrupt social policy to protect their parasitic careers and force welfare mothers to behave this way. Still others see the pervasive poverty in our cities as a result of "bloodsucking" Jews and Asians who operate businesses in inner-city black neighborhoods or perhaps of systematic exploitation planned by a conspiratorial white power structure. If poverty is to be reduced, the "good" people must force the "evil" people to behave differently. There may not be widespread agreement on exactly who belongs in which category, but there is an astonishing degree of consensus that the simple moral explanation is sufficient.

There is at least one important alternative view. In a world as compli-cated as this one, things just do not always turn out as we plan, or expect, or hope. Policy analysts speak of a *law of unintended consequences*. They note that in a world as interdependent as this one, no one can ever do just *one* thing. *Whatever* one does will have unintended, and often unforeseen, ef-fects. If people decide that they should eat less red meat, they will eat more of something else that may be no healthier. If they heed warnings about lower safety standards for commuter airlines, they may put themselves at even greater risk by driving. *Anything* done will affect *other* things in unin-tended ways. That is true of persons; it is true of policies.

If we start our exploration of cities with the primary goal of fixing blame on guilty persons, we may pass by many of the real causes of America's urban problems. There certainly are bad acts in this world and they certainly affect our cities, but we may also need to look at "innocent" acts, under-taken by fundamentally "good" people, that have had cumulative conse-quences for how and where we live today. Cities are the points in space where such disparate elements as the invention of the elevator, the decision to guarantee mortgages for returning World War II veterans, an insistence that all landlords provide indoor plumbing, a commitment to clean rivers, and past investments in transportation networks all come together. In that conjunction there may be as much potential for unintended consequences to be responsible for outcomes as there is for the triumph of overt evil. Simply changing the behavior of the "bad" people may not be enough. Indeed identifying them may not even be possible. Complex interdependent sys-tems will remain. Technology will still evolve; Luddites will always fail. Policies will still be enacted; anarchy is not an option. There will still be consequences for cities, intended and not. Marx was right in noting that while humans do make their own history, they do not make it entirely of their own choosing. It is hubris in the extreme to assume that either we (the good people) or they (the bad people) can control it all.

Perception and Morality

Both of the elements of human perception discussed earlier are connected to our proclivity for imposing moral order on all phenomena. If our prior belief is that all social problems are caused by evil people, we will certainly be able to find sufficient evidence, and interpret it all appropriately, to allow that belief to persevere. That will not make the explanation true, just persis-tent. Good and evil have certainly had a role to play in human affairs, and the development of America's urban structure is no exception. My point is not to deny that but merely to argue that it is too early in our exploration to turn the entire past, present, and future of cities into a simple morality play.

When that morality explanation perseveres, confirmation bias has the added potential of shielding us from ideas we should perhaps confront. Recently there was a debate over immigration policy held on the campus where I teach. After it was over I asked one of my students what she thought of the arguments made by one of the participants. "I knew he was a racist," she replied (without revealing the source of this truth) "and so he had to be wrong." If all social phenomena are part of the eternal battle between the good people and the bad, then ideas and perceptions and evidence do not need to be evaluated in substantive terms. It is enough to see who spoke of them to determine their truth.

It is not just undergraduates who reject messages from suspect messengers. In the opening chapter of his 1987 analysis of urban problems William Julius Wilson recounts how this tendency has affected "objective" social science.[13] He notes historical cycles where certain questions could not be asked, certain issues not explored, because they had become associated with the "bad" people and their "bad" positions. Simply to raise questions previously associated with "evil" people is sufficient to convict the questioner of evil. Our perception of the quality of an answer is often determined by our prior moral placement of the one delivering it. Ideas or insights offered cannot ever be considered if the wrong person offers it. If Newt Gingrich or Louis Farrakhan or Jack Kemp or Jesse Jackson proposed it there is nothing else we need to know.

Exploring Urban Space

To explore the spatial organization of American cities is thus to venture into dangerous territory. Many different pitfalls await the unwary. We are exploring the spatial organization of humans, but, of course, we are, ourselves, human. We may not be up to the task. If we do carry our perceptions with us, and if we act to defend those perceptions even in the face of contesting evidence, we run the risk of following Columbus, being in a place we do not explore and exploring a space where we are not. If we do enter with an open mind we risk finding out that we have long been somewhere other than where we thought we were. In exploring American cities, we need to guard against the dangers of taking *us* along. We may be unwilling to explore with care, and we may not be at all happy with what we find. That is potentially a dangerous kind of search party to join, but it is the only kind available to us. Fairly warned, then, we may as well proceed.

Figure 2.

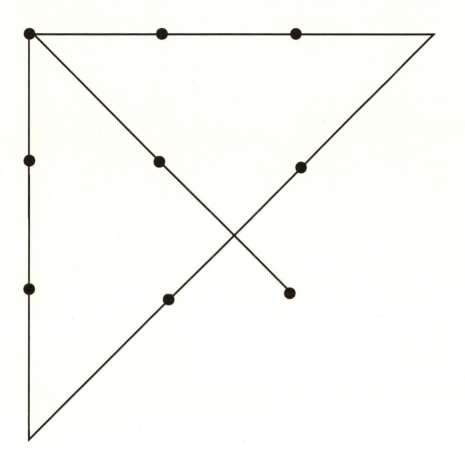

II

The Path from the Past

3

Wind, Wagon, and Water

Cities Before 1830

In 1792 a young man graduated from Yale College at the relatively advanced age of twenty-eight. At nineteen he had decided that he wanted to attend college but he had only a minimal education in a local school. So he had to spend the next several years in teaching himself all that he would need to know to qualify for admission to Yale, and in persuading his family that the endeavor was worthwhile. He wanted ultimately to read for the law, but with mounting debts and no resources as graduation approached, he was relieved to be offered a teaching position at a respectable salary in New York. When the offer was withdrawn at the last moment he was left wholly without prospects until the president of Yale gave his name to a wealthy southern planter seeking a private tutor for his children. With no other options, he reluctantly set sail from New York harbor to begin teaching in South Carolina.

A decade later another young man sought his fortune in the growing regions of western New York State. He and a partner borrowed funds to support a series of commercial ventures shipping flour from the village of Geneseo to New York City. All their attempts ended in financial failure, however, and he was unable to meet his considerable debts. At first he fled the state, but he later returned to face the full legal consequences.

Neither of these events attracted national attention at the time, neither seemed to be of any real significance, but both became part of a vast web of interconnected elements that combined to reshape America. There was no central plan for the transition, no foresight, no intention or understanding of consequences, but once begun, small events like these set into motion inexorable tides of change, for they alter the fundamental logic of location.

The last chapter listed the technical requirements for urbanization. There must somewhere be surpluses of food and resources, there must be effective means of moving those surpluses to the cities, and there must be generated in the cities products, activities, or services that are worth trading for. Within the aggregations themselves there must be means of allocating limited space, providing housing, distributing imported surpluses, supplying water, disposing of waste, and facilitating the movement of people and things within their boundaries. Cities are physical records of how these fundamental problems of urbanization have been solved over time, sized and shaped by what was technologically possible and socially chosen during the period of their development.

Commercial Cities

In the early years, much like today, commerce and services dominated America's urban economies. Cities were collection and transshipment points for goods, often as part of the flow of international trade. City dwellers thus were merchants who bought in bulk and distributed elsewhere; they provided insurance and other commercial services for the dangerous business of ocean trading. They invested in ships and warehouses; they loaded and unloaded ships. Some staffed government offices or provided legal support to commerce. Others developed systems of credit. Some of them produced handcrafted goods displaying skills learned in a formal apprentice system. Some were servants of those who lived by commerce. Early cities did not so much produce goods as distribute them.

There was no real productive advantage to being a blacksmith in a large city, no payoff to farming in the midst of a town, no benefit to weaving one's own cloth in an urban setting. Only commerce and its supporting services made much sense as urban activities. Thus natural seaports facing the European market were the best locations for cities. Smaller towns might survive inland at points along navigable rivers, as secondary collection and distribution points connected to the seaports. For the "common" man or woman, however, there was little reason to be in the city. Their livelihood came from agriculture, and land was still plentiful. The bulk of the population was drawn out to, and held in, the countryside.

"You Can't Get There From Here"

As population spread over wider interior regions while trade goods still had to move through Atlantic seaports, each city's size was determined by distances its merchants could economically reach. Overland transport was thus necessary but it was particularly difficult. At the time of the founding of the nation it was as expensive to ship bulk items a few miles inland from Boston harbor as it was to ship them from London across the ocean to North America!

The problems of inland transportation in this era can be summed up in four words—mud, mountains, water, and woods. Transportation across land could only be accomplished by horse and wagon, and there geography took its toll. Roads do not occur naturally. They need to be constructed. When forests stand in the way, a path must be cleared through timber and brush. Where rivers cross, the route bridges must be constructed, fords discovered, or ferries provided. When snow falls, the route must be cleared. When rain falls, dirt roads become muddy bogs. When erosion and frost destroy the surface, repairs must be made. Where mountains rise, passes must be found or cuts and fills engineered. The growth of the early cities depended on the degree to which they could overcome these obstacles.

The technological possibilities ranged from simple tracks and trails worn smooth by animals and wagons traveling across the country to professionally engineered roadways. The most common surface was, of course, simply dirt—but with rain and snow melt, they became impassable for much of the year. They were often most easily traveled when frozen and covered with a surface of packed snow. In the wettest areas, the surface could be improved by laying logs, side by side, perpendicular to the direction of travel. These "corduroy" roads solved the mud problem, but they were difficult to build and provided an uncomfortable surface. "Plank roads," consisting of sawn planks laid across stringers set directly upon the ground, were another possibility. This created a "boardwalk" or "deck" that was easier to travel on, but the method had its own problems. Contact with the ground and exposure to weather caused early rot, resulting in broken or missing planks, a significant hazard to travelers. The longest lived and consistently best method involved graded road beds with a foundation of stone covered with a gravel surface.

In road construction there was a strong correlation between quality and cost. The better the road, the greater the expense and so the issue was not only what kind of road *could* be built, but what kind *would* be built. Who would undertake the effort and expense? Who would assume the risks? There was a wide network of local, or "common," roads throughout most regions, but they were of low quality and served primarily local routes and needs. They were often built and maintained by local residents "working off" their taxes, designed and built by amateurs and sited for farmers' access to local mills and country stores. They were often no more than tracks through the woods and their quality was uneven at best. To prevent travelers from becoming "stumped," that is, literally and idiomatically unable to continue, the Ohio legislature felt it necessary in 1804 to pass a regulation that stumps left in the middle of roadways must not exceed one foot in height.[1] The common roads were ill-designed and too poorly maintained for long-distance travel. Local communities saw no need to expend their funds to provide roads for the benefit of long-distance travelers and shippers. City merchants and distant customers would benefit from improved roads, but local communities would not pay to build them.

The merchants of Philadelphia came to realize that if they were to continue to thrive they would have to be the suppliers of choice and the port of preference for the increasingly rich and populous growing regions inland from the city. It was clear that without better roads they would not be able to distribute their goods over wide land areas and farmers would not be able to move their surplus crops to the city, but who would provide better roads? Neither local communities nor the state were willing and while a limited liability corporation might, general incorporation laws were not yet a part of the law. At that time it took a special act of the legislature to create one. So in 1792 the merchants of Philadelphia went to the Pennsylvania legislature and persuaded it to grant a charter to a road corporation, allowing for the sale of shares in a private company organized to build and maintain a road between Philadelphia and Lancaster, some sixty miles to the west. That charter solved the problem of capital financing, and it also gave the company the right-of-way privileges necessary to cross large tracts of land.

The company then spent the next two years constructing a high-quality stone and gravel road connecting the two communities. It did some leveling of grade and provided effective drainage, creating a sure and passable route year round. The entire project cost in excess of $300,000, a significant sum for its day, and the company sought to recoup its investment by charging tolls at regular intervals along the route.[2] Collection was accomplished by placing long poles or "pikes" across the road as barriers. Set up to pivot on a standard, they could be turned to allow passage upon payment of the appropriate toll, giving rise to the name of the road, the Lancaster "Turnpike," a term for a toll road that has outlived the particular method of revenue collection. Upon completion, shippers and travelers had a route that permitted consistent movement at speeds averaging two miles per hour. It was a major advance to be able to complete a twenty-mile shipment in a single ten-hour day.

The success of the Lancaster Turnpike stimulated construction of other private toll roads connecting other water port cities with their interior areas. These new transportation channels became important forces in urban development. Cities that invested in road networks to support their commercial base could grow. Those that did not, could not.

Turnpikes could solve the problems of mud and mountains, at least to a degree, but they failed when they came to barriers of water. While smaller streams could be forded, at least in drier seasons of the year, moderate rivers had to be bridged using masonry and wood. Exposure to the elements made these expensive wood beam bridges subject to rot, giving them short-ened useful lives. Builders began covering them in order to protect the beams and extend the lives of their substantial investments. Like turnpikes, bridges were a major expense and were constructed primarily by private companies who attempted to recoup their expense by charging tolls for passage. These companies, like the turnpike companies, usually came into being with charters created by specific legislative acts. The largest rivers, however, were too swift and wide to bridge economically with existing techniques. Ferries were a possibility though they were slow, awkward, uncertain, and often dangerous. Where major rivers ran, roads ended.

Navigable rivers, however, could be travel routes as well as travel obsta-cles, though they worked much better in one direction than the other. Flat-boats, riverboats, and barges of multiple designs could carry goods down river with ease. In the early nineteenth century a load of freight could move downstream from Pittsburgh to New Orleans in as little as one month with minimal human effort, propelled only by the steady current. To travel the same distance by wagon would have taken several times as long, would have required carrying or purchasing along the way extraordinary amounts of feed for the draft animals, and would have resulted in the payment of extensive tolls, *if* there had been a good turnpike covering the same route. Down-river transit was fast, easy, and inexpensive.

Moving goods upriver was another story. If the river was broad, fairly straight, and open to the wind, some sections could be traveled under sail if the conditions were just right. Otherwise, if the current was not too swift, boats could be pushed by poling against the riverbed, a method of propul-sion that worked better on the more solid bedded rivers like the Ohio than on the muddier Mississippi. Where topography permitted they could be towed by horses or oxen walking along towpaths lining the shore. Occa-sionally they would be moved upstream by tying long lines to trees upriver, then pulling the craft forward, fixing it, and moving the rope ahead to another tree. This was slow and grueling work, severely limiting the use of upriver transport.[3] Only the most precious of commodities could justify the cost and effort of upriver shipping. Those journeys were rare. In the very early 1800s, 165 boats came down to New Orleans for every one that left heading north. Most vessels were simply broken up for lumber at their downstream terminus.[4] Thus before 1830, only those cities connected to networks of roads and rivers could capture larger areas as markets, support more commerce, and grow in size and importance. All others were too isolated to grow.

Artificial Rivers

These solutions to the transportation problem were far from perfect. Turn-pike travel, though a vast improvement over common roads, was still slow and tedious. A round trip to a destination one hundred miles distant could still take up to two weeks. The tolls collected at each "pike" quickly added up, and the farther the trip the smaller the effective payload since more feed for the animals had to be carried, displacing other cargo. Even though the expense for shippers was high, the revenues collected by the turnpike companies were often insufficient to cover all of their expenses. The financial success of the Lancaster Turnpike was unusual. River travel was flawed because easy movement could only occur in one direction and effective commerce is by definition two-way. Besides, rivers' flow is highly variable while their routes are wholly inflexible.

What if there were a transportation technology that could combine the energy efficiency of movement over water with the route flexibility of roads? Water can support heavier loads and it presents much less resistance to movement than do wagons on land. Roads, on the other hand, vary their routes to go over or around obstacles and ultimately can connect any two points on land. What if there were a way to create artificial channels of water, free of strong currents, designed to float freight and passengers in both directions, across land or around obstacles, routed exactly where we want them to go?

Europeans had been experimenting with building artificial canals for many years, and while they had many advantages, they were not completely flexible. They required a ready, natural supply of water at the highest point to keep them filled. Both drought and flood could render them unusable for extended periods. They also needed expensive locks to float freight uphill on a series of currentless level steps, with water itself providing the lift to raise the boats. Still, where rivers and roads were inadequate to provide transportation connections between cities and growing inland regions, the commercial interests in those cities began to turn to canals as possible solutions.

In the early 1800s Boston's merchants sought to extend their markets north and west in New England by constructing the Middlesex Canal, tapping the waters of the Merrimack River to reroute commerce with New Hampshire to Boston's harbor. Further south, Charleston's merchants pushed for the development of the Santee and Cooper Canal, as did

Norfolk's merchants for still another one in Virginia. The new canals had many advantages, but low construction cost was not among them. A quality stone-bed road cost between $5,000 and $10,000 per mile to build. A canal cost at least double that amount, perhaps even as much as $30,000 per mile.[5] They remained limited in length. The longest was barely twenty-five miles in distance, and none proved very profitable, though each contributed significantly to the prosperity and growth of their respective cities.[6]

Hawley's Failures, Clinton's Ditch, and the Big Apple

Of the major seaport cities, New York clearly enjoyed the finest natural harbor. Located along the Hudson River it had access via water to a large area upstate, but by the early 1800s the lower Hudson Valley was already well settled and that region had limited prospects for future growth. The center of economic activity was on the move, heading west as population moved out of the Hudson Valley and out of neighboring New England, where thin and rocky soils could not support any more people. The pressure to move on to better land was becoming intense, and the plains of western New York State offered exceptionally productive land, as did the still-wild Ohio and Michigan territories further west. Speculative land companies bought up large tracts and then aided and encouraged New Englanders to relocate to this newly developing region where there was abundant farmland capable of supporting a vast population while still producing significant surpluses, especially of wheat.

If New York City was to maintain its preeminence it needed to develop commercial access to this growing region. It was not the only suitor seeking these markets, however. There were competitors. Products from the Ohio territory could, and did, travel south and west by river, supporting growth in Ohio and Mississippi River towns and feeding a boom in New Orleans. From the whole Great Lakes region and from upstate New York there were two possible paths east to the Atlantic—via Montreal to the north or New York City to the south. Developing access to Lake Erie was the only hope for New York City in this contest. Boats already on Lake Ontario could travel easily to Montreal, and from there up the St. Lawrence River to the Atlantic, but Lake Erie craft could not simply sail onto Lake Ontario. The Niagara River, connecting the two lakes contains the famous falls, later a major attraction to tourists but always a significant obstacle to river transportation. No boat has ever traveled down that route twice. Certainly roads and turnpikes over land were possible, and indeed connecting roads did ultimately link western New York and Lake Erie with New York City, but the travel was tortuous and long. Freight rates were high and long delays were common.

It did not take long for interested parties in New York to begin considering new water connections. The elevation of Lake Erie is only 500 feet above that of the Hudson River at Albany, and discovering that, Gouverneur Morris was probably the first to propose construction of a canal from Lake Erie to the Hudson, binding together the Old Northwest territories, western New York State, and the growing commercial center of New York City. (Gouverneur was his rather presumptuous first name, not his title. He was once a U.S. Senator, "Senator Gouverneur Morris," but he was never "Governor Gouverneur Morris.") His vision was unrealistic and oversimplified, however, imagining a simple "inclined plain" dropping a steady six inches per mile, consistently and gently across the width of New York State.[7] In fact, of course, the landscape undulates and rises over 600 feet to a high point near what is now Rome, before descending again into the valleys of first the Mohawk and finally the Hudson Rivers.

The first realistic vision of a canal came out of the chronic business failures of Jesse Hawley, the failed entrepreneur whose story began this chapter. Deeply in debt and unable to pay, he was sentenced to twenty months in the jail at Canandaigua. With too much time on his hands and a solid first-hand knowledge of the territory through which any such "artificial river" would have to pass, he worked out detailed and realistic plans for a canal and published several treatises outlining his proposal under the pseudonym "Hercules." The essays generated much public debate and ultimately solid support for the idea.[8]

Hercules was an appropriate name for Hawley to use, for a canal successfully constructed across the state would, at that time, have been a feat of mythic proportions. It would have to extend over 360 miles (fifteen times longer than the longest then on the continent), rise over 600 feet and then descend 1,000 more, cross several large rivers, and traverse wilderness territory, and it would cost millions of dollars. With all that against it, perhaps only someone with nothing else to do would invest the time and effort to promote it. What might have been the social consequence had Hawley been more of a business success?

> There I was!—in a Debtor's Prison for the relief of my bail; betrayed and defrauded by my partner; broken down and almost destitute in despondency at the thought that hitherto I had lived to no useful purpose of my own;—accompanied with many pensive reflections that I never want to recall. Recovering myself, I resolved to publish to the world my favorite, fanciful project of an overland canal, for the benefit of my country, and to endure the temporary odium that it would incur.[9]

Hawley's idea took hold and attention shifted from possibility to policy. Who would undertake this task? Who would decide its final form and route? Who would meet the expense? There was no way to aggregate that much private capital, and the federal government refused any support. If it was to be done, the state of New York would have to provide the means. There arose a conflict within the state between those who felt they would clearly benefit economically from the canal and those who feared they would bear more costs than gains. Certainly the merchants of New York City were in the former camp and they turned to De Witt Clinton, ex-mayor of the city, as their primary public spokesman for the proposal. The state finally agreed to the funding, subject to a promise that future tolls would ultimately underwrite the expense.

With financing secured, attention then turned to the question of the best route. New York City interests were firmly opposed to any canal terminating on, or even connecting to, Lake Ontario. They feared that shipping, once on that lake, might never be routed to the canal at all where it would have to be reloaded to smaller canal boats. Any shipping on Lake Ontario could simply continue on to Montreal. By extending the canal along an inland route parallel to the shore, farm surplus brought to canal ports for shipping would never reach Lake Ontario at all and face that temptation. The only logical port left for it would be New York City.

Niagara's powerful falls meant that all eastbound shipping on Lake Erie would always have to off-load at least once, either to portage around the falls or to transfer to an overland canal. If that canal did not connect to Lake Ontario, but only to the Hudson, that would clearly route all freight from the growing west through New York City. It would also assure that New York would be the optimal port of entry for goods headed for the Northwest Territories. New York's merchants considered it a clear victory when the final route of the canal was planned with a Lake Erie terminus and no Ontario connection. To their city, and not to Montreal, would the gains from all this commerce flow. One contest over the canal between *existing* urban centers was settled. There was another between two *potential* cities yet to be resolved.

Where, exactly, would the canal terminate at Lake Erie? There were two possibilities, one a little village of a thousand inhabitants on Big Buffalo Creek and another a few miles away at a place known as Black Rock. Recognizing the potential increase in commerce that would accompany the canal, both villages lobbied vigorously to be selected.[10] One needs to know no history to know how that competition played out, a glance at a modern map will suffice. Buffalo is at the center of a metropolitan area with a population well in excess of a million residents. Black Rock no longer exists as an entity, swallowed long ago by the expanding boundaries of western New York's largest city. The logic of location confers growth on the places that perform the most useful functions. The choice of terminus was certainly beneficial for Buffalo's merchants and probably for music lovers in subsequent generations as well. Schoolchildren learning to sing about that "mule named Sal" plodding the "fifteen miles on the Erie Canal" would have had trouble fitting "from Albany to Black Rock" into the meter of the last line.

The canal was finished in only thirteen years at a total cost of $7.1 million. As sections were completed and opened, traffic built rapidly and tolls from earlier sections helped to finance later ones. The supporters of the Erie Canal proposed still another project to be undertaken simultaneously— a canal connecting the Hudson River to the southern end of Lake Champlain. Not only would this extend New York City's viable trading region into northern New England virtually all the way to Canada, it would also increase the likelihood that the northern regions of the state would support funding for the Erie Canal. By 1819 the Champlain Canal was operating and when the Erie Canal was finished in 1825 a vast new transportation network was completed.

New York City now had low-cost transportation links to northern New England, to the rapidly growing western regions upstate, and ultimately to the whole growing Northwest Territory via the Great Lakes. Freight rates between Buffalo and New York City that had stood at about 20 cents per ton/mile when the canal was proposed fell to less slightly over 1.5 cents upon its completion.[11] Traffic that had been routed south along the Ohio River increasingly moved east through New York.

This meant a vast increase in the business to be done in New York, and a growing need for more people to do it and support it. That quickly became apparent. In a letter written in 1832 Samuel Ruggles observed that "now that Our Statesmen have yoked together the Atlantic and Mississippi Valley by the Erie and Ohio Canals . . . we must forthwith get more hands here [in New York City] to do the work."[12] Only two decades after completion of the canal, the editor of the Albany *Argus* understood its impact and import.

> For only twenty years, the wealth of the teeming West has poured down that avenue, and already it has placed New York on an eminence as the Commercial Emporium of America. . . . So long as New York remains at the head of the western trade . . . it must irresistibly advance in wealth, influence, and population until she will be known not only as the great city of America, but as the *great city of the world.*[13]

There was some hyperbole and a good deal of truth in those observations. New York City had had a population of scarcely 25,000 at the close of the American Revolution. When the canal was completed fifty years later its population had grown to 125,000 and twenty-five years after that it was in excess of half a million.

New York was not the only city affected by the changes in technology and policy. Certainly Buffalo at the other end of the canal experienced rapid growth as did canal ports along the route. Indeed during the 1820s Rochester was, in percentage terms, the fastest-growing city in the nation. Located at the juncture of the Genesee River and the Erie Canal it was particularly well situated. The Genesee Valley produced exceptional wheat yields and had enjoyed a significant increase in population via migration from New England. In what is today downtown Rochester the river drops some 200 feet to the lower elevation of Lake Ontario. The falls provided ample power for a vast milling operation that turned the wheat crops of the region into flour that could be packaged into barrels and shipped down the canal to New York City either for consumption or resale.[14] By the early 1830s a third of all of the flour carried into New York City via the Hudson River trade came from the mills along the Genesee in Rochester.[15]

The financial success of the canal system in New York and its impacts on commerce in its port city led to a boom in canal construction throughout the Northeast and upper Midwest over the next two decades. An extensive system of canals was built through Pennsylvania, Ohio, and Indiana, with lesser systems in other states. When the Erie Canal was begun there were only about one hundred miles of canals in the United States; twenty years after its completion there were over 3,300 miles. Philadelphia and Baltimore, Atlantic seaports in close competition with New York, both realized the importance of having canal systems terminate at their ports and contributed to appropriate segments of the new construction. By 1840, $125 million had been spent connecting cities with hinterlands via artificial waterways. The nation's spatial reorganization had begun.[16]

Agriculture

In contrast to Europe, there was an abundance of land in the young nation, and an acute shortage of agricultural labor; hence Americans were wasteful of the former and conservative of the latter. Land was overcropped and underreplenished. As it was "used up," yields fell and farmers moved westward to new, undeveloped areas. The lands west of the Appalachians were generally more fertile but less accessible. Thus, farming more productive soils also meant coping with greater distances from seaports and markets.

Here, of course, the circle of spatial organization is closed. Without viable access to increasingly distant urban markets and commercial centers, increased yields of cash crops are of little value. Without urban markets the profit potential of rural production could not be realized, and without a growing region in which to sell goods and from which to gather product cities could not expand. Greater agricultural production over wider regions served by better transportation created both the need for, and possibility of, growing cities.

Both North and South were increasingly engaged in commercial farming, but the character of farming differed from region to region. In the North the primary unit was still the "family farm," perhaps with some limited addition of hired labor. Most laborers preferred to work for themselves, however, and so the easy availability of land further west meant that there was always a shortage of labor for hire. There was some early mechanization in terms of wheat harvesting techniques, but all power was still provided by humans and horses. While a few of the best established and wealthiest planters in the East formed agricultural clubs and societies to share new techniques and crop strains in order to farm more "scientifically," the fundamental reason for the increased surplus in the North was the superior quality of the soils in the western region and the increased movement of population in that direction.

This migration was facilitated by large land speculation companies that bought up huge tracts of western land and actively recruited farmers from New England. The companies provided some basic transportation infra-structure, financing, and support to those willing to make the move. As eastern yields per acre fell and population grew, the West provided a neces-sary outlet that was eagerly taken by increasing numbers.

When George Washington took his oath of office, southern agriculture was in a crisis. Organized in a slave-based plantation system needing cash crops to continue, there seemed to be no crop capable of supporting the system. Rice was difficult to grow and required exceptional amounts of labor, indigo was too limited in its market, and tobacco was both destroying the land and falling in price. There were two varieties of cotton available, but only the long-staple variety was commercially viable, and it could only be grown on the sea islands along the Atlantic coast. Short-staple, or "green-seed" cotton, could be grown throughout the region, but its seeds were so sticky and difficult to remove that the fibers were unsuited for use without prohibitive amounts of labor.[17]

Southern planters recognized the potential of upland cotton and desper-ately sought a solution to the seed problem. One of them, a widow by the name of Elizabeth Greene, happened to journey south on the same vessel carrying the aforementioned young Yale graduate to his new career as a private tutor in South Carolina. She urged him to visit at her own plantation and he accepted. Much taken with her, he spent a good deal of time there, and she in turn asked him to seek a solution to the short-staple cotton problem. Over the next few months he devoted much effort to the task, and ultimately he devised a machine that successfully removed the seeds, effectively opening the way for a major alteration in southern agriculture, indeed in American history. The young man was of course Eli Whitney, whose invention took the unusual name of the cotton "gin," shortened from the word "engine."[18]

It would be hard to overestimate the impact that Whitney's invention had on the young United States. In the South, cotton quickly became "king." The expanding textile industry, particularly in Europe, provided a nearly insatiable market. Prices were high and profits irresistible. The output of cotton exploded. Fifteen years after the invention of the cotton gin, total production had increased fiftyfold, virtually all of it for export. By the start of the Civil War, cotton accounted for two thirds of the exports of the entire nation.[19]

Whitney's invention affected the use of space in the South in two important ways. First, there was a major expansion of plantation agriculture further west to virgin lands that were less tired and more productive than the old, worn coastal lands. This, of course, meant an extension of slavery as an institution with the social and political consequences that culminated in the War Between the States. It also meant that the primary cash crop was increasingly distant from southern Atlantic ports. As commercial agriculture shifted west, optimal transport routes shifted to rivers that met ocean waters at Gulf ports. Mobile, Natchez, and New Orleans grew while the older tidewater ports became relatively stagnant. Southern cities, like so much else in southern society, were in the service of cotton exporting. What if that teaching job in New York had come through and Whitney had never met Mrs. Greene? What if he, a native New Englander, had never traveled south? Would the organization of space and history both have been very different? Probably someone else would have found a solution to green-seeded cotton, but it is interesting to speculate on how a seemingly small event can have such large, and unforeseeable, consequences for so many.

Inner Space—The Structure of the Cities

Canals and cotton gins made it possible for larger numbers of people to come together, but there were still other issues to be resolved before they could really live together in larger numbers. First, of course, the competition for city space had to be resolved. Who would be able to use which urban location for what purpose. With no old structure dictated by aristocracies of the past, cities in the new nation developed under the principles of the market alone. Private property rights were well-defined, and contracts were enforced by courts of law. Location thus went to the highest bidder, the one for whom it held the greatest economic advantage, and that advantage was almost always easier access to goods and people when compared with other urban locations. As early cities grew, the problems of access became more compelling.

Both people and goods moved about within cities in the earliest decades of the nation by foot or by wagon. There was no other option. Most people, rich or poor, walked wherever they needed to go within an urban area. Under ideal conditions a journey of a mile would take approximately twenty minutes, but conditions were often somewhat less than ideal. Originally even city streets were plain dirt; they would become mud bogs in wet weather and dust basins in dry. It was not until the mid-1700s that Boston took the radical step of "crowning" its streets to facilitate drainage, an innovation soon copied by other cities. Paving streets was a further step but also an expensive one. Originally the owners of property facing a street were assessed to cover the cost of paving their frontage. In the earliest years, relatively large stones were used, creating a solid surface, but a rough one that was very hard on wagons and passengers. Separate pedestrian walkways provided smoother surfaces, safe from growing wagon traffic, but they added significantly to the expense and were often foregone. As the numbers of pedestrians and wagons, both moving and loading on a city's streets grew, congestion increased travel times and discomfort between any two central points.

Wealthier residents could use carriages to move about, but that only improved comfort at the cost of convenience. Horses needed to be harnessed and cared for each time a trip was taken, a process that consumed time and was expensive. An urgent but unanticipated journey was still faster on foot. The primary transportation advantage of wealth was the ability to afford the higher cost of living in a location convenient to the business center, thus minimizing the need for intracity travel at all.

Bulk items were particularly difficult to move within the city. They had to be transferred by hand from watercraft to relatively small capacity wagons, moved by horse through low-quality streets, often clogged with traffic, and then off-loaded by hand once again. Any business that depended upon moving trade goods any distance from the harbor or riverfront was at a tremendous cost disadvantage. Trading ventures would pay a significant premium for the privilege of doing business at the water transport terminus. Market competition for space thus ensured that commercial activity was packed tightly around the waterfront. Warehouses were built on wharves and cities' commercial and support activities were centered around these harbors. Commerce and trade were why those cities existed. The logic of location, played out in markets, put those two activities at the very center physically as well as conceptually, and located the wealthier participants in those ventures, willing and able to pay a premium to avoid the cost and inconvenience of long travel to their businesses, just beyond the commercial district at the core.

Housing

All of the residents of the growing cities needed housing, and the protections of well-developed laws supported investment in long-lived structures. What kind of construction techniques were then known? City populations could obviously not be housed in the log cabins of frontier design. There were far too few trees within a city, and moving logs any distance over land was prohibitively expensive. Post-and-beam construction was the usual urban alternative. A frame was built from large timbers, joined in a system of mortises and tenons, providing support for a solid house of modest size. It was not practical to build structures on these frames higher than perhaps three stories at most. A great deal of skill was involved in cutting the joints and many hands were needed to place the heavy timbers. Construction was thus more labor intensive, and hence more expensive, than for simpler log structures. The stresses involved required fairly substantial timbers that took a long time to grow and were thus limited in local supply. Too much new construction in any one place would quickly exceed the supply of skilled carpenters and exhaust the local supply of heavy timbers.

Masonry buildings were also possible at that time, though they used both more expensive materials and more overall labor. They had the advantage of being able to be larger, and to be built taller, but since the ground-level walls had to support the weight of all stories above them, they, too, were limited in size. As height increased, usable space on the lower levels decreased as the thicker supporting walls needed at ground level resulted in a diminished interior volume. Masonry structures were also inflexible in design. Since all walls were supporting walls, no rearrangement of space was possible. Still, a few of the wealthiest citizens in early cities built large masonry homes and some commercial and public buildings also used that technique, although most urban housing during this period was post and beam.

What physical structure to a city did all of this generate? For pedestrians, even small increases in distance were a major inconvenience. For moving bulk goods, they were a prohibitive barrier. Hence no urban land was "wasted." It was used either for businesses, houses, or streets connecting the two. As much house as possible was built on each piece of urban land. There were no front yards, entrances were directly off of the street. Houses were built touching each other, sharing common side walls. Building techniques limited vertical expansion and transportation techniques limited horizontal. Cities were compact and low, centered around the harbor with the wealthy in central locations. They were limited in size by walking distance and by the amount of building that could be put on any given piece of land. Even today, a few areas such as the North End in Boston stand as living relics of the city structures that were logical at that time.

Growing Pains

As cities began to grow they faced growing difficulties. There was no central land on which to squeeze more population—it had already been used intensively. There was no way to extend the city vertically by making buildings taller. Any growth had to take place on the periphery and that increased travel distances to central locations. As more and more traffic tried to reach the center, there was increasing congestion on existing central streets. The residents of the older sections still used them and now those of the new sections did as well. Because structures had been built right to the edge of the street, it was not possible to increase street capacity by simply widening central thoroughfares.

Urban growth also brought even more fundamental problems. People need water to live; living people produce waste. Too many in one locale means too little of the former and too much of the latter. City residents, like their rural counterparts, used wells and springs to provide water, privies to dispose of body wastes, and streets to dispose of garbage. These practices are fundamentally inconsistent with high densities of population. More people meant more privies and graveyards, but that led to pollution of local wells and epidemics of disease. Following the European practice, urban dwellers simply dumped their garbage into the streets, making intracity walking considerably less pleasant and effective. Because long-haul bulk shipping was so expensive it was not practical to "truck" it off to some New Jersey landfill. Hogs and goats were allowed to run wild and forage the streets as a way to cope with garbage, but they mostly succeeded in transforming one form of sidewalk pollution into another. If population grew too much, a city could be smothered by its wastes. It was thus becoming clear that public solutions to the organic problems of concentration would have to be developed. Cities were qualitatively different from rural places. Large aggregations were unnatural, and the private solutions of the day were inadequate to support the growing populations.

Philadelphia was the first American city to address the water problem. In 1798 it began construction of a municipally owned system using steam driven pumps to raise water from the Schuylkill River to reservoirs at high spots throughout the city. Water was then distributed via a system of wooden pipes. Within a few years other cities followed suit, though they were divided between ones that chose to charter private corporations (e.g., New York City) and those that opted for municipal ownership. Needless to say the for-profit companies had a worse record of providing water to the poorer sections of town. Cities began to develop primitive sewer systems as well.

The cities that were technologically possible in this era thus faced their own set of special urban hazards. Epidemics of disease were common in dense communities with primitive sanitation systems. Wooden buildings, unseparated by open spaces, heated by fireplaces and lighted by candles, in places with limited water supplies created an ever present danger of catastrophic fire. Many of the young cities of the nation experienced these fires and felt a need to develop policies to control the danger. Volunteer fire companies were established to ensure a rapid response to any blaze, and some cities limited the use of wooden construction in the heart of the city.[20] Other cities imposed nighttime restrictions on open fires. Most cities developed systems of night watchmen in response to the rising fear of crime that came with rising population.

Conclusions

By 1830 America's urban centers had well begun their transition from "Citty upon a Hill" to the place "where we face our failures as a civilized nation." They had grown in size, been located in space, and had taken on shape and form dictated by the technology and policy of the early 1800s. Cities' function then was to provide commercial services to an economy shifting from subsistence toward commercial agriculture. They were dependent on transportation systems made up primarily of water links. In the South, cities formed a perimeter around the region in service to cotton exports. In the North cities were in service to nonplantation cash crops and early manufacturing, located on sea and river ports throughout the growing region. Everywhere cities were low and horizontally dense, with the wealthy living nearest the center. As they grew cities faced growing internal problems of health, safety, and services and had to redefine the role of the public sector in addressing them, but the strongest among them still seemed bright and clean compared to older European cities. The cities that survived and grew most were the ones that made sense in the context in which they were built, but they became fixed structures that perhaps had longer lives than the technologies that defined them.

4

Water, Water, Everywhere

Cities 1830–1870

Even as the canals and turnpikes were being constructed, the seeds of their successors had already been sown. While Jesse Hawley was serving his time in the Canandaigua jail, a failed portrait painter was in London attempting to persuade the British government that submarines offered the best defense against Napoleon's planned invasion of the British Isles. He claimed that he could disable the French fleet while it was still massing in French ports. He had already built and demonstrated a successful submarine in France, but he had become impatient with that government's delay in providing him with funds, a naval commission, and personal protection. Lured to England by a British secret agent's promises of generous support, he had switched sides and was now awaiting his fame and fortune in that country. However, the British government was too slow as well, and so he finally returned home to play a key role in redefining the American transportation system, and the cities based upon it.

While the cotton gin was restructuring southern agriculture and its supporting cities, in the North a dramatic shift in production methods was taking place that would redefine the basic functions of all cities. A new "American System of Manufactures" was introduced by the successful bidder on a government contract for 10,000 muskets. No other bidder had dared to commit to more than a tenth that number. Handicraft production simply could not handle so many different items, but this successful bidder saw the whole process in different terms. He intended to create precision tools that would assure such consistency in the manufacture of parts that they would be interchangeable from one musket to the next. The precision of tools would replace the precision of trained eyes and hands. "In short, the tools which I contemplate are similar to an engraving on copper plates from which may be taken a great number of impressions perceptibly alike."[1] His success in fulfilling that contract marked the beginnings of a shift in the essence of American cities. They would now become important sites for production as well as simply the locus for commerce.

Energy and Motion

By the early nineteenth century Americans had derived just about all the transportation gains they could from muscle, wind, and gravity—the energy sources developed to date. Overland power was supplied by either human or animal muscle, and Americans had already done what they could to increase the efficiency of that source by improving roads, building bridges, and digging canals; there was not much more innovation left there. Gravity, drawing water downhill, could move goods downstream or through locks, but upstream motion still required prohibitive effort. Only in the case of large bodies of open water could the power of the wind be harnessed, and even there the vagaries of weather made transportation uncertain. Significant improvements in transportation could only come from the development of new sources of usable energy.

As early as 1712 simple steam engines were being used to drive mine pumps in England, but they were large, bulky, unreliable, and very inefficient.[2] Steam as a source of power was largely a novelty until late in the century when James Watt, a Scottish instrument maker, built an efficient reciprocating piston engine driven by steam. He also devised a method to transfer the piston's motion into a smooth circular path. It was his engine that first turned chemical energy into usable mechanical power, increasing the energy efficiency of the earliest pump engines by 450 percent.[3] Watt and his partner, Matthew Boulton, realized the import of their invention and fiercely guarded access to the new technology.

The Steamboat

It did not take long for Americans, spreading rapidly across a continent marked by such vast distances and traversed by so many rivers, to see the potential for this technology. If the new engines could be acquired and built, and a way could be devised to apply this source of power to navigation, thousands upon thousands of miles of waterways would be opened for two-directional transport. But first there were monumental technical problems to be solved. The engines had to be relatively light in weight and efficient in operation or the machines and their fuel would leave no room for freight or passengers. Early skeptics joked that a steamboat carrying a load of coal would consume its entire cargo before it reached its destination. To be efficient the engines would have to operate at high pressures, but that increased the danger of boiler explosions and an explosion on a vessel in mid-river would be deadly. To be safe the high-pressure boilers had to be exceedingly strong, but that made them heavier and bulkier.

The vessels themselves had to draw very little water or else they could operate in only a few deep-water channels and even there only at certain times of the year. Finally there was the problem of using the energy produced by the engine to propel the boat forward with enough force to overcome strong river currents. Thus the hull had to provide minimal resistance to the water, be stable and maneuverable, have a large load capacity, be strong enough to withstand the mechanical stresses of the engine and drive train, and still draw minimal water. The problems were clear to all; the solutions were well hidden.

With the advantage of hindsight we know full well what a steam-powered riverboat should look like. Large and elegant, it should be powered by a paddlewheel, usually at the stern, pushing the craft upstream against the currents, probably with a New Orleans jazz band playing on deck. That was less obvious to the first Americans seeking to resolve the dilemma. They tried a number of mechanisms. One of the earliest attempts copied the upstream poling techniques of existing riverboats and attempted to move the craft upstream by mechanically pushing a series of poles against the riverbed itself. Another anticipated the modern JetSki and pumped water out the stern in an attempt to propel the craft forward. Still others tried to use steam to power oscillating stern oars or sets of reciprocating side paddles that mimicked the action of a paddler in a canoe. Needless to say none of these proved to be a viable solution to the complex problem.

That would have to await the return from Europe of Robert Fulton, the failed artist and frustrated submariner. Even though he had built and successfully demonstrated a working three-person submarine, complete with periscope as well as hand-cranked propulsion and dive control systems, he could get neither side to commit to its use.

While waiting in vain for Napoleon to realize the genius of his invention Fulton became acquainted with Robert Livingston, the new American minister plenipotentiary to France. Livingston was a prominent New Yorker with a distinguished history, including administering the Presidential oath of office to George Washington. Livingston was wealthy, a bit of an eccentric, and an amateur mechanic who, like many others, was convinced of the great potential of steam-powered navigation.[4] Clearly, steam-powered vessels plying the Hudson River would be a significant transportation improvement that would generate exceptional profits, but no one had been able to figure out how to make them work. Hoping to accelerate development of the technology, the state of New York in 1787 had granted a fourteen-year monopoly on steam travel on its waters to John Fitch, but he had been unable to build a viable craft.[5] Before leaving for France, Livingston, promising success, had convinced the state legislature to transfer the monopoly to him. When he met Fulton in Paris he quickly realized that this might be the man who could finally help him realize the gains from his new franchise. Livingston had the monopoly; Fulton had the skills.[6] Working together, by 1803 they had built a working model of a steam-powered boat and successfully demonstrated it on the Seine, both up- and downstream.[7] Still the Hudson River project had to wait until Fulton was finally convinced that his submarine ventures with the British would never come to pass.

In 1807 Fulton returned to the United States and was finally ready to demonstrate a steamboat on the Hudson River. His craft was 146 feet in length with two side paddlewheels and a Watt and Boulton 24–horsepower engine amidships. It made the round trip from New York City to Albany in just over sixty hours, averaging better than four miles per hour. In later years the boat was given the name *Clermont* after Livingston's Hudson River estate, but to Fulton it needed no such name. At that time it was simply known as *The Steamboat* because, of course, there were no others.[8]

Soon, however, steam-powered vessels were plying both river routes and coastal waters. In 1811 a craft of Fulton's traveled the 2,000–mile route from Pittsburgh to New Orleans. Four years later a vessel built in Pennsylvania made a complete round trip to New Orleans. Two-way traffic over the whole network of the nation's major rivers was quickly established. Eastern seaports could now be reached from the vast interior of the nation without ever having to go over land. Shortly thereafter the U.S. Supreme Court invalidated state grants of monopoly for steam travel if they affected interstate commerce, and the use of steam power on the nation's waters was opened to all comers. For the next several decades, navigable rivers and lakes became inland highways for both passengers and freight. To be a river port was to be squarely in the path of all this travel. To be a seaport at the mouth of a major river, as were New York and New Orleans, was to be doubly blessed.

The Coming of Railroads

The extra advantage that steamboats and the Erie Canal conferred on New York City was immediately apparent to the other eastern seaport cities. By

the mid-1820s so many of Baltimore's merchants had moved their operations north that the Baltimore newspapers bemoaned the " 'gone-to-New-
York' spirit among its businessmen."⁹ Geography had not graced those
other cities with the same potential for exploiting the new transportation
technologies. Boston was at a disadvantage because New England's major
rivers, all of which lay to its west, ran north and south while the more
rugged topography of New England made construction of an east-west
canal connecting to the Hudson River prohibitive. Baltimore and Charleston
were equally disadvantaged. Water transport to their west was blocked by
the multiple ranges of the whole Appalachian mountain system. Philadelphia tried to build its own canal system to compete with the Erie, creating a
"Main Line" through to Pittsburgh and the Ohio River. The intervening
mountains required a much more complex system, however, with twice as
many locks as the Erie and even a segment where the boats had to be taken
out of the canal and hauled up a series of inclined planes. That complexity
added to the expense of construction and delays in travel.

Disadvantaged by topography, merchants in all those cities were quick to
recognize that if the power harnessed on water by Fulton could be adapted
to overland transportation whole new networks connecting their cities to
interior regions could be developed. Their growth depended upon the development of steam power in a land system to rival the water routes of canals
and steamboats. They were rescued from their geographic disadvantages by
the arrival of the railroad.

The first commercial railroad in the world began operations in England
in 1825. Barely three years later the merchants of Baltimore, in an attempt
to stem the "gone-to-New York" movement, successfully petitioned the
Maryland legislature to charter the Baltimore and Ohio Railroad. Boston
was quick to follow, and by 1831 Massachusetts had chartered several rail
branches to connect its capital city with other parts of New England. It was
clear that a line through to Albany, and thus to the Erie Canal and the
Hudson River, would be crucial, though that connection was not finally
completed until 1841. Further south Charleston's merchants pushed for a
rail connection with the Savannah River in order to provide access to the
growing cotton regions inland.¹⁰

As with steamboats, however, there were a number of technical problems
to be overcome before railroads could become a viable transportation alternative. First, of course, was the fundamental mechanical problem of how to
build an engine on wheels powerful and efficient enough to carry a payload
other than just itself and its fuel. That, of course, meant fairly heavy weights
and high-pressure boilers, and if these were to be produced in large numbers the reliance on Watt and Boulton and the English monopoly had to be

broken. America had to build its own railroads and there the fact that economic development is a seamless, interdependent web became apparent. To build the engines and rolling stock there had to be prior development of basic mining and metal industries. There had to be new machine tools and skilled craftsmen. And of course, those industries could only develop in America when there was a large enough market for heavy products like railroad engines. The development of capital-intensive transportation systems and basic industry went hand in hand. These were not shoes and hats that could be produced in a cottage industry. Railroad engines needed large concentrations of capital equipment and skilled labor at central locations. The logic of location dictated that this production take place in cities. Manufacture of rolling stock became a new heavy industry, concentrated largely in the Middle Atlantic states, that provided something new for cities to export and trade.

Steam engines powerful enough to propel heavy-wheeled vehicles on land were of no value without good operating surfaces on multiple routes. What kind of surfaces would work best and who would provide them? Certainly existing roads and turnpikes were not viable; a more stable surface was needed. The earliest experiments were with granite blocks or simple wooden beams as rails, but they were either too rigid or too fragile. The most common early solution was to use wooden rails, capped with iron for added strength.[11] These, of course, had their own shortcomings. Iron weathered rapidly, often leaving the countryside marked by "parallel ribbons of rust." Iron is also relatively weak, and the weight of passing engines was enough to cause occasional "snakeheads" where the iron caps worked loose and bent upwards, sometimes even piercing the floor of other coaches in the train. After several years the T-shaped, solid iron rail secured to wooden sleepers embedded in gravel became accepted as the best platform. However, only after the productive capacity of iron mills increased was it possible for that standard to be adopted throughout the system.[12]

Is That Any Way to Run a Railroad?

The construction of the early railroads was a monumental task fraught with monumental risks. Who, in a nation of craftsmen and commercial partnerships would be willing and able to undertake it? The capital and conceptual requirements for creating a national network were staggering. No one had enough private resources to build even a modest rail system. No one knew how to manage any endeavor on that large a scale. Private companies, chartered as joint stock companies might be able to amass enough capital to build a small railroad covering a distance of perhaps one hundred miles, and most potential investors thought that an operation of that scale in an industry with untested technology and little history was plenty to manage as well. At the beginning the railroad "network" was really just a group of uncoordinated investments undertaken by relatively small investors pursuing local interests. Even then, they needed significant support from government.

It came in three forms. First, of course, was a willingness to grant liberal corporate charters to private railroad companies. Limited-liability, joint-stock companies were, in that era, still an unusual form of business organization. Each one required a special act of the state legislature before it could form. Most states were willing, indeed anxious, to provide that support to railroad companies, but of course each state's jurisdiction was limited to its own territory. No state could grant a company the right to operate outside its borders. That reinforced the prevailing practice of constructing local and regional systems serving limited areas. State governments also aided railroad construction by allowing the creation of new modes of financing as well as by actually building segments in some places.

In the very earliest years some of the companies perceived themselves as analogous to the turnpike operators. They would provide the track and right-of-way while anyone who wished to travel over it would provide their own vehicles and pay a toll for the use of the track. The traffic control problems soon became obvious, especially along routes with a single track serving both directions of travel. Before long the railroad companies saw the advantage of owning and operating the rolling stock, and they began to move passengers and freight only under their own control and conditions. The advantages of railroads were quickly apparent, and new ones were built with astonishing speed. In 1830 only thirteen miles of track existed in the whole nation. By 1840 over 3,000 miles had been laid. By 1860 the network had grown to more than 30,000 miles. That was an astonishing accomplishment, but taken alone, it overstates the scope of the national railroad system. What had been built was a series of small regional lines that were connected, but were often inconsistent. They were not a coherent whole by any means.

The "gauge" or distance between the two rails is not too important, as long as it is always the same. Like competing computer operating systems, it does not matter so much which one becomes the standard as that all users adopt the same one. Since each rail company built to its own specifications, unless the connecting lines had by chance chosen the same gauge, at the end of one company's track goods had to be transferred to another company's cars in order to "fit" the next segment of track. When the Civil War began there were still at least eleven different gauges of track in the North and several others in the South. A shipment of freight moving from Philadelphia to Charleston ran up against *eight* changes in track width in a journey of less than 700 miles.[13] Long-distance shipping by rail still faced significant problems to say the least. Every company recognized the advantages of a shared standard gauge, and each one was convinced that the gauge in use on its own considerable investment should be the standard.

Steam-powered transportation opened the way for urban growth. It allowed cheaper and easier two-way travel and shipping to the interior. It allowed cities to connect with much larger trading areas. It also created new industries in urban areas that provided the materials used to build and operate the new transportation system and its extensions. Cities were changing in size. They were also changing their function.

Urban Production: The Need for Power and People

In one of the most extraordinary ironies of American history, Eli Whitney, the same man whose cotton gin was responsible for saving plantation agriculture in the South, was also the man who first implemented an innovation that propelled the North toward a growing dependence on urban manufacturing. In fact, to the extent that the Civil War was caused by economic differences, no individual was more responsible for the growing sectional conflict than he. That war was no part of his intention, but it was clearly partly a result of his inventions. A reorganization of space in the United States was not part of his intention either. Just as surely it, too, was a result.

After he built the first cotton gin and its use spread rapidly throughout the South, he spent the next several years engaged in legal battles over patents and licensing fees. Frustrated with the pace of the legal proceedings, he returned to his native New England and sought his fortune in other endeavors, leaving his lawyers to defend his interests in the cotton gin. It was Whitney who first conceived and put into place a manufacturing process using precision machines to create interchangeable parts. It was he that bid on and successfully fulfilled that government contract for 10,000 muskets.

The significance of Whitney's innovation should not be underestimated. He changed forever how work is done, and crucial to our exploration, *where* it is done. He fully understood the challenges of his concept. "I have not only the *Arms* but a large proportion of *Armourers* to make," he wrote.[14] He would not simply buy the output of skilled craftsmen. He would completely change and standardize production processes instead. He would hire workers and teach them the skills necessary for his technique. ". . . [T]he tools themselves shall fashion the work and give to every part its just proportion—which when once accomplished, will give expedition, uniformity, and exactness to the whole."[15]

The increase in productivity and the attendant decline in unit costs arising from this new method of manufacturing quickly became apparent and
the approach was widely copied. Indeed Whitney's concept became known
as the "American System of Manufactures" and by mid-century it was
being studied by delegations of visiting Europeans who sought to adopt it at
home. Soon the whole industrialized world would be reshaped by
Whitney's innovation. He was a central figure in the developing nation, but
the process should not be over-personalized. There were fundamental historical forces pushing for a solution to the problem of upland cotton. There
were many different people experimenting with manufacturing innovations.
Almost certainly others would have stepped in to fill those voids if Whitney
had not, but it is interesting to speculate on how the course of American
political and economic history might have been changed if he had not lost
that first teaching job.

Once firmly established, the requirements of this new method of manufacturing dictated a new logic of location. Large-scale production in a factory setting, using workers with general rather than specific skills, required
a large pool of labor to draw upon. Isolated rural sites had too few people to
satisfy the labor requirements. Only urban ones had enough. The production
of consumer goods collapsed from dispersed household manufacture to
central factories built, most often, in cities. The new, larger factories also
had to ship large quantities of raw materials in and finished product out.
Thus ready access to transportation networks was a major advantage, and
what was already located at the chief nodes of these networks but the
existing commercial cities that felt a new impetus to further growth.

Not all of the newer factories were built in existing cities and towns,
however, for there was one other factor to the new logic that sometimes
brought factories to lightly settled sites and then caused new aggregations to
form and grow up around them. All of this new precision machinery needed
an energy source to drive it. Factories thus needed to be located not only
where there were ample people and ready access to transport; they needed
to be where there was power. That brings us back still once again to the role
of water in shaping urban space.

Water, Water, Everywhere, Nor Only Just to Drink

Water has always been a key element in the logic of location. Biology
dictates that human aggregations can only remain where there is access to
sufficient water. That has always been so. Water had been a key means of
transportation for moving food in and goods out of cities for centuries.
Now, for the first time, water's incredible power potential, when converted

to steam, was being used to drive boats up rivers and move trains over land. When Whitney and his industrial progeny needed power to drive their new machines they turned once again to water, extracting kinetic energy from it as gravity drew it inexorably downhill. It was not only fundamental to new transportation technology, it now became the basis for new forms of manufacturing.

As Whitney designed his new factory, he had two choices for power. He could have driven his "precision" machines with one of the new steam engines, but that would have required the constant purchase and transportation of fuel at considerable expense. His other option would be to use the power of falling water. Millers had used "free" water power to grind their flour for hundreds of years. If Whitney could devise systems of belts and gears to distribute the energy captured by a waterwheel to the various machines he had designed he would avoid these recurring fuel costs.

The most efficient and reliable power came from "breast" wheels where water was captured behind a dam, raised, and then channeled onto the backside of the wheel. This captured energy both from the weight of the water pushing down via gravity and the current pushing forward. Such wheels worked best in midsize rivers. The biggest channels carried so much water it was hard to maintain control; the smallest ones did not deliver a reliable flow. Whitney recognized the advantages of water power over steam and the ready availability of appropriate streams drew him back home to New England. He built his factory in New Haven, Connecticut, because there he found an ample supply of labor, ready access to water transportation, and a stream site well situated to take advantage of water power.

As with most successful innovations, Whitney's approach to manufacturing and his method of harnessing water power were copied in many other industries. As more new machines were invented to reproduce the work of skilled craftsmen in a variety of products, the iron and machine tool industries grew to supply them. More efficient, hydraulic turbines were soon developed, and much of the production of consumer goods in the nation "collapsed" from dispersed households to the new urban factories whose productivity was much higher and whose prices were much lower. Geology and technology combined to define the optimal locations for factories. Cities were not just for commerce anymore. People now gathered in unnatural aggregations in order to produce, not just to trade. Ironically, much of that new production was destined for the farm.

As You Sow . . .

This growth of manufacturing and the increase in the urban population was possible only because of technological improvements in agriculture. There was nothing happening on farms to rival the drama of the new steam engines and their adaptation to railroads and riverboats. Still there was a steady improvement in productivity, made up mostly of incremental changes that cumulatively, over a few decades, changed both farm and city life forever.

The biblical admonition, "as you sow, so shall you reap," is really only qualitatively true. Quantitatively, you may be able to do much more of one than the other. Farming is made up of a series of steps and operations. Ground must be broken, seed planted, weeds controlled, and crops harvested and stored. If they are for market rather than consumption, they must be processed, preserved, and shipped. The output of each farm, and hence the total agricultural surplus available, is limited by the productivity of labor in the least productive phase. In makes no sense to plow more land than you can plant or to sow more than you can harvest unless there will be an assured supply of extra labor to help at crucial times. With abundant land and limited labor for hire, most farming households in this era had to depend upon themselves for the tasks of all seasons. Only if they could somehow accomplish more in a day could they produce more crops in a year.

Busting Sod

The farm cycle begins with preparing the soil, and for thousands of years that has meant some type of plowing. At the beginning of this period plows were heavy, fragile, awkward to operate, and difficult to repair. Many were made of wood and were simply ineffective in the heavier Midwest soils. They required strong draft animals and skilled handlers. Farmer after farmer spent the time walking behind the plow thinking about ways to improve the implement. By 1855 over 350 different improvements in the basic plow had been patented and a number of new urban manufacturers had begun producing a variety of new models for sale.[16] As early as the 1830s individual factories in Pittsburgh and Worcester were turning out 15,000 to 20,000 cast iron plows a year.[17]

Further west, in the village of Grand Detour, Illinois, a blacksmith by the name of John Deere began building polished-steel plows that were lighter, easier to handle, and yet strong enough to break even the thick prairie sod. By 1847 demand for his plows was so great that he relocated his operations to a new factory in Moline on the Mississippi River. There he had a ready flow of water to power his precision machines and easy access to water routes for bringing in bituminous coal for his forges and hardwood for frames. Finished product could be shipped out via the same river routes. A decade later he was employing sixty-five workers and shipping over 13,000 polished-steel plows a year. Eventually "sulky" models were added, where the farmer rode the plow and used levers to adjust depth and angle. They were so efficient that significantly less animal power was needed to pull them. Each farmer could now plow a much larger area, and with the development of seed drills and broadcast spreaders, could plant much more. John Deere changed, for thousands upon thousands of American farmers, what they could sow.[18]

... So Shall You Reap

It took the efforts of another tinkerer to change what they could reap. In the first years of the nineteenth century a young boy living on a farm in Virginia watched his father experiment with a variety of mechanical devices for harvesting wheat. By the time he had reached his adolescence he found himself spending long days under a hot sun swinging a heavy scythe. His interest in perfecting a mechanical reaper was by then personal as well as financial. Cyrus McCormick was as anxious to avoid the hard labor as to make a fortune. He tried several different designs for a mechanical reaper before, in 1831, he was finally successful. His contribution was not really a new invention but a clever combination of seven different elements into a single horse-drawn machine that vastly increased the amount of land that could be harvested with a given amount of labor. McCormick's innovation raised the productivity of the most labor-intensive part of agriculture. Each farmer could now provide daily bread for a much larger number of urban workers, for now he actually could reap as much as he could sow.

There was a close tie between changes on the farm and in the city. The increase in the agricultural surplus could be realized, of course, only if the plows and reapers were widely available and easily affordable by most farmers. That meant they had to be inexpensive to manufacture and to ship. Here, of course, the circle is again closed. Using the "American System of Manufactures" with precision machines producing interchangeable parts at low cost, McCormick in 1848 established a reaper factory in Chicago, a growing urban area. Chicago was a big enough city to assure a steady pool of labor to operate the machines. From Chicago he could ship his products throughout the nation via rail or the Great Lakes, in turn connecting with major river routes or canals.

Further downstate John Deere's factory had became a beacon to easterners and even Europeans seeking employment, attracting them to Moline. His factory produced something new for the city to trade and allowed it to support a growing population. By 1880 the Deere Company had over 800 employees producing and selling machines to farmers all over the nation. Other urban factories produced other implements that raised the productivity of agricultural labor. With improved transportation, no farm was beyond their reach. The nation was being reorganized.

The three conditions that permit cities to form and grow—an agricultural surplus, an ability to produce ample trade goods, and a transportation system to move people and things—are all parts of the same whole. They feed off of each other. None develops without corresponding changes in the others. Technology in all three areas combined during this period to allow larger and larger aggregations to form and be sustained. Machines produced in cities raised the productivity of American farmers, releasing labor from the land to fill the new industrial jobs. The new transportation systems allowed farm and factory output to move over great distances while the production of the components of those systems added new industries, based on the new American System of Manufactures, to urban areas. When all were added together the United States was well on the path to becoming an urban nation.

Getting Around in Town: Intracity Transportation

As more and more people moved into the major cities they found it harder and harder to get around within them. These were still walking cities, and in even the biggest ones development had rarely extended more than two miles from the center. As population grew, more people crowded into, and tried to move around within, the same area. Urban streets were still mostly unpaved. Signal lights and traffic cops were unknown; the right-of-way simply went to the most aggressive. Indeed one contemporary wrote that to cross Broadway in 1837 ". . . you must button your coat tight about you, see that your shoes are secure at the heels, settle your hat firmly on your head, look up street and down street, at the self-same moment, to see what carts and carriages are upon you, and then run for your life."[19] Urban traffic was becoming a major problem.

In 1827 Abraham Bower added a new ingredient to the urban transportation stew. He began running a stagecoach along Broadway offering rides for a fixed fee to travelers wishing to move up and down Manhattan, and intracity public transportation was born.[20] The advantages of a public wagon over a private carriage were clear; there was a significant increase in convenience and a decrease in cost for any single rider. There was no need to harness up a team and carriage whenever one wanted to travel, and no need to "store" them at either end of the journey. This "omnibus," as it came to be called, proved so popular that before long a multitude of others had joined Bower traveling up and down streets throughout American cities. Twenty-five years after that first run, over 120,000 passengers a day were riding omnibuses on the streets of New York.[21]

Abraham Bower had barely harnessed his horses to that first omnibus when John Mason came up with an improvement. By first laying special tracks in the road, the speed and comfort of the trip could be increased. Because there was less drag, the same horses could pull twice as many passengers so operating costs would be lower. However, the initial costs were far higher than simply starting an omnibus route, and like the omnibuses it had to share the right-of-way with all other traffic. Still, after the canal and steamboat, the explosion of commerce in New York was so great that the growing need for improved transportation seemed certain to justify the capital expense. By the mid-1830s Mason was operating the nation's first horse-drawn, street railway, again in Manhattan.

At the time of the Civil War, horse/rail networks were operating in eight different cities. Because of the heavy investment in rails their routes were inflexible, and because commuters traveling longer distances came to rely so heavily on them, they developed fixed and regular schedules.[22] They were more reliable than omnibuses and thus commuters came to rely more heavily on them. With dependable travel at average speeds in excess of six miles an hour the borders of a city could easily expand wherever street railways were laid. The horsecar increased the effective radius of development by at least 50 percent. However, the costs of a daily commute were high compared to wages, and it was the wealthy who were most likely to take advantage of this easier transportation to move to lower cost land farther outside the city. People began to build new neighborhoods of larger homes connected to the commercial areas via the new transportation.

There was, of course, one mode of travel far faster and more comfortable than even the horsecar. Initially built to carry freight between cities, by mid-century steam-powered railroads ran into the center of all of America's major cities. Small towns along the line that had been effectively isolated from the central city now were regular stops along a new and vastly more efficient pathway. Because they required a separate right-of-way, railroads were ill-suited to moving passengers within a city on a grid of tracks, but they were ideal for moving them into and out of the city. The Boston and Worcester pioneered special annual commuter tickets in 1838, and five years later it was running several special commuter trains a day between Boston and outlying towns that quickly became the first real "suburbs."[23] Now the central city was accessible to a much larger area. Almost immediately contemporary observers recognized that this would change the shape and scale of the city. One predicted that "[i]f by horse one can go eight miles per hour, the diameter [of the potential city] becomes sixteen miles, and area two hundred and one square miles; and if by railroad he moves thirty miles per hour, the diameter becomes sixty miles, and the area 2,827."[24]

There was an element of truth in this observation, but its author was better at arithmetic than he was at urban analysis. Besides the obvious fact that most major cities were water ports, thus limiting development on at least the water side of downtown, a city commute was still not possible from most points within that thirty-mile circle. The usable area was only the accessible area. Cities still could not sprawl. They could only extend themselves in linear fashion along the rail lines, for while steam trains were fast once a traveler was on board, he or she still had to walk to the station. The new urban development was like the addition of strings of beads, joined in the center of the city and extending out beyond the old urban boundaries. Along the way, scattered, relatively dense nodes grew up around rail stops, but a location some miles from the city that was not within walking distance of a rail line was no more likely to be developed now than before. The expanding cities looked more like long-legged spiders than evenly spreading orbs. The usable area around a city was greater, to be sure, but it was still only a fraction of the whole circle.

One-Way Development

Intracity transportation investments changed the character of cities as well as their size. For cities to expand beyond walking scale they had to embark on a one-way journey of development, and they had to sign on for a package tour. More population could reside in a city only if it grew to include more space, but that edge space was usable only when it became accessible as the new transportation systems connected it to the rest of the city. The significant investments in extended transportation were only sustainable if urban development at their outer end followed. Of course, once relocated there the new residents were wholly dependent upon the transportation systems.

What began as a new convenience that allowed people to live in previously inaccessible places, became a necessity to prevent them from being isolated there. Access to the central city then depended on the continued availability of the new transport modes. To eliminate transportation would have been to choke off the community. A twelve-mile walk to work down the railroad tracks was not feasible. Once built up around it, transport was the lifeblood of the new developments.

New Urban Housing

With the growth of commerce and expansion of industry it now made sense for more people to live in urban settings and for much of the expansion to take place in those areas at the edge of the older cities. The growth of population meant a need for much more new urban housing as well, and that new demand could only be met by changes in construction technology. Large timber, post-and-beam construction requiring highly skilled carpenters could not have kept up with that need. Large timbers take time to grow. They are expensive to transport and hard to join. Especially in the newer communities to the west, there was a shortage of beams and of skilled workers. If the new residents were to have houses they would have to be built with different techniques. There is some disagreement as to who was the very first to devise the "modern" solution, but starting in the 1830s Chicago builders pioneered a new method of construction using a network of much smaller pieces of lumber—the forerunners of the standard "2 by 4." They joined them with nails rather than intricate mortises and tenons. Known as balloon-frame construction, this technique significantly decreased both the labor and material costs of construction and made use of much more abundant small-dimension lumber.[25] The houses thus built were "as firm as any of the old frames of New England with posts and beams sixteen inches square."[26] Indeed, by mid-century the practice was so widespread that contemporaries would claim that "[i]f it had not been for the knowledge of balloon frames Chicago and San Francisco could never have arisen from little villages to great cities."[27]

The ability to utilize this technique on a large scale depended of course on the simultaneous increase in the industrial capacity to produce nails and woodworking machinery, which in turn depended, of course, on growth in the "American System of Manufactures." In his fascinating account of modern construction, Tracy Kidder noted that in the early nineteenth century each nail was made by hand and was so valuable that records can be found of their explicit inclusion in wills and estates as important treasures.[28] Only when the costs fell and availability of materials rose sufficiently could this new form of construction be used to produce enough new housing for the increasing urban populations.

In the center of some cities land was so expensive that it justified the cost of putting more building on each lot and larger and higher masonry and brick buildings were added downtown. The burden of having to balance increased height with greater wall mass was finally overcome in 1848 when

James Borgardus designed a five-story building in New York supported by cast-iron columns rather than masonry walls. He and others quickly developed construction techniques using frames of cast iron to support higher and larger buildings in the centers of these newly growing cities.[29]

However, even after all this, cities' horizontal expansion was still limited and taller buildings were still expensive to build and impractical to use. As more and more people kept moving to cities the only way to fit them all in was to increase crowding in existing buildings. That was especially so for poorer migrants and immigrants now coming to the city seeking work in the new urban industries. Land and housing were scarce and expensive and the costs of the new transportation prohibitive for the poor. Thus the density of central places like lower Manhattan doubled from early to mid-century. By 1815 the very first urban slums appeared in New York, and after 1830 all of the major Eastern cities began to develop neighborhoods of high-density, low-quality housing, occupied by the poor.[30] That crowding plus the availability of cheaper land on the fringes of the city and easier transportation to it encouraged more and more of the wealthier citizens to vacate the oldest neighborhoods. "Filtering," the process whereby housing deteriorates in quality, is broken up into higher density units, and passes down to lower income groups, had begun, and American cities would never again be the same.

Industrial employment, located within cities, attracted to the city both surplus farm and foreign workers seeking better lives. In industries like clothing, subcontracting led to a growth in sweatshop labor that took advantage of growing populations of desperate workers. Industrialization did not create poverty; for most of human history poverty had been the normal condition for the vast majority of people. It did relocate it, however, and served to begin concentrating it in particular urban neighborhoods.

Living Together

The biological stresses and social conflicts associated with high-density living remained and intensified as cities grew. They could not be ignored much longer. Even though water systems were being extended, they often remained inadequate and unsanitary. During his first months in office, Abraham Lincoln was devastated when his son, Willie, sickened and died from typhoid fever, contracted through contaminated water in the White House. Even the president of the United States was not exempt from the fundamental dangers of aggregated living.[31] By 1849 New York City still had only seventy miles of sewers. By 1857 sewer mileage had doubled, but it still served less than one quarter of the total population and that system consisted only of pipes to move raw sewage to the river. There was still no attempt to treat it. Not until 1866 was the New York Metropolitan Board of Health established, and then only in response to a deadly cholera epidemic. Only when the population was approaching 1 million did the new board finally move to rid the city streets of the hogs that had been the primary sanitation crews and to adopt a more systematic approach to public health.[32]

City government was thus also being transformed. It was becoming apparent that some kind of collective response to the problems of concentrated living would be required. In addition to simple sanitation, the growth in numbers and the concentrations of poverty contributed to a rising concern with urban crime. The old system of community "watchmen" was inadequate and major cities began forming professional police forces. New York City was again first in 1844, followed over the next decade by Philadelphia, Boston, and Baltimore.[33]

High-density, wood frame houses, each set close by its neighbors, in areas where water supplies were limited increased the dangers of fire, and growing cities increased the areas over which fires could rage. In 1871 Chicago's Great Fire consumed all of the buildings within a 1,700–acre area.[34] Two thirds of the city was leveled and 100,000 of its citizens were left homeless.[35] The following year Boston suffered a catastrophic conflagration. Fear of fire in dense wooden cities of that size created a need for a governmental response. To prevent fires from spreading destruction and death over wide areas, cities began to implement systematic fire codes affecting the construction and maintenance of urban buildings. To combat fires once started, they abandoned the old volunteer companies and replaced them with professional firefighters under city employ. This meant more complex administrative structures and a need for tax revenues to support them. As they became bigger spatially, cities were pressed to become more complex politically.

An Aggregating Nation

As the Civil War era was drawing to a close, the spatial structure of the nation had been as dramatically redefined as had its political and economic systems. By 1870 fully 25 percent of the entire nation's population lived in urban areas, compared with less than 5 percent a century before. The urban population had increased fiftyfold over that period and was now two and a half times the population of the whole nation at the time of the American Revolution. Major cities like New York and Boston had grown very rapidly, but much of the urbanization had taken place in smaller communities along rivers and streams. In the Northeast, waterpower drew people from farms to mill towns like Holyoke, Chicopee, North Adams, and of course,

Lowell. Indeed Massachusetts and Rhode Island, reflecting the abundance of viable waterpower sites, were already half urbanized as early as 1850. Further west other smaller cities along rivers now opened to trade by steamboats flourished. St. Louis, Pittsburgh, Wheeling, Natchez, and Louisville had grown rapidly, and the seaports at the end of each river's run shared in their growth. Mobile and New Orleans boomed.

Railroads defined which of the inland cities would prosper and which would not. While railroads, especially in the early part of this era, mostly served as regional systems in service to water transportation, wherever rail lines met people aggregated. Early "boosters" of individual cities recognized this connection and sought to profit from it. William Ogden, the first mayor of Chicago, was instrumental in creating the conditions for its phenomenal growth in the mid-1800s. He and his partners built over one hundred miles of city streets, constructed numerous bridges, promoted canals, and founded both a medical school and the University of Chicago. They built railroad companies and rail networks connecting the new city to vast areas of the country. Ogden became the president of the Union Pacific organized to construct the first transcontinental railroad, and he made sure that its route would go through Chicago.

His aggressive foresight gave that city a competitive advantage over other growing midwestern aggregations, such as St. Louis, that mistakenly hitched their futures to continued river travel.[36] The results of his efforts were phenomenal. In 1830 Chicago had a population of less than one hundred. Forty years later the population was approaching 300,000 people, housed in new balloon-frame structures, moved about by horsecars and railroads, employed in or supporting new industries connected to their resources and markets by a vast network of rail and water.

Changing Cities

The shift to industrial production did not just change the number and size of cities in America, it caused fundamental qualitative change as well. There was now a growing spatial separation between production and residence. With craft production, master and apprentice often lived in the same household and worked there together. In industrial cities, workers and owners lived separate both from work sites and from each other. As cities and factories grew in size, these separations, in every sense of the word, increased. Members of a household were now likely to scatter during the day, performing their various functions in diverse locations throughout the urban area, often having to rely on the new transportation networks to carry them back and forth.

These growing aggregations and the qualitative changes in their character were the immediate result of individual efforts, but they were the inevitable results of collective forces. In each city there were significant decisions made by individuals who saw the future of urban places and acted to shape their towns accordingly. We live today in cities that reflect actions taken a century or more ago by a multitude of these identifiable people, but the broad dimensions of their future (our present) were determined long before they, individually, saw it. If Deere or McCormick or Fulton or Ogden or Bowers had not acted, someone else would have. Conditions were ripe for urban change; those people saw the forces but they did not create them. There is little to be gained, therefore, by our seeking to place credit or blame for the changes they wrought in America. The consequences that their actions have had for cities today were beyond their ability to foresee or understand. They were part of a larger current.

Cities at Their Limits

All these American cities were still horizontally dense and relatively low in height. In the mill towns, dense housing for the workers was clustered tightly around the factories, minimizing the time it took to walk to and from work, often in the dark and cold. In the larger cities new intracity transportation systems had extended their spread and for the first time some of the wealthier citizens had taken advantage of this mobility to escape the crowding of the city. Frederick Law Olmstead, the famous landscape architect who had designed New York's Central Park, was later hired to design "Riverside," a new planned suburb of Chicago. In reaction to the regimentation of regular grids he envisioned a more rural and irregular arrangement that would recapture some of the aesthetic appeal of village life. To "waste" space was a luxury only the wealthy could afford, however, and the developers could only survive by limiting construction to upper-income housing. Back in the city, the middle class and the poor lived in houses more closely built and densely occupied. Few tall buildings existed, and those that did were limited to five or six stories.

Urban space was being used about as intensively as was possible. By 1870 the largest cities already held as many people as could reasonably fit. It would not be possible to grow much more without expanding the usable urban area. The population of the mill towns was limited by the amount of power that could be derived from any given water site. They could not grow bigger as long as falling water drove their machines. Cities could not grow further and reorganize again until there were fundamental changes in the way urban structures were built, urban populations were transported, and urban production was powered. Those changes were just around the corner.

5

Electricity and Steel

1870 Through the First World War

Railroads: From Fragments to a Whole

In February of 1861, with secession fever spreading through the South, Abraham Lincoln set out from Illinois to travel to Washington, D.C., there to take the oath of office as the nation's sixteenth president. He and the nation faced problems of staggering proportions, but before he could engage them he first had to solve the lesser problem of how to travel. He wanted to "meet the people" all along the route and reassure them of his commitment to the Union and the Constitution. It was important that he begin his administration with an air of confidence and dignity. Yet the state of the nation's transportation systems at that moment was indirectly responsible for causing him to fall short of that goal. When it came time for him to leave Illinois there was no longer any question as to the fastest and best mode of transportation. Riverboats were too slow and indirect and, given the weather at that time of year, too uncertain. The Erie Canal would have been slow even if it were not still clogged with ice, besides its very narrow corridor would have prevented him from making politically important stops in scattered key cities along the way. Long-distance travel was clearly best accomplished over the nation's patchwork system of rail lines that by then were partially joined though not yet fully integrated.

Each railroad had been built as an investment by a company of modest size, and each company had built its line to serve a local need. No one had tried to build a rail *system,* and what had resulted was something less than the sum of its parts. Typically, where one line ended, passengers and freight had to transfer to another in order to continue their journey. Indeed that often meant having to transfer between two different rail stations in the same city. To reach Washington in February of 1861 Lincoln had to travel through Baltimore, a city rife with secessionist sentiment and Southern sympathizers, served by separate and independent rail lines. He would arrive from Philadelphia at the Calvert Street Stadium on the Philadelphia, Wilmington & Baltimore and would have to leave on the Baltimore & Ohio, departing from the Camden Street Station across town. There were no bulletproof limousines or presidential helicopters in his day. The president-elect of the United States, like everyone else, had to get off of one train and walk across town to another to complete a through journey by rail.

Allan Pinkerton, the head of a private detective agency, uncovered evidence of a plot to assassinate Lincoln as he walked through the streets of Baltimore between train stations. Unwilling to cancel his scheduled appearances along the route and thus avoid Baltimore altogether, Lincoln reluctantly compromised with his advisors and agreed to change the timing of his arrival and to wear a disguise as he transferred between stations. So at 3:30 in the morning, after traveling incognito in a compartment that had been reserved for an unnamed "invalid passenger," the president-elect and his personal bodyguard walked through downtown Baltimore, with Lincoln abandoning his trademark stovepipe hat in favor of a soft cap and cape. When news sources reported that the new president had arrived to assume power in the troubled nation in such an undignified fashion his prestige clearly suffered. It took some time to undo the damage to his stature.[1] It took even longer to meld the various bits and pieces of the railroad network into a unified national system. That consolidation came not from any single change but as the cumulative result of a series of developments.

Railroads: Coordinated and Consolidated

First, of course, was the need to settle on a standard gauge so that the costly delays of transferring from one line to another could be reduced. The rail companies in New England had recognized the potential advantages of using the same gauge and had laid their tracks a uniform 4 feet 8–1/4 inches apart. After the Civil War rail lines in other parts of the nation began adopting that standard, and when Southern railroads finally acceded in 1886, one of the main obstacles to a national rail system was finally overcome. While a major expense, the relaying of track lines with the new gauge was not quite as burdensome as it may, at first glance, appear. Iron rails with limited life spans were still the norm as this period began, and they had to be replaced at regular intervals anyway. Once the companies were committed to the new gauge, it could be modified as the rails were replaced, either with new iron, or increasingly with stronger steel. The new agreement on a standard gauge was not enough to complete a national rail system, however. What advantage is to be gained from standardizing the gauge on all tracks if they never physically meet? Someone would have to overcome the reluctance of competing companies to merge into a single system.

Cornelius Vanderbilt was a man who always liked to be in control. Starting as a ferryboat captain in New York harbor, he went on to make a great fortune in trans-Atlantic steam shipping before turning his attention to consolidating the small regional railroads of mid-century into a coherent system. He gained control of the New York Central and soon ruled over a vast transportation empire. His breadth of experience led him to see transportation as a system needing coordination, though he generally preferred that that occur under his personal direction. Seeking that end, he helped close another gap in the rail network shortly before his death in the 1870s.

Independent railroads were still entering cities in both the North and South without joining anywhere. Philadelphia, for example, was the junction point of four separate rail lines entering the city, but no two of them ever physically met. In Richmond, Virginia, the old capital of the Confederacy the situation was the same. This proliferation of unconnected rail lines entering major cities was the norm. As inconvenient as it was for travelers and shippers, that situation provided a great deal of business for local interests. Porters, wagoneers, teamsters and cab drivers, restaurateurs and innkeepers, merchants and shopkeepers, all made a living from passengers and freight forced to disembark and pass through town between train stations. They clearly saw that if passengers did not have to get off, they would not leave much money behind. It took someone as determined as Vanderbilt to overcome strong local resistance to through connections. In the early 1870s he finally persuaded the other rail lines serving New York City to share the terminal facilities of his New York Central in a newly built Grand Central Depot.[2] Other cities reluctantly followed and by the end of the decade a *Union* Station was the norm, though it came too late to spare Lincoln his ignominious early morning walk through the streets of Baltimore.

Lowered Cost—Increased Revenue

At first new railroad profits could be made by building new lines—using standard-gauge tracks joined to the existing network. In the quarter century after the Civil War an additional 140,000 miles of track was laid. By then the basic network for the whole nation was in place, and increased profit from the system could only come from cutting the per ton/mile costs of operation or increasing the use of existing lines. Lower costs allowed cheaper rates and a chance to capture business from competing water routes. Several developments contributed to the ascendancy of rails. The old iron-capped wooden rails and even cast-iron T rails were limited in their durability and carrying capacity. While initially more expensive, steel T rails could carry much heavier loads and had a useful life more than ten times longer than iron ones.[3] As steel production grew and the old iron rails were replaced by steel, set at the now standard gauge, railroads provided rapid, reliable, all-weather transportation throughout the nation. The new rails could carry heavier loads pulled by more powerful engines. The development of safety couplers and air brakes allowed the safe operation of much longer trains.

Key trunk lines like the New York Central expanded their capacity by laying four complete lines of track along their right-of-way for separate freight and passenger traffic in each direction.[4] The development of the telegraph and of signal systems allowed centralized traffic control, permitting the safe operation of more trains on the same tracks at one time. Before that, information about trains' movements in the system could not travel any faster than the trains themselves. Consolidated ownership also contributed to the ability to provide more efficient planning for through routes. There was still one more obstacle to be overcome before a truly national system was in place.

Bridging the Final Gap

Trains were fast overtaking river steamboats as the prime moving force for the nation. Once the track network was in place, trains were faster, surer, and safer. With all of the new improvements they were now becoming cheaper as well. But rivers were not just alternatives to rail, they were also barriers to it. Heavy bridges over the nation's largest rivers taxed materials and building techniques to the limit. They were expensive to construct and difficult to maintain, yet without them a train reaching a large river either had to transfer its payload to riverboats or shuttle the rolling stock across the river on special ferries resulting in extra expense and delay. Without bridges, key river ports were central locations providing necessary transportation services, but ones the railroads would have gladly foregone. A conflict between river communities and railroads was inevitable.

The first bridge over the Mississippi was built by the Rock Island Line in 1856. It was a cumbersome wooden affair, built in sections across a series of rocky islands. River shippers saw it as a clear danger to their economic vitality as well as a potential hazard to navigation. Shortly after it was completed, the steamboat *Effie Allen* rammed the bridge and set it afire, damaging it beyond any possibility of repair. The owners of the boat then sued the railroad for damages, and sought a legal prohibition against any further attempts to build bridges across the river. The railroad hired a down-state lawyer to defend it in the lawsuit. The lawyer, of course, was Abraham Lincoln who could not seem to extricate himself from the transportation problems of his day. He won the suit when he convinced at least some members of the jury that the collision was an intentional act of sabotage by the shippers. The U.S. Supreme Court later took the case on appeal and ruled in favor of railroads' right to bridge rivers.[5]

As engineering skills improved and the availability of better construction materials increased over the next decades, the glory days of many of the river towns were numbered. When the Missouri River was bridged at Omaha in 1872 there was finally an unbroken rail link from the Atlantic all the way to the Pacific. As more spans over the major midwest rivers were constructed and the broad coastal mouths of eastern channels were bridged, the rail network became complete. By the turn of the century there was a coherent national system that allowed shippers and passengers direct access between virtually any two points in the country.

The use of trains for both passengers and freight grew at a phenomenal rate during the late nineteenth and early twentieth centuries. In 1850 ton/miles shipped by rail were perhaps one tenth the total for water. Forty years later, rail shipments were twice the total for water—a twentyfold increase in relative terms. In absolute terms the growth of rail was vastly greater. Total freight shipments were approximately 350 million ton miles in 1850. They had grown to 80 billion ton miles by 1890, and by 1910 they were over 250 billion—a 71,000 percent increase. Freight rates fell consistently throughout this period. By 1910 they had fallen by two thirds relative to their level in 1870. Passenger rates fell by one third over the same period.[6]

Testing the Nation's Metal

The expansion of the rail system, the shift to steel rails, and the construction of bridges over the major rivers that had separated the land into self-contained regions—none of that would have been possible without significant advances in practical metallurgy. For thousands of years humans had known about the basic properties of iron and had tried to develop techniques to exploit the metal to their advantage. Commercial production came to North America almost with the first Europeans. The first iron works in colonial America was built in Saugus, Massachusetts, in 1645. Because the basic materials for iron smelting, ore and fuel, are widely distributed and because the costs of shipping bulk items over land were so high, small firms tended to develop, supplying mainly local needs.

In 1860 there were 268 small furnaces in operation, scattered widely throughout the nation, employing nearly 16,000 workers and producing in the aggregate just under 1 million tons of iron. Steel has greater strength and resiliency than iron, but it is much more difficult and costly to make. In 1860 there were only thirteen American establishments making steel and their combined output was less than 12,000 tons, barely 1 percent of the total iron produced that year.[7]

By the 1880s the huge deposits of higher quality ores in the upper peninsula of Michigan had been developed, and as transportation evolved to make bulk shipments feasible, ore was shipped to sites where it could be easily combined with the bituminous coal. Cities in western Pennsylvania, particularly Pittsburgh, became concentrated centers of steel production, combining their coal deposits with the "imported" ores, shipping resources in and product out via easy river and rail transportation. They had something new to trade in order to support their own growth.

Bessemer's Bombs

Pittsburgh owes much of its economic reorientation from river commerce to steel production to the efforts of an English inventor. Henry Bessemer was typical of innovators of the nineteenth century. He worked in a variety of fields and had already been granted a number of patents while he was still a young man. He began his search for improvements in steel making techniques almost by accident. He had devised a method of building elongated projectiles that could be fired from existing smooth-bore cannon. By providing carefully placed vents in the shells, he believed he could induce rotation in flight, greatly improving accuracy without undertaking the expense of cutting rifling grooves into the barrels of the guns. He persuaded Napoleon III to finance prototypes and tests of his concept, and in 1855 he carried two of his projectiles to France to be fired from a standard 4.75–inch smooth-bore cannon. The test was a success in terms of projectile behavior, but Bessemer was confronted with a new concern. The French commander felt that even though the shells worked as predicted, their use would be too dangerous because the guns themselves might be unable to withstand the stresses of firing such heavy projectiles. He questioned Bessemer about the possibility of making guns stronger than the existing cast-iron ones. Bessemer had no immediate answer to this query, and so to further the use of his new bombs he had to turn his attention to questions of basic ferrous metallurgy.[8]

Steel of sufficient quality and affordability to meet his need was difficult to produce because two fundamental problems were unsolved—how to generate heat in excess of 2,500° Fahrenheit and how to build a crucible able to contain material at that temperature without melting. Bessemer was able to devise a method of forcing heated air directly into the molten metal contained in furnaces made of special clay. There the added oxygen increased the rate of combustion and hence the temperature to levels sufficient to boil off remaining impurities. Finally pure carbon or other metals could then be added to form different grades of alloy steels. In 1864 the first Bessemer converter in the United States began operating, and it was soon copied many times over. Bessemer's process, coupled with improvements in the machinery needed to shape steel and iron in rolling mills, lead to an explosion in the nation's capacity to produce, and effectively use, both iron and steel.

It also lead to a concentration of production into fewer and larger facilities. A Bessemer furnace requires too much investment for a small operation to be run profitably. Thus the average size of blast furnaces rose as rapidly as did the total output of the nation. In 1900, the one hundred Bessemer converters in operation yielded a total of 7.5 million tons, an average annual output of 75,000 tons each, twenty times that of the average iron smelter forty years earlier.[9] A number of newer open-hearth converters were also operating at this time in firms of increasingly large size. Iron and steel made by individual entrepreneurial firms were things of the past. Corporate structures and large, integrated operations were the norm.

There was a circularity in all of this. The increased capacity of the iron and steel industry was necessary for the creation of a complete national rail network. That network in turn allowed for easier distribution of bulk products like steel and allowed each production facility to serve a larger area. That, in turn, allowed the capture of economies of scale in production, lowering the costs of iron and steel. Finally it was the cheaper metals that made the construction of the expanded rail system affordable. By 1900 total track in the United States had grown to over 258,000 miles, with only 7 percent still iron rails.[10] In thirty years the steel plants of America had produced enough steel to cover the whole nation with a fully joined and interconnected web of rails.

Westinghouse's Fair Play

As those strands of steel were being smelted in Pittsburgh's converters and laid across the land, a World's Fair celebrating American progress was being planned and constructed in Chicago, one of the cities most affected by the rise of railroads. The Columbian Exposition of 1893 was, among other things, a showcase for George Westinghouse's system of electric power and light. Scientists and inventors had been trying, literally for centuries, to understand the fundamental nature of electricity and to explore its practical uses. Only recently had they begun to be successful.

In 1831 Michael Faraday had built a device using wire coils and magnets that transformed mechanical energy into an electrical current. It was clear even then that this was a form of energy that could perform useful functions, if only a series of practical problems could be overcome. First, of course, was how to build large-scale generators that could reliably produce electricity in consistent quantities without overheating. Then there would have to be some way to transmit the power generated to user sites, and finally some way to turn it back into useful work once there. What Westinghouse demonstrated at the fair was a complete system that had solved all three of those problems.

Westinghouse installed twelve separate generators, each standing ten feet tall, each powered by a steam engine. He added transformers, a network of switches and wires, and a quarter million incandescent lamps. His system also powered a moving sidewalk that carried over 600 seated passengers at a time. It provided motive power to a street rail system that carried over 6 million passengers during the course of the fair. The use of electric power was not entirely new to Americans, but never before had they seen anything on this scale.[11]

Thomas Edison had been selling electricity for home lighting from his Pearl Street station in New York since 1882 but his system had serious flaws. It used direct current that could not be efficiently transmitted much beyond a mile, and then only over expensive "large" wires. To provide lighting for a growing city, his system would have to keep adding new generating plants, scattered uniformly throughout the urban area, each serving only a small number of customers. Costs would be high because of limited scale and because each plant would have to be built right in the middle of a high-density residential area where land costs would be prohibitive.

Edison, the inventor of the incandescent bulb, saw electricity primarily as a substitute for the gas lighting that predominated in American cities of the day. His system was meant to help promote sales of his new light bulbs. He catered primarily to his residential customers. That meant that demand for Edison's direct current power was very uneven, peaking in the early evening, then falling off significantly later at night and during the day. As a result, generating plants had to be built to cover the peak loads, but they operated well below capacity most of the time. He was stuck with the high fixed costs of providing abundant current in the evening, yet to compete successfully with gas he needed to keep the price to consumers low.

The Westinghouse system, on the other hand, used alternating current and thus had several advantages. By using transformers to step up the voltage, current could be transmitted over longer distances at lower cost and with greater efficiency, and then be stepped back down for end users. He could thus generate power in larger plants on cheaper land located farther from end customers. Westinghouse also saw the prime function of electricity differently. With the recent development of efficient alternating current motors by Nicola Tesla, he was designing a system to provide power, with the ability to provide light as a convenient supplement. Power by day and light by night would result in a more even demand for electricity and a more efficient use of the generating equipment.

Edison's electric company (General Electric) had been the only other bidder on the contract to provide lighting for the World's Fair, but Westinghouse, realizing the potential long-term gains from a successful demonstration seen by millions of people, underbid General Electric by more than half. This was not so much a competition between companies as between different visions of the future of electricity. Westinghouse would lose money on the fair, but he hoped to win converts to his alternating current system, and indeed he did.[12]

Power to People

The reliance on water power for manufacturing in the mid-nineteenth century meant that factories had to be located where nature had provided appropriate conditions. Labor had to be brought to the power source and small manufacturing cities grew up around water sites. If some method could be devised to transport the energy available at these sites over extended distances, the machinery would not have to be located at the river. Power could be brought to people rather than the other way around.

Ever since the rise of water-powered production, practical Americans had been troubled by the "waste" of energy at the falls of the Niagara River. There an extraordinary volume of water flowing between lakes Erie and Ontario tumbles over high cliffs. How could that energy be captured? By 1861 a canal around the falls had been built and water to power mechanical wheels was being delivered to several mills along the route. Some even began to use their waterwheels to power internal dynamos. It was not long before the New York legislature, in order to support more industry, chartered a special Niagara Commission charged with exploring ways to extract still more energy from the falls. There was great controversy among the engineers and politicians of the day about the best way to achieve this, but finally plans to divert part of the flow from the upper river through a set of turbines in an underground tunnel were approved. On the basis of his successes at the Chicago World's Fair, George Westinghouse was chosen to build and operate the alternating current generators to be driven by the flow. His investment in the fair had paid off.

By 1895 Westinghouse's company had installed three 5,000–horsepower dynamos at the falls and quickly began generating electric power. The Niagara Falls Power Company, the operator of the system, owned a square mile of land surrounding its plant and offered lease or sale to companies that wanted guaranteed access to efficient electrical power at low rates. A number of companies, starting with the Pittsburgh Reduction Company (later to become Alcoa, Inc.), soon relocated their production facilities next to this new source of extraordinary power. Not having to transfer power mechanically from river to machine meant that many more machines could draw upon the energy extracted from a single site. This resulted in a major industrial park growing up around the power station.

The final stage in the development of electricity as power for industry came with improved systems to move it over long distances. No longer was there reason to locate even at Niagara Falls. With improved transformers and better controls, high voltage step-ups and voltage step-downs at substations and at end-user facilities were feasible. It became cost effective to move electricity tens or even hundreds of miles. For the first time, it was economically feasible to bring the power wherever people and production facilities were. Even hydroelectric power did not have to be used anywhere near the stream. It, like the nation's population, could move with ease into larger and larger cities.[13]

The advantages of centrally generated electricity soon became clear. In 1900 perhaps 2 percent of the industrial horsepower in America was being provided by electric motors. Twenty years later nearly a third was.[14] In 1900 the nation's power companies generated 6–billion kilowatt hours. Twenty years later they produced ten times that amount in power plants that were on average six times as large.[15] By then long-distance power grids were in place. Los Angeles was using power generated 240 miles away and sent over high-tension lines at 230,000 volts.[16] Steam and water no longer powered industry directly. Their days of dominance were past. They were used instead to generate electricity that could then be sent virtually anywhere, and the decision about where to locate factories would never again be quite the same.

Down on the Farm

Between 1870 and 1920 the combined population of America's cities grew from less than 10 to over 50 million people. This would not have been possible without steady growth in the agricultural surplus. Each decade the average American farmer became able to feed more and more of the city dwellers who were now working for wages in the new urban industries. There were no dramatic technological leaps in agriculture during this time; the improved productivity was the cumulative result of many small steps. First, of course, was simply an improvement in the soil. The center of agricultural activity was shifting inexorably west, from less fertile New England and tired tidewater soils to the more fertile lands of the vast Midwest. That alone accounted for some of the increase in average yields. Of course, these productive western farms could help feed those in the population centers far to the east only because of the new, integrated national rail system.

In terms of mechanization, the period saw improvements in animal-powered sulky plows, planters, and harvesters and thrashers, especially for grain crops. Some new huge Pacific coast farms were mechanized to the point of using massive steam tractors to power early combines capable of harvesting, thrashing, and bagging nearly 500 pounds of wheat a minute.[17] Steam tractors were not well suited to the scale of most farms though. Steam engines had been mounted on farm tractors almost as soon as they had been developed for trains, but they never really caught on. They were massive and extremely heavy, and thus they often acted as steam rollers, compacting the soil wherever they were driven. To reduce those effects they were fitted with huge wheels, occasionally as wide as eighteen feet, in order to spread the weight load and reduce compaction. The biggest tractors consumed enormous amounts of water and fuel and often required separate teams of horses and men simply to keep them stocked and running.[18] They were awkward to handle and maneuver. By 1917, even though the earliest gasoline-powered tractors were being built, there were over 6 million farms in America and still only 51,000 tractors.[19]

In the aggregate, the gains from improvements in agriculture were significant. In 1898 the U.S. commissioner of labor published a comprehensive study of the labor requirements for various farm tasks, comparing necessary labor in the 1830s with that in the 1890s. While the gains were much greater in some crops than others, for twenty-seven different crops, average labor requirements had been cut in half. For grains, where mechanization was most complete, the gains were extraordinary. The labor required in 1890 to grow and harvest wheat was barely one twentieth that required in 1830.[20] By at least one estimate, had farm technology stayed fixed at its 1860 level, 18 million more persons would have had to have worked in agriculture to feed the nation's population in 1900. It was improvements in productivity that "released" these people from farms and allowed them to move into cities.[21]

Urban Space Redrawn

The improvements in transportation, the expanded industrial capacity, and the rising agricultural surplus over those fifty years acted together to propel a reordering of American space. By 1910 the population of New York City was 20 percent greater than the population of the entire nation had been in 1790. Ten years later the nation passed a milestone when more than half of its population lived in an urban area, though there were strong regional differences. The South would not become half-urbanized for another thirty years; the Northeast had been so for over forty.

It was industrialization that drew people to America's cities, from its own farms and from the European continent. Surplus agricultural population had to go somewhere, and increasingly, that meant to jobs in the city. That was true for rural whites, and for the first time it became true for southern blacks who were drawn to northern cities in significant numbers by much higher wages and lesser social oppression. Regular steamship service across the Atlantic and improved rail networks across Europe provided easy access to American labor markets for millions of Europeans. Foreign immigration into the United States grew to record levels, and most of the new entrants landed and stayed in cities.

The jobs they found were not just in the newest industries. Urbanologists speak of a job "multiplier" in a city's economy. Some of the work force is employed in "basic" industries that export to the rest of the nation or the rest of the world. Without these industries, there can be no city. But for each job in them, there are others that arise from housing, feeding, clothing, entertaining, and educating those in the basic jobs. The growth of new urban industries over these years also created a growing need for urban grocers, teachers, doctors, retailers, streetcar drivers, sanitation workers, police, and bankers. It was the growth in the industrial base that supported, directly and indirectly, so many new people in so many unnatural aggregations.

But not all American cities grew in this era. The cities that thrive are those that best fit the economic logic of their time. If technology undercuts their particular advantage, the tides of change are difficult indeed to resist. This was a period that favored large-scale manufacturing centers and good rail connections. The water-powered mill towns of the Northeast lost much of their edge. With the advent of alternating current systems capable of delivering electricity over long distances, power for manufacturing became as cheap and available in the larger cities as in the smaller river towns. Large cities also offered mass markets right at the factory doors and ready supplies of labor to man the machines.

Port towns along the Ohio, Mississippi, and Missouri Rivers lost much of their reason for being as the rivers were bridged and the rail network was completed. Transportation, in every sense, passed them by. No longer did regional railroads have to off-load at the riverbank. They just kept going and going. Wheeling, Marietta, Vicksberg, and Natchez diminished in importance while Chicago, Detroit, Denver, and New York boomed. St. Louis, which had staked its future on river transport while Chicago was building itself into a rail hub, slipped into the shadow of its northern rival. Chicago became the dominant city in the region and indeed the second-largest city in the nation by the close of the century. Denver and Seattle eclipsed Cheyenne and Tacoma as they became the regional rail centers. Of the largest cities in the nation at the close of the Civil War, only New Orleans fell significantly in national ranking as north-south river traffic was replaced by east-west rails.[22]

Giving Growing Cities a Lift

Those cities that found themselves joined to the new technology faced their own special difficulties. How could hundreds of thousands, indeed for several millions of people, all live in a single city without crushing it under their own weight. How could they gather so many more people into a coherent whole? Several of the forces fueling the industrialization and urbanization of the era also combined to reshape the internal structure of cities. It was clear that in order to fit more people in, cities had to go up, out, or both, but how could they?

On a spring day in 1854 an event took place at the Crystal Palace Fair in New York City that changed forever the face of the modern city. For centuries people had used hoists of various types to raise and lower heavy objects. All used some kind of rope and pulley system and all had one significant flaw. If anything happened to the rope, the payload would plummet to earth, to the serious detriment of any freight or passengers on board. On that day in 1854 a composed and distinguished-looking gentlemen climbed onto a platform lift contained in a narrow shaft. Before a large audience he stood calmly while the platform was raised higher and higher. Suddenly he cut the rope, only to have the platform quickly stop as spring-loaded safety latches engaged ratchets attached to the walls of the shaft. The passenger, who was also the inventor of this new device, had successfully and publicly demonstrated his invention, and safe vertical transportation systems were born. Elisha Graves Otis, whose name can still be found on the walls of most elevators operating today, created a new industry and contributed to a new profile for cities.

Otis's first elevators were powered by steam engines that turned drums upon which the rope was wound and unwound. The earliest models were used to move freight, but by 1857 his first passenger elevator was operating in a five-story building. As their use spread, both the use and perception of vertical space changed. The higher floors in a hotel that had been considered the least desirable, now commanded a premium. Offices at the top of commercial buildings that had been rented at a discount now were sought after as symbols of prestige. People's willingness regularly to climb stairs had before placed a practical limit on building height of four or five floors. A new limit of perhaps ten stories was now established by the capacity of a winding drum and the weight-bearing capacity of ground level walls under then current construction techniques.[23] Only when Otis's invention combined with two other developments over the next years did the use of vertical space really "take off."

A separate steam engine dedicated to each elevator was impractical at best. If a head of steam was kept up at all times, there was a significant waste of fuel when the lift was not operating. If the engine was only heated to steam when there was a demand to ride, the delays would be substantial. But when electricity became available as a source of power, generated at a distant, high-capacity plant servicing many customers, the energy costs of operating an elevator were much reduced. When a counterweight suspended in the same shaft was added, the capacity of a winding drum no longer became an effective limit on height. Here was a new form of intracity transportation that operated vertically. Cities could hold more people by going up rather than out. Many thousands of square feet of building could be placed on a few square feet of land. Then the limit on the use of vertical space was only the inability to construct taller buildings, and that was about to change.

To Scrape the Sky

In the fall of 1885 the first tenants of the Home Insurance Company on LaSalle Street in downtown Chicago moved into their new offices. Standing eleven stories high, the main entrance brought visitors face to face with a bank of ornately decorated elevators, powered by electricity, carrying passengers at vertical speeds of 500 feet per minute. With lavatories on every floor, both gas and electric lighting as well as central steam heat, the new building was fully modern. It had been designed by William LeBaron Jenney, an architect of some renown. It looked much like other structures of its day, but within its solid appearing masonry walls it held the secret to the future of urban architecture.

Jenney had designed an iron skeleton to carry the full weight of the building. The masonry walls served only to shut out the elements, not to support the upper floors. Indeed the interior of the building could be reconfigured with ease simply by moving around nonbearing partitions. When Jenney first proposed this radical departure from accepted technique, the officers of the Home Insurance Company were resistant. When the president found out that no other iron framework buildings existed anywhere, he originally rejected the proposal. Insurance companies tend to be conservative. Jenney was able to prevail only when he brought in bridge engineers, who had considerable experience with iron frames, to validate his design.[24]

The building was a major success, even a sensation of sorts. The modular framework design could be expanded indefinitely. Buildings of almost any height were now conceivable, and maybe even practical. They could be constructed of iron and steel whose ready availability would change the skyline of cities as much as it changed the rail lines in the country. They could be made accessible by safe elevators powered by electricity. Central cities could house a much denser population without any increase in crowding. Cities could grow in population without adding land area. Over the next decades the central area of America's largest cities rose to unimagined heights, but not everyone chose to live higher up.

Getting Urban Transit Back on Track

It was not enough for cities to rise vertically as they grew. To accommodate the huge increases in population they also had to grow out, and that was possible only because of advances in intracity transportation systems. These were of two types—improvements in motive power and speed, and exploitation of new spaces for travel. Steam engines were early adapted to intracity travel, but the engines themselves were too bulky to travel with the cars. They stayed in one place while passengers rode along in cars connected to them. In 1873 San Francisco was the first city to offer cable car service; today, of course, it is the last to still do so. A continuous wire loop underneath the street was pulled by a powerful engine at a central location. Individual cars would grip the cable and be pulled along, releasing it and applying brakes when they needed to stop. Within twenty years there were cable car systems in place in over a dozen major cities in virtually all parts of the nation. Chicago alone had eighty-six miles of cable car tracks in operation by 1894.[25]

The drawbacks to such a system are obvious. It was expensive to build and maintain the underground cable network. Since the entire system ran from a single power source, any failure of the central engine or the cable itself paralyzed the entire operation. When Frank Sprague, an engineer working with Edison, devised an electric-powered streetcar and installed his system in Richmond, Virginia, in 1886, a strong competitor was born. Sprague's carriages each contained a separate motor that was powered by contact with an overhead wire via a flexible connector, or "troller," that lead to christening the carriages "trolleys." His original system operated off of Edison's direct current, but he soon adapted it to alternating current when that prevailed. Four years after Sprague's first trials there were already 1,200 miles of electric trolley tracks in American cities compared to 5,700 miles of horse car tracks. Just a dozen years later, animal-powered systems were all but completely gone while electric trolley track mileage had grown to exceed 22,000.[26]

Wherever trolley lines were built, longer distance commuting to downtown became feasible, at least for those who could afford the fare. As the center of town became more crowded with the newly arriving poor, the middle class sought to recapture the amenities of village living by moving out to developments of single-family homes with yards and open spaces in new suburbs. Quiet, cleanliness, and safety were increasingly just a trolley ride away from the bustle of the city. Suburbs were, of course, still restricted to areas served by rail and trolley service. Where no transit company was willing to invest in expensive infrastructure no suburb could thrive, but the companies were willing to make a great many such investments. By 1900 the edges of urban development tied to the city of Boston extended ten miles from the core. Fifty years earlier the walking limit of two miles had marked the edge of the city.[27]

Trolleys, however, had to travel in the same space as pedestrians, wagons, omnibuses, carriages, and, by the end of the period, cars and trucks. As urban populations swelled, more and more people were trying to move in the same narrow channels. Trolleys let them move faster in theory, but as traffic grew, increased congestion clearly reduced their advantage. More building per lot was being added in the older central areas. There was no room to widen streets and increase their capacity until, like Otis, planners started thinking in vertical terms. The possibility of running steam trains on elevated tracks, supported by iron and steel frameworks, was exploited in a few places, but the dangers of heavy locomotives suffering derailments or other accidents above heavily traveled urban streets was a deterrent to their widespread use. Once electric trolleys were devised, several cities saw the advantages of building an elevated right-of-way above the traffic for lighter and safer electric rail systems. New York and many other cities did that, but New York also went deeper—literally. By the turn of the century it had begun operation of electric subway trains running on tracks beneath the city's streets. The expense of building such a system prevented most other American cities from following, but it was probably necessary for New York that by then had reached a population size simply unimaginable a generation before.

Housing Patterns

With literally millions of new residents arriving in American cities there was tremendous pressure on the stock of urban housing. The new residents had to live somewhere. The middle class was increasingly moving outward to neighborhoods of newer and nicer housing, trading off the higher costs of commuting for greater space and comfort. Their employment, however, was still highly centralized. Retail outlets, and especially the new all-purpose "department" stores, had to be accessible to vast numbers of customers and where better to locate than where all transit lines converged—downtown. The increasing numbers of lawyers, financiers, and managers had to be accessible to each other in order to conduct their daily face-to-face business. Indeed, it is during this period that a dominant "central business district" came to predominate in the core of cities.

Manufacturing, while outside of that commercial core, still needed a central location. Bulk goods still moved within urban areas by horse and wagon. There was nothing comparable to the electric street car or subway for them. Long-distance shipping by rail was essential for access to large-scale markets and proximity to rail lines was a necessity. Where did rail lines now meet? In the central city, of course. Both white- and blue-collar jobs were heavily concentrated in the central city. By 1900, 90 percent of all industrial production in the nation took place in urban factories.[28] Most of the new suburban communities regularly sent their residents back into the city to work, shop, and seek entertainment.

The urban poor could not afford either the commuting costs nor the price of the spacious housing being built at the city's edge. Even though the per-square-foot cost of living space in the suburbs was, and still is, much cheaper, it was not sold in small enough increments to be of use to the poor. Occasionally fringe communities of shantytowns like those that typify urbanization in contemporary Third World nations would spontaneously develop. More commonly, needing to be nearer jobs and labor markets, low-income households and individuals flocked to the central city in need of housing, only to find that there was not enough of it for all of them.

The Growth of Slums

The filtering process that had begun in the prior era accelerated, and older middle-class housing was broken into smaller units, housing more and more people. In New York the standard residential lot laid out several generations before measured 25 by 100 feet, adequate for a small house, perhaps with a yard in back. As housing pressure grew, owners increasingly added more structure onto the back portion of the lot, squeezing ever more building and more people onto the same 25 by 100 feet. Even that proved inadequate to the demand, and they began razing old structures and replacing them with four- to six-story "tenement" houses containing as many units as possible. Lots were soon filled front to back and side to side so that most interior units had no windows at all. Sanitation facilities were minimal. Even that was "too rich" for many of the poor and families often shared individual units or took in lodgers to lower their costs. Extraordinary concentrations of poverty resulted. By the time Westinghouse was illuminating the future at the Chicago World's Fair, the density in the poorest parts of New York was over 700 persons per acre.[29]

New York's extreme crowding was not matched in most other cities, but in all of them the logic of location dictated higher density housing for the poor. As more and more people tried to live in the same space, increased crowding was inevitable. Lots containing even partial open spaces filled in. In cities like Boston new multifamily triple-deckers were built to house working-class families, but they were often subdivided to hold far more than the originally intended three families.

As urban slums developed the social consequences of so much concentrated poverty became apparent to all who chose to see them. Reform movements grew apace with slums; virtually all were destined to fail. They rightly abhorred the worst consequences of the changing spatial organization, but they simply could not overcome the fundamental logic of the urbanization of their day. Vast numbers of people—persecuted Jews in Russia, poor peasants in Poland and Italy, displaced farmers in Ireland, poor blacks caught in sharecropping in the South, and excess farmers from all parts of the nation—now felt that their best chance to escape from poverty was to seek industrial employment in American cities. Urbanization per se did not cause an increase in poverty. Most of the new entrants to the city were poor before they arrived. What urbanization did was to concentrate them in large numbers in very high densities and make them more visible.

What Else Could They Do?

As more of the poor were drawn to cities by the prospect of industrial employment, they all had to be housed. The question was how. Many of the reformers of the day felt that nothing short of detached single-family homes on spacious lots would save the poor, and the nation, from the depravations of the slums. Lawrence Veiller, though best known for pushing New York to create its first comprehensive tenement code, was opposed in principle to tenements in any form.

> It is useless to expect a conservative point of view in the workingman, if his home is but three or four rooms in some huge building in which dwell from twenty to thirty other families, and this home is his only from month to month. Where a man has a home of his own he has every incentive to be economical and thrifty, to take part in the duties of citizenship, to be a real sharer in government. Democracy was not predicated on a country made up of tenement dwellers, nor can it so survive.[30]

It was really the modern and much maligned suburb that Veiller sought, but that pattern could not fit into the logic of location when urbanizing so many poor. How much space would it take to house millions of people, all in single-family detached houses but all focused on a common core? How far from the center would the city have to extend? How expansive and expensive a transportation system would have been required to move people over such a vast, but lightly occupied space? How much would it have cost to build that many separate houses? Who would have paid for them? Certainly the poor could not have and even the middle class was stretched to meet the costs of larger homes and longer commutes. Large cities and low-density housing for the poor were logically inconsistent.

George Pullman, the inventor and manufacturer of the Pullman Palace railroad car, responded to some of the reformers by building a model town outside of Chicago, consisting of single-family homes owned by the company and rented to the employees of his factory. On the surface, the town seemed a model for manufacturing communities without urban slums. It soon became apparent to the residents/employees that in fact it created double dependence on the company. If they were fired, they immediately lost their home as well. If they wanted to stay in the home, and indeed the community, they had only one choice of employer. When widespread depression in the early 1890s caused Pullman to reduce the wages he paid, but not the rents he collected, the resulting labor troubles lead to the infamous Pullman Strike of 1894, one of the bloodiest confrontations in American labor history. In the aftermath, the "clear" social benefits of such a solution to urban housing ills were no longer quite so obvious.

For better or for worse, growth in large industrial cities meant using the space more intensively by adding higher density structures. Most of the practical reformers of the day took less extreme stands and made concessions to reality. Many sought to regulate the amount of housing that could be placed on each piece of central-city land. Where they were successful they reduced the crowding of structures on some lots, but the displaced poor were not gone, they were just more desperate. The reduced supply of housing raised its price for those able to find it, and they often took in more boarders to help cover the cost. Fewer housing units without any reduction in the number of people to be housed was not the answer.

Some of the reformers sought regulations to eliminate the worst characteristics of the tenements. They sponsored competitions for improved structural designs that would use space intensively while still providing light and ventilation to all units, without raising construction costs unreasonably. Certainly new skyscrapers with steel frames and elevators, "Trump Towers" for the poor, were not economically viable. Something less extravagant would have to do. The result was the development of "dumbbell" tenements, so named because, while front and back walls stretched the full width of the lot, there was a pinched-in waist creating internal shafts between the center sides of adjoining buildings. In principle these seemed an improvement, but they became dumps for refuse, breeding grounds for vermin, and chimneys to feed and spread fire in far too many cases.

There also arose a model tenements movement where reformers tried to demonstrate that it would be possible to construct and maintain low-income housing superior to typical tenements. Many such projects were initiated. Virtually all failed. Most found that to succeed they had to limit occupancy of model tenements to model tenants, that is, those with stable incomes and employment. If they admitted the poorest and most insecure, rent collections fluctuated too much and revenues failed to cover costs. If they tried to maintain high standards in their buildings they had to charge rents beyond the reach of the very poor. If they kept costs down to promote affordability, the buildings quickly deteriorated.

The Growth of City Government

As cities' populations grew and the use of their space became more intensive, the basic problems of aggregation intensified. The need for a more active public sector grew apace. When skyscrapers brought hundreds of office workers together each day and tenements crowded over 700 persons onto an acre of land, upgraded water and sewage systems became absolutely essential. As the basic causes of infectious disease came to be understood, public health became a legitimate concern for local government. As the need for building codes to ameliorate the worst excess of slum construction were enacted, new officials were needed to enforce the regulations. As the miles of city streets multiplied over and over again, some coordination of construction and maintenance became necessary. As more and more people crowded into cities, more police and firefighters were required to maintain order and safety.

In combination, these contributed to significant growth in the scope and power of local government throughout this period—and also to a significant increase in its cost. Real per capita expenditures by New York City's government more than tripled between 1850 and 1900, and continued to rise apace through the years of World War I.[31] The higher taxes were a further incentive for the middle class to move out. The increased need for services, and the problems faced by so many of the newly arrived poor in getting them, created a fertile environment for the growth of big city "machine" politics. The rise of bosses and the subsequent development of the reform movement can be attributed to these changes in the organization of space.

Cities on the Eve of the Modern Era

By the end of the First World War, the structure of America had been irreversibly changed. Over half of the nation's population lived in cities, and growth in the economy now came from the new factories and industries located there. It was no longer a nation of farmers. Agriculture was in support of industry rather than the other way around. The biggest cities had achieved a scale unimaginable, and certainly insupportable, just a few decades before. Water-powered mills no longer anchored smaller cities in the Northeast. River ports no longer dominated transportation. Electricity allowed factories to move into larger cities and railroads dominated the movement of goods and people throughout a national economy that bridged the continent, shore to shore.

Cities had grown both up and out, but still they were at the center of commerce and production. Vast numbers of factory jobs requiring minimal skills, as well as many secondary jobs supporting them, were created and located in cities. Vast numbers of poor from within and without the borders of the United States had aggregated in those same cities to be close to those jobs. The growing middle class had moved out from the crowded center but was still tethered to it by the lifelines of the new public transit systems. The wealthy had their own enclaves, either in exclusive neighborhoods within cities or in expensive suburbs beyond them, but their business was still downtown. The nation's cities would have been unrecognizable to those who had founded them. As extraordinary as the changes had been there would be still more restructuring of space in the decades ahead. The transition to modern times was not yet done.

6

From the Great War to the Great Society

Mr. Edison's Engineer

In 1891 Thomas Edison hired a young man as the mechanical supervisor for his Edison Illuminating Company in Detroit. Once the generators were set up and operating there was little for him to do, so he used the time to tinker in a machine shop that he set up in a corner of the plant. In early 1896 he came across a two-part article in the *American Machinist* containing plans for a simple gasoline-powered, internal combustion engine built from scrap parts. Excited by the challenge he soon had one built and running. Then, bitten by the automobile bug that was infecting machine shop denizens around the world, he installed it onto a frame that he built from two bicycles to form what he called a "quadricycle." After several weeks of work the vehicle was completed and it was time to test his horseless carriage on the streets of Detroit. Only then did he discover that it would not fit through the door—an inauspicious beginning to a test of engineering skill and foresight. Not one to be thwarted by so small a problem, he tore out enough of one wall to push the car into the street where he started the engine and drove off, accompanied only by one observer on a bicycle who had no difficulty keeping up with the slowly moving vehicle. The car traveled only a few blocks before it broke down and a spare part had to be retrieved from the shop before the quadricycle could complete its first trip.[1]

This was not the first successful automobile in the world. That had been built in Germany a decade before. It was not the first successful one in the United States; that had been built in Springfield, Massachusetts, three years before. It was not even the first successful automobile in Detroit. Earlier that same year one had been built by Charles King, the observer on the bicycle.[2] The significance of this car's success was that it brought into the competition a new player who would come to see the automobile and the business of producing it in a new light, and would ultimately transform both the American economy and its whole spatial organization.

Once begun, the development of the automobile proceeded at an extraordinary pace. Only nine years after the quadricycle broke down within a few blocks of its starting point, Dwight Huss and Milford Weigle drove another automobile into downtown Portland, Oregon, a spot reached exactly a century before by Meriwether Lewis and William Clark. Lewis and Clark had spent two long and torturous years crossing a vast unknown from St. Louis to the Pacific Northwest. Huss and Weigle had set out from New York City and in just forty-four days had traveled coast to coast—in an automobile. In Portland they claimed a $1,000 prize for being the first to successfully cross the continent by car.[3]

The automobile had gone from tinkerer's concept to working reality in a very short period of time, but still it was an expensive novelty. Before it could achieve its full impact there had to be a change in how it was perceived and produced. The first commercially built cars were custom built and made to order. Even though they used Whitney's system of interchangeable parts, the process of assembly was still done by groups of skilled mechanics who transformed each one from a pile of parts into a finished car. The earliest car companies manufactured nothing. They simply assembled parts that they ordered from a series of suppliers. Ransome Olds, whose Oldsmobile was one of the first commercially successful cars, was the production giant in the first years of the century. In 1903 his production teams assembled 4,000 new, and expensive, cars.[4] His company was the largest of twenty-four car companies competing for business at that time. Every year there were more entrants to, as well as a few dropout from, the industry. Still, at that rate of production it would have taken generations for cars to have become a pervasive element in transportation and industry.

His success with the quadricycle led Mr. Edison's engineer to seek a piece of the business as well as a slice of the glory. In 1899 he put together sufficient financial backing to establish the Detroit Automobile Company. Two years later it had failed completely. Too much attention had been given to design and mechanical improvement. Too little had been given to producing and selling cars. No sooner had his first company failed than he was drawn into another. Capitalizing on his name recognition arising from the success of his cars on the race course at Grosse Pointe, the new firm was organized as the Henry Ford Company. Once again though, Ford paid too much attention to the cars and the races and not enough to the business. He parted ways with his backers and left his second car company a short time later.

In 1903, already a two-time failure, Ford was ready to try his third automobile company, now organized as the Ford Motor Company. This time production and sales would be central. There would be no third failure and the shape of American society would be forever changed. Initially Ford, like Olds and all the others, used stationary assembly teams to produce each vehicle, and so to increase production he had to hire enough new assembly teams to recreate the efforts of the existing work force. Twice as many cars required twice as many workers. Ford's innovation came not from changing the design of cars but from changing the production process itself, a change precipitated by a new vision of the potential role of the car in American society.

Of all the automobile pioneers, he alone saw the car as an item of mass consumption. He saw that a basic car, priced appropriately, had millions of potential customers among the middle and working classes. The automobile need not be just a luxury of the rich, but to realize mass potential he had to find a way to get the price down to a level affordable by the bulk of the nation's population. To do that he had to find a way to lower the costs of building them. Ford started on a modest scale. He began by urging design for efficient production as much as for performance. His single-block engine design was much cheaper to produce than his competitors' engines, but it performed as well. He devised powerful machines to stamp out all the parts of a radiator in a single step, lowering costs again. The cheaper parts did lead to a cheaper car. By 1910 he was producing 18,000 cars a year. In 1911 his output doubled, but so did the number of employees. The next year both doubled again.[5] He was producing more, but cheaper parts alone were not enough to penetrate the mass market.

Putting It All Together

The winter of 1913–1914 was a time of dramatic change. The Ford Motor Company doubled its output once again, but this time it did so with fewer employees than it had had the previous year. It was not the invention of a new car but of a new assembly *process* that led to Ford's greatest success the third time around. He first began experimenting with a moving assembly line to build some of the key parts of the car. The resulting increase in production soon threatened to bury the final assembly plant in parts, so in 1913 he experimented with the first moving assembly line for cars themselves. At first each chassis was simply pulled across the plant floor by a rope while a team of assemblers moved with it, taking successive parts from piles placed along the route. Average labor/hours to assemble each vehicle fell from over twelve hours to less than six. Then a line with stationary workers, each performing specialized tasks as the body passed by, was tried. The labor/hours per vehicle fell to barely one and a half hours.[6] He made cars much cheaper to build when he found a way to put much less labor into each one.

Ford, like many of his contemporaries, was a disciple of Frederick Taylor, the original industrial efficiency expert. Taylor recommended careful "time and motion" studies to break complex tasks into smaller components that could be managed for efficiency. The job assigned to each worker along the line became more and more specialized and demanded less and less skill. Neither mechanical experience nor knowledge of internal combustion technology was required of workers whose job was simply to place bolts in engine mounting brackets, to be tightened by another worker at the next station along the line. One of the crucial outcomes of Ford's innovation was that as less and less skill was needed for these new industrial jobs, newly arrived, even illiterate, immigrants and uneducated migrants from the countryside could step into the line and quickly learn to do most of the necessary jobs.

While workers on a Taylorized line could be more easily replaced, there were still advantages to continuity and costs to continually having to find new employees. Thus when Ford reorganized the plant he also reorganized the system of compensation. To the astonishment of both his board and his employees, he announced that all workers at Ford would, after six months, receive a daily wage of $5 for an eight-hour day. In the rest of the industry the standard was half that for a nine-hour day. When Ford announced the new wage policy in January of 1914 there were riots at his Detroit plant as crowds of job seekers showed up hoping to be hired. In fact the nation as a whole was in a period of high unemployment, and soon applicants for $5 jobs flocked to Detroit from across the nation seeking work with Ford. The success of his innovations was a beacon drawing more and more people into the city in search of industrial employment.

No one has ever uncovered evidence that Ford was a soft-hearted utopian reformer. By going to an eight-hour day he could operate around the clock using three shifts, using his expensive but productive equipment to the fullest. By paying wages in excess of the market, he could be assured of a ready and steady labor force, even though the work itself was unpleasant. Ford was confident that labor productivity would rise so dramatically that the cost of assembling cars, even while paying those much higher wages, would fall significantly. He was right.

What Ford was producing by his new method was known simply as the Model T. He did not have the advantage of a modern marketing staff to create catchy names like Mustang or Taurus. When he started producing his cars the first one was called simply the Model A. The second version was known as the Model B. When he switched to the assembly-line method of production he was up to the Model T. Basically unchanged in design for the next nineteen years it was designed as "everyman's" car. In 1909 he had sold 12,000 Model T's at a price per vehicle of $950, accounting for approximately 10 percent of the total U.S. market. By 1915 the new production technique allowed him to lower the selling price to $440 and he sold 342,000, accounting for nearly 40 percent of the total U.S. market, making record profits in the process. In 1923 the price was down to $295 and he sold 1.6 million, just under half of all cars sold in the country that year.[7] When he first started the line it took the average American worker nearly two years to earn enough to purchase a Model T. By the mid-1920s, that worker could earn enough in less than three months.[8]

Ford had a much better grasp of manufacturing than he did of marketing. While more affordable, his cars were still too expensive for most families easily to buy for cash. His original marketing idea was to establish the Ford Weekly Purchase Plan. Interested buyers would register with a Ford dealer and make payments until finally they had enough in their account to cover the purchase price. Only then would they take delivery of the car.[9] It was the reverse of the modern come on—pay everything now, get nothing until later. Needless to say there were not many takers.

Others soon proposed a different solution, and soon car purchasers began to borrow and to buy "on time." The size of the monthly payment became the crucial determinant of affordability. In the mid-1920s Ford was finally persuaded that he would have to allow installment purchases of his cars, and before long he was involved in financing as well as production. By the close of the decade well over half of all the new cars purchased in America were bought on installment plans, and one of the more ubiquitous elements of modern life, the monthly car payment, had become well established.[10]

The Road to the Modern City

The fact that it took Huss and Weigle six weeks to cross the nation by car in 1905 says more about the state of the roads at that time than the speed of the automobiles. Cars capable of speeds in excess of sixty miles an hour had already been built and tested on race tracks under ideal conditions. If their vehicle had been reliable enough to sustain that speed for long periods, then even stopping each night, the journey should have taken only four days. In fact the much slower average speed was not caused as much by the unreliability of the car as by two other factors—the abominable condition of the nation's roads and the drivers' penchant for taking lots of time to "show off" in each town they passed through. It was not so much a race as a performance.

Still the utility of the new cars depended on the condition of roads. The practice of having local roads constructed by citizens "working off" their taxes was ill-suited to highway improvement. Good roads required professional engineers and builders and those cost money. In 1916 the first federal allocation of funds to states for the explicit purpose of improving highways was made. States established construction standards and helped with funding. But what kind of system was to be built? Any complete transportation system has three elements: *collection* where goods or passengers are brought together, *line haul* where they are moved over some distance, and *distribution* where they are delivered to their final destinations. Railroads are primarily line haul modes of transportation. Freight must be brought to and distributed from rail terminals via some other mode.

At first the railroads tried to make highways perform collection and distribution functions for them just as they had done in service to steamboats a half century before. The other option was to construct a network of high-quality roads directly connecting cities to each other, providing an *alternative* to rail transportation. Once there was a widespread network of roads everything changed. Rather than trucking goods to the railroad, transferring them to a train to be hauled some distance, and then transferring them back to another truck to distribute, shippers increasingly opted to have the first truck just keep on going.

The Road More Traveled

Today there are nearly 4 million miles of public roads in the United States, and it is estimated that total miles of travel by motor vehicles exceed 2.2 trillion each year. That means that, on average, each mile of road is traversed by a motor vehicle over half a million times each per year.[11] Most of these miles, of course, are concentrated on a few of the roads. The Interstate Highway System in total has less than 50,000 miles but carries a high proportion of the traffic. Other main arterial roads make up less than 10 percent of the total but account for a much larger share of the total miles traveled. Over three fourths of the roads are local or collector routes that carry only a small proportion of the total.[12]

Faced with this extraordinary network, the railroads were no more successful in their attempt to make the new technology support the old than the riverboat operators had been. Cars and trucks became powerful competitors, rather than subservient feeders, to the railroads. At the turn of the century virtually all overland shipping was by rail. By mid-century trucks had captured 16 percent of the total intercity freight and railroads were down to 57 percent. Today trains carry approximately 37 percent of the intercity freight while trucks' share has risen to nearly 28 percent. Surprisingly, 15 percent of the total freight shipments are still by river, canal, and Great Lakes shipping.

For passengers, the advantages of travel by automobile are even greater than for freight. Cars go whenever and wherever the driver chooses. If he or she wishes to take others along there are no extra tickets to buy and no extra costs. If he or she drives to another city the car is available for transportation around that town as well. Railroads are hard pressed to match those advantages, and by 1950 their share of intercity domestic travel had fallen below 7 percent, by 1970 it was below 1 percent, and today it is lower still. With the development of the interstate highway system and the ready availability of cars, intercity passenger travel by that mode grew at a phenomenal rate, peaking at nearly 90 percent in the late 1950s. The introduction of relatively inexpensive jet air service has cut into that so today 80 percent of those miles are traveled by car and 18 percent are by air. The rather tiny remainder is shared by trains and buses.[13]

In 1895 there were four known automobiles in the United States. When the U.S. entered World War I two decades later there were nearly 5 million.[14] By 1930 total registered cars exceeded 22 million, enough so that the entire population of the nation could all have gone for a ride at once.[15] By the start of World War II there were nearly 30 million passenger cars on the nation's roads. At its end, production really exploded. By 1967 there were 80 million registered passenger cars in the United States and today the number is approaching 150 million. There are today over 190 million registered motor vehicles, enough so that if every licensed driver in the nation decided at the same moment to go for a drive, there would be enough vehicles to accommodate each and every one—with 17 million left over.

The impact of the automobile on the industrial structure has also been immense. In 1900 the industry was too small to have any noticeable effect on the national economy. When the Great War ended less than two decades later it was the country's third-largest industry, and it had propelled other industries like oil, steel, and rubber to new levels of output as well. By the 1980s one out of every six jobs in America was dependent, directly or indirectly, on cars![16] Cars are how Americans now move around between and within their urban aggregations, and they are now one of the fundamental things that cities produce and trade. They are industrial base and transportation system combined. The automobile has driven Americans to a restructuring of their space.

The Internal Combustion Engine Takes Off

The automobile offered speed and convenience, door to door, unmatched by any other mode of transit—until air travel became widely available. Just sixteen years after Huss and Weigle first crossed the continent by car, coast-to-coast airmail service was established. Huss and Weigle's journey had taken six weeks. The initial airmail run, flown in relay fashion by teams of pilots, made the trip from San Francisco to New York in just over thirty-three hours. Air navigation was still so primitive, however, that adding overnight routes to the mail network had to wait until a system of ground lights could be installed along the route to guide the pilots.[17] By the 1930s passenger traffic was becoming well established. In 1936 American Airlines inaugurated nonstop service between New York and Chicago, and the same year regular coast-to-coast service, though with stops, was established. Flying time was down to sixteen hours.[18]

It was not until the advent of the jet age that air travel really took off. Larger and faster planes lowered the per seat mile cost and made all destinations closer. Transatlantic jet service began in 1958, and by the next year it was becoming common on domestic routes as well.[19] Cities were closer to each other. National markets could be administered from one central location. No city in the nation was more than a few hours from any other. Today, nearly one in five intercity passenger trips is made by air, a fraction of 1 percent is made by rail. Access to the airport is more important that proximity to the train station.

As with other major transportation innovations, new manufacturing industries developed hand-in-hand with the new modes of transportation. Specialized companies with valuable technical expertise hired more and more workers to produce equipment for the new system. By the 1980s the entire aerospace industry was producing over $100 billion of product each year. That supported a vast network of basic urban jobs and many more nonbasic ones in servicing the needs of aerospace workers. The air-travel system itself also requires labor. Transportation, in all its new forms, gives cities something else to trade in support of their survival as unnatural aggregations.

Driven off the Farm

The internal combustion engine could not only move passengers and freight over the new roads and through the air, it could power and propel machinery across the fields of America's farms. There was no need to start a fire and build up a head of steam. Now a tractor's engine, like a car's, could be started and stopped in an instant. Lighter, more efficient engines and large rubber tires overcame the soil compaction problems of the early steam tractors. Gas and diesel tractors became necessities on every farm. At the close of the Great War there had been nearly 120 farms for each tractor in existence. By the 1980s there were more than two tractors for every farm. The largest farms had whole fleets in operation. Power from the tractors' engines drove all kinds of new machines capable of performing virtually all of the heavy labor tasks needed on the farm. Greater yields with less labor was the result. There simply was not the demand for farm workers that there had been, and the displaced workers had to go somewhere.

When Nicholas Lemann wrote his account of the massive movement of African Americans from the rural South to the industrial cities of the North in the years after World War II, he began the story with a description of the first successful test of a mechanical cotton picker on Howell Hopson's Mississippi plantation in October of 1944.

> The pickers, painted bright red, drove down the white rows of cotton. Each one had mounted in front a row of spindles, looking like a wide mouth, full of metal teeth, that had been turned vertically. The spindles, about the size of human fingers, rotated in a way that stripped the cotton from the plants; then a vacuum pulled it up a tube and into the big wire basket that was mounted on top of the picker. In an hour, a good field hand could pick twenty pounds of cotton; each mechanical picker, in an hour, picked as much as a thousand pounds.[20]

The company that Silas McCormick had brought to Chicago to manufacture his reapers a hundred years before had by then grown into an industrial giant, developing and producing all kinds of heavy equipment. The prototypes tested that day had been built by McCormick's old company, now renamed International Harvester. Each one did the work of fifty people as it picked each bale of cotton at one eighth the cost of hand labor.[21] With productive efficiency fueled by Eli Whitney's interchangeable parts and Henry Ford's assembly lines, International Harvester's machines soon penetrated deep into the heart of southern agriculture, eliminating the jobs of hundreds of thousands of farm workers, most of whom were black. With the growth of industrial employment in the North, and to a lesser degree in southern cities, a massive aggregation of people began. In 1950 the Southeast finally became one half urbanized, fully a century after the more industrialized Northeast had passed that mark.

It was not just new machines that were raising farm productivity in these years. "Scientific Management" also moved from industry to agriculture. Factory modes of production and Taylorized processes penetrated even farms. New seed strains and fertilizers, along with expanded use of pesticides raised average per acre yields dramatically. Improved breeding raised the average annual milk production of America's herds year after year in a treadmill race no dairy farmer could afford to ignore.[22] Starting in the 1950s larger scale chicken farms began raising broilers in individual cages with automatically delivered and carefully measured feed. Between 1940 and 1970 the human labor required to produce a pound of chicken fell by 95 percent and the real cost to consumers fell by two thirds.[23]

In short, agricultural surpluses became so great that there was little reason for so many people to stay on the farm. The question was not so much "how you gonna keep 'em down on the farm?" as it was "what will you do with 'em if they stay?" Labor was no longer needed in agriculture and was in short supply in the industrial centers of the nation. Employment opportunities at good wages were a gravitational attraction pulling more and more of the nation into these unnatural aggregations. At the nation's founding 95 percent of the American population was engaged in agriculture, and collectively they produced very little surplus indeed. Today barely 1.6 percent of the nation's labor force is engaged in agriculture and yet collectively they produce enough food to feed all 270 million Americans with enough left over to export tens of billions of dollars worth each year. Getting that food to market takes more labor than growing it. It now has to be processed, preserved, increasingly prepared, and packaged. It has to be transported, distributed, and sold. More and more of those jobs are in the urban aggregations. By the time Lyndon Johnson declared that America was to become the Great Society, it was clear that, great or not, its future would be as an urban society. It was equally clear that our cities were suffering massive social problems, in large part because of how the space within those growing aggregations was being reorganized.

Suburb and Sprawl

The internal combustion engine changed not only agriculture and industry, it changed the whole spatial organization of cities. It affected where people live, where they work, play, learn, and socialize. It changed how they move between those activities and places. It reshaped space. Southern and western cities that experienced most of their growth during this era were built differently—they are car cities. Older cities built under the logic of preautomobile technologies adapted and restructured as much as their old forms would allow. In all American cities though, old and new, the appeal of space drew more and more people into the suburbs and drove them, more or less, to "sprawl."

Urban space, of course, is only as valuable as it is accessible. If cut off from the rest of the region it is of little use. If well connected there will be competition for it. Cars connected all parts of the metropolitan area with all other parts. There was no longer any place so isolated that "you couldn't get there from here." Cars are the only short or long distance, all-weather form of urban transit in which all three elements of transit systems are combined in a single mode—collection, line haul, and distribution. They can take you door to door whenever you choose to go. There is no need to follow some common route, no need to transfer from one mode to another, no need to travel only when others do. They are ideally suited for low-density suburban living.

Suburbs had been part of the urban landscape for a long time, but before the car they had been limited to those places where transit lines—commuter railroads or trolleys—had been installed. Suburbs followed those lines, leaving large tracts of open land between. With millions of American families driving Ford's new, affordable Model T and earning industrial-level wages the entire plain surrounding a central city became open for development. It was no longer important to live within walking distance of a rail or trolley line. If suburbanites needed to go anywhere they could drive.

The nation had been aggregating for a long time, but beginning in the 1920s the nature of urbanization changed. While the population of central cities continued to increase the most rapid *rate* of growth was no longer in the central cities but in the new suburban rings. According to census data, in nearly three fourths of the nation's metropolitan areas the growth rate of the suburbs in the 1920s exceeded that of the central cities. A few experienced very large imbalances. In Boston the suburbs grew five times as fast as the city; in Cleveland, ten times; and in St. Louis, twenty times.[24]

This rapid development of new suburban communities soon exposed the problems inherent in uncoordinated growth. Beautiful new homes lost much of their appeal, and perhaps more significantly their value, when a hog slaughtering plant opened across the road. Supermarkets were good to have nearby, but not too near. Along with food they brought noise, traffic, and clutter to the neighborhood. Arterial roads made the suburban community accessible to the central city, but they also brought noise, pollution, and danger to the neighborhood. Where exactly did the different activities belong?

Planning from the Start

Large-scale real estate developers in every major city saw the gold at the end of the automotive rainbow, and many saw the conflicts arising from uncoordinated growth as an obstacle to attaining it. Jesse Nichols built the first successfully planned suburban community and so produced a model for the whole nation. A graduate of the University of Kansas and Harvard, in 1921 he bought a vast tract of land south of Kansas City, Missouri, and developed it as a planned community. He introduced private deed restrictions to provide use zoning, high-quality construction standards, building cost minimums, lot set backs, and the preservation of open spaces. In order to provide retail services to the community he conceived and built the first suburban shopping mall in 1922. American culture would never be the same. His successful Country Club District was widely studied and soon became a model for suburban planning throughout the country.

The adoption of Nichols's system of high-quality construction standards on large lots did two things. It defined the character of the suburban community as it developed, assuring the kind of decentralized housing that earliest urban housing activists had advocated. That was a large part of its purpose, but that also meant that only those above some minimum level of resources would be able to afford the new housing. It was, and still is, economically impossible to build new, high-quality, *high-density* housing that the poor can afford to rent or buy. High-quality, *low-density* housing is just that much more out of reach. As if the restrictions on quality were not enough of a barrier to low-income suburbanization, Nichols also inserted into his deeds racial restrictive covenants that forbade the resale of any property in the District to other than white, Christian buyers.[25] Because they were private contract provisions rather than governmental laws, the racial restrictions were initially deemed legal and their use spread rapidly to new developments throughout the nation. Until they were finally declared unenforceable in 1947 they presented a legal barrier to suburbanization of those minority households that could overcome the economic obstacles.[26] The new suburban communities begun in the 1920s were predominantly wealthy and white.

This was the first wave of automobile-generated development, and by the end of the 1920s new suburbs made up of nice, new homes occupied by relatively well-off residents had appeared around every major city. In the 1930s restrictions on immigration significantly slowed the overall rate of population growth and that, plus the hard times of the Great Depression, brought new housing construction, and with it new suburban development, nearly to a halt. Then came the Second World War, and construction resources were diverted from civilian to military uses. Despite rising population and growing real income, suburbs were not allowed to grow. Thus after the war there was a terrific backlog of demand. GIs returning to a now prosperous economy, armed with discharge papers and government mortgage guarantees, demanded housing. As always, it was cheaper to build new housing on vacant land.

The older central cities of the North were already "full." There the only land available for development was outside the city limits. In some of the newer cities of the "sunbelt" not all of the urban space had already been filled with structures left over from a preautomobile era. There it was still possible to build some new low-density housing within the political boundaries of city. In all cases, however, the urban aggregation spread outward— older housing in the center, newer housing on the edge. For the nation as a whole, the suburban growth rate was four times that of cities. In the older Northeast, central cities began to lose population even as their metropolitan areas continued to grow. Only in new cities like Los Angeles, Dallas, and Denver, all of which covered vast geographic areas, did central cities continue to increase in population, but they did so in suburban-style neighborhoods that happened to lie within their broad city limits.[27]

Commuting by Car

In the immediate postwar period suburbanites still mostly found employment within the central city, and thus they needed to commute from their dispersed suburbs into the city. Increasingly the preferred mode of travel was by private car. Each day more and more cars were being funneled from a wide area into the congested center where they competed for space. Ways to improve traffic flows were desperately needed. In 1924 the electric traffic light was introduced, and with careful coordination it allowed a smoother flow of traffic along surface streets. Lights at sequential intersections could be coordinated and timed to pass along traffic at a specific speed.

Most cities welcomed the shift to the automobile and invested significant amounts of public money in urban street improvement. Ironically the current environmental concern over automobile pollutants is a late development. Originally cars were welcomed as an environmental improvement because their emissions were seen as cleaner and much less noxious than the cumulating emissions of the many horses then traveling city streets.[28]

It did not take long for automobile advocates to recognize the speed and convenience advantages that would come from a separate right-of-way for suburban commuters, isolated from slower forms of travel and local traffic on cross streets. Separate parkways limited to automobile traffic and crossing above or below local streets via tunnel or bridge were first tried in the New York City area. The first, the Long Island Motor Parkway, was built even before the First World War. As the suburbs expanded during the 1920s other parkways and bridges were built to serve as feeder routes for automobile commuters traveling into the central city.[29]

As with so many things associated with cars, urban expressways achieved their highest form of expression in California. Cities and freeways grew up hand in hand. Surrounded by marching bands and balloons the governor cut the ribbon opening the Arroyo Seco Parkway, later to be renamed the Pasadena Freeway, just hours before the start of the New Year 1941. The road had first been proposed even before Henry Ford threw the switch starting his moving assembly line, but the idea languished until the downtown department stores started to feel competition from suburban retailers. They began to push for its construction in order to defend the location of their businesses, and it soon became a reality. Those downtown merchants became the first of many, however, who would experience the harsh reality about the symmetry of freeways. Roads that make it easier for people to travel into the city also make it easier for them to move out of it! Los Angelenos were able to travel through the heart of the urban area at a mile a minute. Living a few miles from town was no inconvenience at all. Even through the heart of a major city, a five-mile drive took less time than a half-mile walk—unless of course too many other people tried to undertake the same journey at the same time. The solution to overcrowded expressways connecting suburb with city was obvious—build more expressways. The race was on. Each new freeway led to further and farther suburban development and more development increased the need for more freeways.

Much of the rest of the nation followed California's example. Newer cities were constructed along with their expressways. In the older cities the expressways were retrofitted, cutting swathes through existing urban neighborhoods to provide access into the central city from the newer suburbs. Impressed by the logistical advantages conferred on the German military during the Second World War by its Autobahn system, the Eisenhower administration proposed in the mid-1950s a major national investment in an Interstate Highway System for the United States. Much of the system was to connect distant cities to each other, but at each end it supported new construction of intraurban expressways as well.

Population, like any fluid, changes its shape whenever the constraining forces on it change. Cars and highways in combination shifted the constraints limiting urban space much farther outward from the central city, and population flowed outward as a result. Table 2 shows the impact on central-city and suburban ring populations over a fifty-year period. In the older, preautomobile cities of the Northeast and Central regions, central-city populations declined in absolute terms as suburbs grew. New York's fell slightly, Boston's by a quarter, and St. Louis' by over half. The newer postautomobile cities did not at first experience an absolute decline in population—they were still filling in. However, by the latter part of the period, 1970–1990, half of even the automobile-age cities in the sample had begun to experience an absolute decline in population—while their suburbs con-

Table 2

Central-City Population 1940-1990

Selected preautomobile cities	Total population			Percent change	
	1940	1970	1990	1970–90	1940–90
Atlanta	302,000	497,000	394,000	−20.72	30.46
Dallas	295,000	844,000	1,007,000	19.31	241.36
Denver	322,000	515,000	468,000	−9.13	45.34
Houston	385,000	1,233,000	1,631,000	32.28	323.72
Los Angeles	1,504,000	2,816,000	3,485,000	23.76	131.72
Seattle	368,000	539,000	516,000	−4.27	40.22
Selected postautomobile cities					
Boston	771,000	641,000	574,000	−10.45	−25.55
Chicago	3,397,000	3,367,000	2,784,000	−17.32	−18.05
Detroit	1,623,000	1,511,000	1,028,000	−31.97	−36.66
New York	7,455,000	7,895,000	7,323,000	−7.25	−1.77
Philadelphia	1,931,000	1,949,000	1,586,000	−18.62	−17.87
St. Louis	816,000	622,000	397,000	−36.17	−51.35

Source: Chudacoff, pp. 274–75 and Downs, *New Visions,* table 5-1, pp. 62–65.

tinued to grow. In 1940, less than a third of the total population of these twelve metropolitan areas lived in the suburbs; by 1970 that proportion had risen over one half, and by 1990 it was approaching two thirds. The population of all of America's urban aggregations has reorganized into a low-density sprawl.

Meanwhile, Back in the City

The changes in the total population numbers fail to tell the complete story, however. Over this period a major alteration in the composition, as well as the size, of central-city populations was taking place. There was migration in as well as out. As the upper and middle classes increasingly moved to the suburbs, more and more of the nation's poor were moving to urban areas to seek industrial employment. International Harvester's mechanical cotton picker was demonstrated on the Hopson plantation right on the eve of the great wave of postwar suburbanization, setting off a corresponding wave of mostly black migrants from the rural South into cities in the North. Chicago's experience was typical.

> During the 1940s, the black population of Chicago increased by 77 percent, from 278,000 to 492,000. In the 1950s, it grew by another 65 per cent, to 813,000; at one point 2,200 black people were moving to Chicago every week. By 1960, Chicago had more than half a million more black residents than it had had twenty years earlier, and black migrants from the South were still coming in tremendous numbers. The mechanical cotton picker was now in use everywhere in the South and the Sharecropper system had been phased out on most plantations.[30]

All of these new city arrivals had to live somewhere, and the workings of urban housing markets meant that most would only be able to find suitable housing in the central city. Most new arrivals came with high hopes and low finances. The prevalence of high construction standards meant that new housing could not be constructed for them at a cost they could afford. If the market was to provide any housing at all, it would be filtered-down housing—older, higher density buildings broken up into more and more units. Only in central-city neighborhoods developed under older technologies was there a significant pool of old, high-density buildings. When the middle class moved to the suburbs it left behind block after block of apartment buildings that could be broken up into one- and two-room units with central bathrooms shared by several tenants per floor.

Central location made sense to the new migrants for other reasons as well. They had been drawn to the city by the prospect of industrial employment, and for much of the period those jobs were still concentrated in the central city. The cars that made the suburbs accessible to the middle class were still beyond the reach of many of the new city residents. Low-skill, entry-level jobs accessible via older-style public transit modes were features of the cities, not the suburbs. Finally, of course, for those residents of the growing black communities in the inner city who had the financial resources to move out, their options were limited by racial discrimination. The ubiquitous restrictive covenants were only the most formalistic obstacle to black suburbanization. Discrimination by mortgage lenders, real estate brokers, and opposition from potential neighbors foreclosed the suburban option for most.

The black urban migration was largely completed by the end of the 1960s. Blacks were followed into central cities by a wave of new immigrants from Latin American countries as they too found filtered housing to be the only form of low-income shelter made available by the market. Black and Hispanic households have not been exempt from the lure of the new technologies that have drawn white families into the suburbs through-out this century, however. They too have sought better quality housing with more space when it was attainable. The first trickle of black suburbanization began as early as the 1930s, but it involved only a minority of families. Most were restricted by low incomes and the overt hostility they faced in many communities. As family incomes have risen for black and Hispanic households, and as overt discrimination in housing and lending markets has become more difficult to maintain, the pace of minority suburbanization has increased in recent years. By 1990 two thirds of the whites living within Metropolitan Areas resided outside the central city, but so too did nearly a third of all blacks, 43 percent of all Hispanics, and half of all Asians and Native Americans. As members of minority racial groups attained middle-class status many responded just as the white middle class had done—by moving to the suburbs. They often remain segregated in suburbs that are identifiably "their own," and often in older ring communities, but they too have left the central city and its concentrations of extreme poverty behind.[31] Increasingly it is only those unable to leave that are being left behind.

Suburbanizing Jobs

As urban populations moved out to these new suburbs they, of course, took with them the market for many retail goods and services. Most residents of the metropolitan area now lived a considerable distance from downtown stores and theaters. They lived in the low-density patterns made possible by the automobile and thus when they went shopping they could not just take trolleys or trains directly from their houses to the downtown stores. They either had to drive to the public transit lines, find parking, and change modes before riding into town, or else drive all the way in by car, confronting the traffic and parking problems that ensued. Retail outlets with ample free parking close to the suburban majority began to enjoy a significant advantage over central-city competitors. Moreover, with land prices in the center of town still much higher per square foot, downtown stores faced higher operating costs along with a declining customer base. Movie theaters, doctors offices, community hospitals, schools, police and fire services, all followed population out of the central city. Those employed in providing those services increasingly both lived and worked in the suburbs; all of their ties to the central city were largely severed. New suburban business districts became growing subfoci as "edge cities" began to develop.[32]

The internal combustion engine whose widespread use was only made possible by mass production techniques went on to change the logic of location for its own mass production and that of other products. Large assembly lines like Ford's operate most efficiently in large, low buildings that occupy a lot of space. Multistory urban factories built at the turn of the century could not accommodate this kind of production. Horizontal space was needed and that space was much cheaper per square foot in the suburbs. Of course space had always been less expensive on the periphery, but the necessity of locating near rail lines had been so compelling that it overrode any land cost savings—until trucks and highways provided a new and more efficient means of distribution for many goods. Then both production *and* distribution costs fell for plants that located outside of central cities and the exodus was on. As large manufacturers and assemblers moved their facilities to the rings, the firms supplying them with parts found it beneficial to follow. Their land costs were lower in the suburbs and, located near their major buyers, so too were their distribution costs. Adam Smith's "invisible hand" pushed production to the suburbs.

In an earlier era, central-city locations for manufacturers had also been important because of their need to be near, or at least accessible to, large pools of labor. If workers did not live in the immediate vicinity of the factory, they had to be connected to it via public transportation, and those networks focused on the central city. As population suburbanized and came to depend upon the automobile, the labor supply shifted out of the central city and away from its dependence on public transit. Industrial workers could drive from their homes in the suburbs to plants also located in the ring. Suburban industrial parks came to be a standard element of all cities. Employment decentralized right along with population as jobs moved to the suburbs too. By the era of the Great Society the vast majority of workers who lived in the ring area also worked in the suburbs and a significant number of residents of the central city had even begun to commute out to suburban jobs. They primarily traveled to and from work by car. Today 85 percent of all urban trips to work are by car. Even in New York, the quintessential preautomobile city, nearly 40 percent of commutes to work in the metropolitan area are by car. In newer cities like Fort Worth, the ratio is well over 90 percent.[33]

The Rise of the Central Business District

Central cities did not just close down when retail stores and large-scale goods manufacturing moved toward the suburbs. There was still a need for the direct face-to-face personal interactions that characterize top management functions, the law, advertising, government, and finance. In this period there was a major expansion in central business district functions. The management functions of large companies became physically separated from their production facilities, and company headquarters moved into the business center of cities into higher and more impressive office towers. Architects took Jenney's steel skeletons to new heights, literally. The Empire State Building was opened in the 1930s, and an era of super office skyscrapers followed. There, professional-level employees could physically meet and interact with the occupants of other managerial, legal, and governmental offices without spending their expensive time on intracity travel. There were not many jobs for the urban poor in these new office towers, however.

In the thirty-five years after the Second World War the six largest cities of the North and East saw central-city jobs in the services sector double, even while they experienced a 20 percent net decline in total central-city employment in four major industrial categories. In retailing, total central-city employment fell by 35 percent, in wholesaling by 38 percent, and in manufacturing by an astonishing 54 percent. Those cities were undergoing a fundamental change in their economic functions. The six largest cities in the South and West experienced their greatest period of growth during those years and central-city employment grew in all areas up until the 1980s, but the rate of growth in services was twice that of the other industries. Growth was even greater in the ring areas, however, so that in relative terms central-city employment, even in the Sunbelt, fell from over two thirds of the metropolitan area total at the beginning of the period to less than half by the end.[34] By the 1990s Sunbelt automobile cities, too, were beginning to experience absolute declines in central-city employment.

Even though overall service employment continued to rise, northern central cities were beginning to lose their grip on even the core central business district jobs as early as the 1960s. In 1954 the General Foods Corporation moved its headquarters from Manhattan to suburban White Plains. Over the next twenty-five years more than fifty other corporations followed, relocating their central office functions from New York City to suburbs up the Hudson, in New Jersey, and especially in Connecticut. By 1984 Fairfield County, Connecticut, had more corporate headquarters than any other American city except Chicago and New York.[35] Interestingly, the key determinant of where a corporation relocates its offices seems to be the residence of the chief executive officer at the time. If his or her commute is too long, he or she seems to prefer moving the office out rather than the residence in.[36]

The Look of the Suburbs

The face of urban development has been forever changed by the car. Contrary to popular perception, the car has actually *reduced* the total share of urban land that must be devoted to streets. For example, in Sacramento, California, in the parts of the city developed around 1850, 38 percent of the land area is devoted to streets, in the parts developed between 1900 and 1950, that proportion is 21 percent, while in the portions developed since 1950 it is only 15 percent. With cars as the standard mode of travel, blocks can be bigger and cross streets farther apart. When people walked everywhere, the distance around the block had to be small enough to be covered in a few minutes. Now that they are likely to drive, a half mile between cross streets in some suburban developments seems perfectly reasonable.

Of course we again come face to face with the circularity of urban development. Once physical structures have been built to take advantage of a new transportation technology, that technology is no longer just superior, it is essential. What was convenience becomes necessity. When the car is the norm, large grocery stores are built miles apart. Because they are miles apart, a car is necessary for most people to reach them. As a result the purpose of trips using transportation changes. As recently as 1950 over half of all urban trips involved commuting either to or from work. By the 1970s that proportion had already fallen below one quarter. It is because we have cars that we can live in low-density settings, and it is because that is how we live, whenever we go to the store, to school, to the doctor, to the hair salon, to the movies, or even to pick up a copy of the local newspaper, we drive.

In modern automobile-based suburbs a majority of American city dwellers have precisely the separate "homes of their own" that turn of the century reformers hoped would make them "full sharers" in the community. Ironically, current reformers see that outcome as a modern curse. What seemed "idyllic cottages" to one generation became "ticky-tacky little boxes" to the next.

> In an automotive age, cities have become the negation of communities—a setting for machines instead of people. The automobile has taken over, motorist and nonmotorist alike are caught up in the congestion, and everyone is a victim of the damaging effects of the conflict between the car and the community. The automobile is an irresistible force that may become an immovable object, and in the process destroy the city.[37]

The benefits and costs of automobiles are two sides of the same coin. There is no known way to have one without the other. There is no way to gather several millions of people into a single city, have them live in their own low-density dwellings, and still all be close enough to walk most places, or all to be within walking distance of some mode of efficient mass transit that connects to all other parts of the metropolitan area. Large cities contain many residents. Living space for residents requires dispersion. Dispersion requires transportation. Sprawl is the logical outcome and that is what those with the means to choose have chosen.

Those Left Behind

This long technological evolution explains much of the 200–year transformation of central cities from sanctuaries for the wealthy into the places "where we face our failures," and of suburbs from enclaves of filth and squalor to places of wealth and privilege. Because so many people were no longer needed on farms they were drawn into cities first by the prospect of commercial, and later of industrial, employment. The technology of intra-city transportation combined with the economics of housing construction to concentrate the lower income arrivals in the core of the city where, incidentally, employment opportunities were then also best. Once there, high-wage manufacturing jobs in mass production factories requiring minimal skills provided an avenue out of those enclaves for several generations of American workers. But then changing transportation technology allowed first the wealthy, then the middle class, and finally much of the working class to move outward from the crowded core of the city. The same changes in technology also made it economic to relocate much of the retail, industrial, and even service employment to the fringes of urban areas.

Rising incomes and changes in the logic of production have now shifted employment away from factory assembly and toward service sector jobs—some of which require high education and offer high pay, some of which both require and pay very little. Neither offers a realistic way out of poverty for today's inner-city poor. Those able to leave the central city, no matter of what race, have increasingly done so. Those left behind find that there is a shortage of high-wage, low-skill manufacturing jobs anywhere, and that they are spatially separated from those that still exist. They are educationally separated from the high-wage jobs in the central business district. Locked into neighborhoods of increasingly concentrated poverty, they see little prospect for improvement and increasingly theirs is an accurate perception.

In times past, changing technology gave central cities and their residents economic viability. Today changing technology has taken from central cities much of their economic logic for being. They were built around technologies that no longer prevail, and their aging structures have little use but to contain what some have called the "urban underclass" or what William Julius Wilson has defined as the "truly disadvantaged."[38] Jobs and economic activity continue to move out of the central city and those left behind are, in every sense of the word, isolated from the worlds of work and success. The organization of space and the perpetuation of poverty are intertwined.

Distorted History

The story told over the last four chapters has traced key developments in the evolution of technology and their impacts on the organization of space in the United States from its founding to the present day. It is time to confess that there have been two fundamental distortions in the telling of that tale. First, history has been too personified. As it has unfolded in the chapters just past, key individuals stepped forward in each era to alter the course of technological development. It makes for a compelling story when change is the chance result of special individual accomplishment. A strong case can be made, however, that larger social conditions precipitated and motivated the innovations. Had those particular individuals not come forward, others inevitably would have. If, in some time-travel experiment, we could go back and kidnap at birth Henry Bessemer, Eli Whitney, Robert Fulton, Cyrus McCormick, and Henry Ford, the course of technological history would not be materially changed. The details and timing of innovations might vary, but the main flow of spatial history would not.

Each of those men produced their innovations in competition with others addressing the same problems. They worked on their problems because there was a clear socially recognized need, and because there was by then available to them enough of the component pieces to make the problem seem solvable.[39] No one devoted much effort to powered human flight in 1645. There was no foundation to support a solution; it was not seen as a possibility. There was no basis upon which to develop it. By 1900, however, the pieces of the puzzle were all there, and many people saw that the problem could be solved if only the right combination could be devised. Wilber and Orville Wright were simply the first ones to succeed, but they were certainly not the only ones to try. Nearly all of the successful innovators in the chapters past had to fight for recognition of their contribution as the crucial piece in an unfolding chain of events. The chance event is less the innovation itself than it is the determination of which individual is remembered for it.

Innovation is seldom epiphany. It is more often accretion—a slow reordering of known ideas and elements to address a problem that has come to be seen as important by a large segment of the community. As long as the problem is real and clear, and as long as the necessary prior elements have accumulated, a solution will be found by one or by another. The evolution of spatial organization in the United States has not been by plan or conspiracy. It was not foreseen, and was certainly not intended, by those who played key roles in moving it forward. Like natural evolution, the process moves not by conscious prior design but *ex post* environmental survival.

The story reads better as a tale of individual achievement but it is more accurately one of social inevitability.

Having so confessed, it is perhaps ironic that an emphasis on inevitability has itself been the second distortion, for not all elements of the current organization of space are equally dependent on major technological innovation. In fact the technological imperative has shaped only the general direction of change while human policy choices have greatly affected the particulars. The invention of the automobile set in motion the inevitability of sprawl, but the location of the poor within that spreading metropolis has also been affected by decisions about the construction and placement of public housing. It was cars that drove the middle class out to the suburbs, but the rate of movement has been affected by decisions about tax policy and mortgage guarantees. Policy choices, too, matter.

Navigating the River

Those who successfully navigate rivers understand two fundamental principles. The first is that the current *will* flow and that it *will* carry along with it any vessel that ventures onto its waters. The stronger the current, the more powerful the forces it exerts. If we simply drift with the current we *will* get downstream, but then we will have to take rocks, sandbars, whirlpools, rapids, and waterfalls as we meet them. We can be passive passengers, simply going with the flow. The second principle is that if we wish to influence the path we will take, we must add some other force of propulsion to that of the current. We cannot eliminate the current, nor can we escape it, but we can react wisely to it and affect where it takes us. In order to steer, we must paddle. Only then can we move *within* the current to different parts of the river's flow.

That does not mean that we can go just anywhere. We cannot paddle out of the river's banks and over a nearby hill. If the current is strong enough, we cannot paddle back upstream. If we face in that direction and exert exceptional effort we may slow our progress downstream, but we will arrive at each new destination facing backwards and unaware of where we are going. We cannot prevent the current, and us along with it, from proceeding down the riverbed path. Generally we cannot foresee the path too far ahead, but rest assured, that is where we are going. The skillful application of the paddle influences the safety of the trip but not the direction.

Navigating the Future

The evolution of our urban space, too, is a river. Humans, collectively, but not consciously, have created dramatic changes in the viability and shape of our unnatural aggregations. Technological change is the current that *will* propel us forward. It defines the overall pace of change and the parameters within which we *will* travel. In that we have no real choice. We cannot go back to some other point in the past and change the path of the river. There is no way to purge the human mind and experience of all reference to automobiles and the ability to reconceive of them. There is no way to return to an economy in which industrial jobs located in the central city dominate the economy. To try would be to paddle against the current and be carried downstream anyway—blind and facing backwards.

Nor is there much to be gained by spending energy organizing the past in some moral space, fixing events and actors in the "good" territory and the "bad." The past is past and unchangeable. Knowing how we got here may help us navigate ahead, but wisdom dictates that we face forward and focus our attention and our energies on the future of American cities. We cannot choose any future we might like, of course. The current is too strong for that, but we can influence where within the boundaries of the stream we will pass by the careful selection of policies. They are our paddles and they can help us find a safe passage or they can propel us toward the shoals. In the next few chapters we will examine our policy paddles and how we are using them. It is our current policies, along with the powerful flow of the past technological current, that determine where we are. If we can fix our position and define our strokes we can influence our future. To do so, however, we must face downstream and move forward. We cannot escape our past. We cannot negate the present. We cannot avoid the future. We are going along for this ride.

III
The Role of Policy

7

Urban Housing

Markets, Rules, and Regulations

Ruby Daniels was just one of the millions of African Americans who made the journey from the rural South to industrial cities in the North during the great postwar migration. In his book about that period Nicholas Lemann used her story as a case study personifying that movement. She, like all the other new arrivals, had to find housing in her new city.

> In 1946 Ruby Daniels moved . . . in with Ceatrice at 3666 Indiana Avenue, in the poorest part of the black belt. Ceatrice lived in what was known as a 'kitchenette' apartment—an apartment in a building that had been chopped up into one- or two-room flats each outfitted with an icebox and a hot plate. All the residents of the five or six apartments on each floor shared a common bathroom. Established middle-class black Chicagoans regarded the kitchenettes with something close to horror, as breeding grounds for immorality and ruiners of good neighborhoods . . . [but inevitably] 'once stable middle-class areas gradually become spotted with kitchenettes'.[1]

First individual buildings and then whole neighborhoods changed.

Twenty-four years later Colin and Joan Diver moved into a four-story house in the South End of Boston. He was a Harvard-trained lawyer who had turned down high-paying jobs at prestigious law firms in order to work on urban problems as a member of the mayor's staff. She worked for a progressive charitable foundation known as the Hyams Trust. The Divers were one of the three families whose experiences with court-ordered busing made up J. Anthony Lukas chronicle of Boston during the tumultuous 1970s. They were part of a small flow running counter to the dominant trend of the period—a middle-class family moving into the central city rather than out to the suburbs. They were drawn there by proximity to their jobs and the city's many cultural attractions, by the abundance of old Victorian town houses, and by "the racial, ethnic, and class mix to be found only in the inner city."[2]

The South End had seen many different residents come and go over the years. In the early to mid-nineteenth century it had been a residential neighborhood for wealthy merchants and commercial families. As the century waned and waves of poorer immigrants entered the city, old houses were converted for higher density occupancy and increasingly it became a neighborhood of boarders and poorer tenants. By 1900 the South End of Boston had the largest concentration of rooming houses of any urban neighborhood in the nation, with tens of thousands of poor people crowded into old, architecturally interesting buildings. By the 1960s a trickle of middle-class families had begun to move back into the community, attracted by the advantages of urban living and the special qualities of the old buildings. With great effort and expense, architectural gems could be made to emerge from the shells of the old rooming houses. By the time the Divers started looking for a house in the area, the South End Historical Society was already sponsoring an annual tour of the most impressive restorations.[3]

The house they finally found at 118 West Newton Street had been built in 1855 as the home of a prosperous merchant, but by 1970 it

> was a total disaster. . . . The old spruce floors were rotting, the window sashes were splintered, the plaster ornaments had fallen from much of the parlor ceiling. The bottom two floors were livable, but the top two looked as if they had barely survived a hurricane—wooden lath showing through the walls, wire and cables trailing along the halls, two bathrooms with exposed plumbing and uncovered plasterboard.
> . . . What particularly intrigued Colin was the interior detail—the Italian-ate marble fireplaces, the ornate plasterwork on the high ceilings, the cornice moldings, and the medallions in the center of each parlor from which chandeliers had once been suspended. . . . The house would take a lot of work, but that was precisely what Colin wanted, a tough job he could get his fingers into.[4]

At one level these are the stories of two families, but they are also stories about their houses as well—two long-lived structures that changed both form and function as the demand for them changed. The houses were there long before Ruby Daniels and the Divers moved in; they will be there long after they have moved out. The dynamic nature of urban populations requires both the total number and the composition of households to be in a constant state of change. Housing must somehow adapt to the changing needs, whether for an increase in suburban houses or for an increase in the number of low-income, central-city units—else the city will cease to function adequately. Thus the solution to present need comes out of the past. It is not possible to erase the existing city and build a wholly new housing stock each year, constructing exactly what is needed by the current population. In any given year only a small percentage of the total housing stock can be made up of new units. Most of the urban housing stock has been there for a long time. Most of the urban population, therefore, always has to live in older, existing structures. Indeed, even the president of the United States lives in used housing.

The shape of American cities today reflects the interaction of special markets for urban housing and a series of policy initiatives. Some of these policies have established rules about where, when, and how housing can be built, some have affected the prices of housing, and some have changed the processes of financing housing. In combination they have had a major impact on housing markets and on the organization of urban space. Policies have been, and still are, important, but an understanding of their full implications can only come after an examination of the workings of housing markets themselves.

Housing as a Package Deal

A "house," unlike a bushel of number two hard red winter wheat, is not a single thing. Any one bushel of graded wheat is indistinguishable from any other. With the possible exception of a few new developments filled with mass-produced structures, no one house is a perfect substitute for any other. Each is, to some degree, unique. While some other units may be close substitutes, none will be completely identical. To buy housing is to buy the right to live in a structure with its own particular architectural style, quality of construction, current condition, amount of space, and features. It is also to buy the right to a particular location with its varying degrees of access to other parts of the city and of proximity to the city's various amenities and hazards. It is to buy the right to live in a particular neighborhood and to experience its unique blend of public services, risk of crime, and schools. It is to buy the right to live close to, or far away from, various other people. It is to buy the responsibility for a capital structure whose length of life will be affected by how much is spent over time on maintenance.

The cliché that a house is not a home is thus accurate, but often misconstrued. In fact a house is much more than just a home, it is a complete package of elements that together define the quality of its residents' lives. It is a package that comes all together with no prospect of "unbundling." With the exemption of the rare case where a structure is physically moved, one cannot buy the house without getting the location and neighborhood as well.

Submarkets for Shelter

The market for these multidimensional "houses" is best understood not as a single market but as a series of interconnected submarkets defined by variations in size, quality, location, and cost. Different groups of urban residents compete in the short run for different segments of the total housing stock. There is a market for small, low-income apartments close to bus lines that is related to, but distinct from, that for detached single-family homes close to good schools. Different groups of persons look at different segments of the market. They are not in direct competition for the same structures, at least in the short run. However, over time the *characteristics* of a particular unit can be changed so that, even without any construction of new units, the stock of housing for low-income, or middle-income families can be changed. Housing units "filter" between submarkets. The building into which Ruby Daniels moved was filtering down. The building into which the Divers moved was filtering up. The same structure can serve many different uses over its total lifetime.

It is the relative prices in the various submarkets that act as the driving force in readjusting the number of units in the various submarkets, not administrative decrees. As the middle class was leaving Chicago and poor blacks were arriving in record numbers, the demand for units affordable by the new migrants exceeded the supply and the prices per unit rose to reflect the shortage. As the middle-class blacks moved farther out, there were fewer takers for the larger inner-city apartments and their relative price fell. When it became more profitable to rent forty kitchenettes than ten four-room apartments, buildings began to be converted. At one level this was, of course, a case of landlords "taking advantage" of an urgent need on the part of the new arrivals, but it was also the only way for the market to provide for that urgent need. If private landlords had not done so, the need would still have been there, but the housing would not. It was the only way in which more affordable housing was going to be made available at all. Without that conversion in response to price, there would have been no increase in low-income housing even though there was a greatly increased low-income population.

One of the common experiences of adulthood in this high mobility age, is to return after many years to the neighborhood where one grew up, only to be astonished by the change. Most of the same buildings are still there, but the character of the community is undoubtedly different. The buildings have deteriorated or have been renovated. A few have been added or demolished. The people living there are of different races or income classes or ages than they used to be. Every urban neighborhood is constantly changing, perhaps only an imperceptible amount each day, but over time the cumulative effect can be dramatic. Because I look in the mirror each day I can never see myself age, but when I go to my high school reunion the process is apparent to all. Because I live in my neighborhood I cannot see the changes day by day, but over time it too becomes apparent to all. All urban neighborhoods evolve.

The Role of the Rules

Today, of course, there are comparable mass migrations of the poor from rural areas to the cities in places like Brazil, Mexico, India, and Nigeria, but in those countries the new arrivals are not moving into kitchenettes in older structures in the center of town. Instead they create new "developments" consisting of owner-built housing on the edges of the cities—shantytowns made up of the poorest of shacks constructed from whatever materials can be salvaged. In those cities the poorest of slums are where the wealthiest of suburbs "should" be. Why is their twentieth-century urbanization experience so different from ours? They have access to the same technology. They are experiencing the same kind of population movement. Yet their cities are structured much differently than ours. There must have been other defining factors at work when Ruby Daniels moved to Chicago, and of course there were. Shantytowns are a viable "solution" to the needs of urban migrants only under certain rules of the game—specifically that there are no officially enforced building standards and that ownership rights to all of the urban land are not established and well enforced. In colonial America there was a similar absence of rules, and our suburbs then were also synonymous with squalor. Although on a smaller scale, those suburbs looked more like Mexico City's poorest neighborhoods. Since then, however, there has been a steady progression of more and more stringent rules about housing construction in the United States, and shantytowns have disappeared as an urban housing option.

The first restrictions on building quality were imposed in response to the dangers of fire in high-density cities. In 1871 virtually the entire city of Chicago burned to the ground as flames spread rapidly from one wooden building to another, each one built right to the property line. In a city, how your house is built and where on the lot it is located changes the probability that your fire will spread to my house. In a city, though the rain may fall on the just and unjust alike, if the unjust try to drain their land, they are likely to channel water onto that of their more just neighbors. It was recognition of interconnectedness of risk and damage in urban settings that led to the first building codes in American cities. At first they were seen as public safety measures concerned with fire and flood. Later, building regulations were expanded to address issues of public health. The density of population, poor ventilation, and inadequate sanitation of early tenements made them breeding grounds for disease. Under the recognized authority of its police powers, minimum standards of light, ventilation, and sanitation for all buildings came to be seen as within the jurisdiction of local government. The classic form of the "dumbbell" tenements at the turn of the century was a design response to the new regulations.

Building codes have been both a blessing and a bane to the poor. They have improved the quality of the buildings in which the lowest income urban residents dwell, but they have also raised the costs of providing that housing and they are responsible for the complete reliance on filtering as the source of increased supply. In Third World nations today, new housing for the poor is built by the poor. It is often of abominable quality, but it is affordable. In the United States, more privately provided housing for the poor comes only from existing housing filtering down. It is of better quality than shantytown structures, but it is seldom truly affordable, and because it derives from the old, existing housing stock it is largely limited to the older neighborhoods of the central city. Building codes also mean that the poor will be dependent on landlords for that inner-city housing. Unlike the urban poor in the Third World, they cannot provide it for themselves.

Poor Housing, Poor Landlords

In one episode of the popular television show *LA Law* the wealthy owner of a decrepit inner-city apartment house was sentenced to serve time in his own building for repeated violations of the building code. That episode was modeled on the case of a real-life Beverly Hills neurosurgeon, Dr. Milton Avol, dubbed by some of his tenants as the "Ratlord." For failing to keep his buildings in good repair despite numerous orders from the city, he was forced by Judge Veronica Simmons McBeth to move from his expensive suburban mansion into an apartment in his building for thirty days. That event and the news coverage of it made for good drama. What could be more illustrative of social injustice than the contrast between his own housing and the housing he provided for the poor? There was a fundamental misimpression created by the TV drama and the news coverage of the actual event, however.

It was not rents gouged from the poor that made Dr. Avol rich. They did not provide him with his expensive Beverly Hills home. His neurosurgery practice did that. He was a wealthy man who sought an investment outlet in low-income housing, not a man who became rich by providing it. His real problem with the law came because he was unwilling to use some of the profits from his medical practice to rehabilitate and maintain his investment. The final result of his experience with the law was a desire to rid himself of the building as quickly as possible, and his selling the building did little to improve the quality of the apartments.

An individual who seeks to earn a living providing low-income housing that meets high building code standards is typically destined to earn a very modest income indeed. According to Irving Welfeld, a majority of New York's landlords own but a single building, live in it themselves, and support it largely through their own unpaid labor. Most have not finished high school. They are increasingly immigrants and members of minority groups seeking to gain a foothold stake. The poorer their tenants, the lower the rents charged in dollar terms but the higher the rent burden as a percent of tenants' incomes. Those landlords cannot cover higher costs by raising rents; there is nothing more there in most cases. Yet over recent decades their costs have risen steadily and most are always on the edge of bankruptcy.[5] Strict building codes improve quality, but they force a reliance on filtered housing and they also make the long-term financial health of that housing more tenuous.

Conflicts over the Uses of Space

As cities have grown ever denser and ever bigger it has become clear that what happens on one piece of property affects the ability of its neighbors to enjoy theirs, and not just in terms of fire, flood, and disease. When Jenney and Otis and Bessemer combined to make the construction of very tall buildings both possible and practical they changed urban space for everyone. To own property on the north side of a skyscraper was to be plunged into perpetual shade as the new tower rose to block out the sun. Thus to protect abutters' property rights cities began to place restrictions on the height of new buildings in various parts of the city. In 1909 the Supreme Court upheld Boston's authority to limit building height for the "public good," but it quickly became apparent that that restriction alone was not enough.[6] Multistory, steel-frame buildings of even modest height, rising straight up from the edges of each lot blocked all air and light from adjoining buildings and turned narrow streets into dark canyons. Further restrictions requiring setbacks for upper floors were enacted, and urban skyscrapers began to display a stepped profile.

Those rules addressed the harm that a *structure* could do to adjoining property holders, but there was still the issue of inconsistent *uses*. A factory generating toxic waste, even if done in a tasteful and unobtrusive building, would be harmful to a neighboring day-care center. A foundry operated around the clock would make sleep difficult for its residential neighbors, even if the structure it was housed in cast no shadows on adjoining land. A busy commercial center would create traffic hazards for children living nearby, even if the building itself was quiet and safe. As cities grew, and especially as they spread to envelope surrounding communities, conflicts in the use of land multiplied. When Jesse Nichols faced problems of inconsistent land use in his vast new development in Kansas City he was able to solve them by writing restrictions into the deeds. His solution was viable, however, only because the whole community was being built and planned all at once and under consolidated ownership. In older communities, most of the property was already platted and owned and it was impractical, if not impossible, to get all existing land owners to agree on a single set of covenants to bind them all in the future. If areas already developed and under fragmented ownership were to control land-use conflicts they would have to turn to government and public policy.

In 1916 New York City enacted the first American municipal zoning ordinance. Some portions of the city were set aside for residences, some for commercial activity; industrial plants were limited to certain areas. Restrictions on building sizes and setbacks for various types of buildings were established for each zone. For the first time in the United States a city government placed comprehensive controls on the use and organization of the space within its jurisdiction. Over the next decade American cities grew at an explosive pace. The first wave of automobile-induced suburbanization began spreading population into previously rural areas outside of central cities. Everywhere conflicts followed development and communities sought to contain them. Within a decade over 400 municipalities had followed New York's example, enacting general zoning ordinances that brought over half the nation's population under zoning controls.[7]

Zoning's Day in Court

At the turn of the century, Euclid, Ohio, was a small village, near, but clearly outside of, urban Cleveland. Farming was its central activity. By the 1920s Cleveland's edge was creeping ever closer, however, and the quiet lives of Euclid's residents were being threatened. Some looked to the future's changes with fear and others with anticipation. The Ambler Realty Company was one of the latter. Between two already developed residential areas of single-family homes it bought a sixty-eight-acre tract of land, accessible by both highways and railroad lines. The company saw in the rapid expansion of Cleveland and the transportation convenience of their land the potential for industrial development and significant profit. The prospect of busy factories in their quiet neighborhood horrified many of the village's residents, however. Industrial development so close to their homes would clearly lower the value of their houses. More significantly it would damage the quality of their lives. Yet the law was clear. Ambler could do as it pleased without regard for its neighbors. After all, it *owned* the land.

Or so it thought until the village of Euclid adopted a general zoning ordinance that prohibited industrial development on their tract. According to Ambler this reduced the value of its land by 75 percent, and so it sued the village on the grounds that its regulations violated the constitutional prohibition on the taking of property without compensation. The case went to the U.S. Supreme Court where the constitutionality of municipal zoning was tested for the first time. Ambler lost. The Court recognized that while in the past such regulations "probably would have been rejected as arbitrary and oppressive . . . under the complex conditions of our day . . ." they must be sustained.[8]

> Until recent years, urban life was comparatively simple; but with the great increase and concentration of population, problems have developed, and constantly are developing, which require, and will continue to require, additional restrictions in respect of the use and occupation of private lands in urban communities.[9]

Since then markets have resolved the inevitable competition for urban space, who will use what property and how, but only within the limits established by zoning regulations.

"Nonconforming" Neighbors

The ordinance in Euclid, and in virtually all other communities, not only dictated separations between industrial, commercial, and residential districts, it also created different types of residential neighborhoods. Open spaces, high-quality public services, limited traffic, and minimal crowding all make a community more appealing as a place to live, but that very appeal can be its own undoing. If more and more people move in to take advantage of the attractions, they collectively overwhelm and destroy them. Then neither the old nor the new residents can enjoy them for the benefits are then gone.

Euclid's zoning ordinance thus sought to protect low-density residential areas from "overdevelopment" as well as from incursions by commerce and industry, and the Supreme Court validated that protection as well. It made much of the safety of children playing in open neighborhoods, the health of residents in uncrowded environs, and the tranquillity of life in low-traffic areas.

> [T]he development of detached house sections is greatly retarded by the coming of apartment houses, which has sometimes resulted in destroying the entire section for private house purposes; that in such sections very often the apartment house is a mere parasite, constructed in order to take advantage of the open spaces and attractive surroundings created by the residential character of the district. . . . [A]partment houses, which in a different environment, would be not only entirely unobjectionable but highly desirable, come very near to being nuisances.[10]

That is strong language. Apartment houses, though desirable elsewhere, in Euclid would be "parasites" and "nuisances," and surely as such, the village should have the right to exclude them. Of course excluding high-density nuisances also means excluding all people who cannot afford low-density, high-standard living. What of them?

To Protect Is to Exclude

The statutes granting zoning authority to cities usually require that they use it to promote the "general welfare," but there is little guidance as to what that phrase means. Whose welfare is to be included in the "general?" Courts and legislatures must still decide that. May zoning be used solely to protect the interests of those currently in a community or must it also take some account of the interests of those currently outside of its jurisdiction? There is no way to make that conflict disappear. The only question is how those interests will be weighed and balanced. In the Euclid case and most of those that followed, communities have been allowed to make that choice for themselves.

Is that clearly a "wrong" principle? Should not the interests of current residents of a community or neighborhood have priority? Should not they have the right to preserve their community as it is? Should not they be allowed to control their own future? Should not new arrivals accept things as they found them? That has some appeal, but in strict application it must always fail. First, of course, it is too static a principle for a dynamic society and is thus fundamentally unrealistic. As population grows the "new" people all must live somewhere. As industry and commerce develop it all must be located somewhere. Some degree of change is inevitable and some reorganization of space will occur somewhere. Like a balloon being filled with air, increased resistance to growing pressure in one place only leads to bulges in others. Zoning regulations clearly affect a wider public than just the current residents of a municipality. They cannot prevent change in the larger society, they just help locate it. Should not the welfare of that larger public be a part of the "general" welfare as well? In recent years a few courts have begun to adopt that position.

Legal versus Illegal Exclusion

All zoning, to one degree or another, excludes. The question is, how exclusionary can it be? The answer remains somewhat fluid. Some forms of exclusion are clearly illegal. In 1917 the U.S. Supreme Court invalidated a Memphis ordinance designating certain blocks for "white" or "colored" residence only. Since then there can be no explicit zoning by race.[11] Similarly *purposeful* exclusion of low-income people is not a valid end for a city government. No ordinance that boldly stated that "no persons with incomes below the poverty line may live in this area" could survive a court challenge. However, if the good-faith pursuit of a legitimate end, such as environmental protection, has the *effect* of excluding poor people, the dominant rule is that the zoning is presumed valid. If a prohibition on wetlands development prevents the construction of low-cost housing, that exclusion is legal. Thus challenges to the exclusionary effects of zoning turn on proof of the *intent* of those in the municipal government rather than the effect of the regulations themselves. If the end sought is legitimate, so too is the zoning.

Exclusion may be, and often is, an unintended consequence of seeking perfectly legitimate ends. Excessive growth clearly creates problems for a community. It creates costs for the local government, congestion for the residents, and strain on the environment. Over the last twenty-five years increasing numbers of jurisdictions have taken steps to control or limit their growth.[12] Large-lot zoning is perhaps the most widespread of these. Many local governments have also declared periodic limits, or even moratoria, on new connections to city water and sewer services. Many have restricted the number of new building permits they will allow each year, with the result that builders feel they must use them for the highest profit, highest priced houses local zoning will allow. Some have imposed direct "development charges" on new construction so that all of the costs of new roads, utilities, schools, and fire protection will be borne by the new residents and not burden the old.

Strict regulations requiring extensive environmental impact statements and design reviews can create lengthy and expensive delays in development, and provide points of legal attack for opponents of growth as well.

Indeed, the Stanford Environmental Law Society prepared a handbook encouraging environmental lawsuits against development, not because they could all be won but because the process of delay would be so expensive that many projects would simply have to be abandoned.[13] The handbook took no notice of the impact on the availability of affordable housing. It contained no suggestions about where a growing population might live if all new developments are prevented. It expressed no concern over a slowing of the filtering process. Its concern, and undoubtedly a sincere one, was to promote environmental protection not to restrict the availability of housing for the poor. Zoning regulations enacted by local governments are generally afforded the same flexibility in defining goals and priorities. Within certain limits, if the end can be reasonably seen as neighborhood preservation, capital cost control, or environmental protection, then exclusionary effects will generally not be sufficient to invalidate zoning and use regulations. Doing good with respect to one commendable end may often do harm to another. Local governments have mostly been left to weigh these tradeoffs as they have seen fit. That is a clear policy choice with real consequences for cities.

Mount Laurel and the Fair Share Principle

At the close of World War II, Mount Laurel, New Jersey, was a quiet little town on the edge of the Greater New York metropolitan area. In 1950 it had fewer than 3,000 residents, but with the great wave of postwar suburbanization that quickly changed. By 1960 the population had nearly doubled; by 1970 it had doubled again. By 1980 there were six times as many people in the town as had lived there thirty years before. Public services were severely strained, and the quiet character of the town was being irrevocably changed. The local government felt that it had to gain some control over this extraordinary growth and change, and the obvious medium for that was to use municipal zoning regulations. So in the midst of this period, the undeveloped land within the town was all rezoned for large-lot, low-density, single-family development only. There would be no more "parasitic" apartments built in Mount Laurel.

The town, of course, was not alone in experiencing growth and change over these years. The whole region was experiencing the same thing. New people and new industries were moving out from the city, and many of the new people in the region were members of racial minority groups. There was little question that the zoning in Mount Laurel had the *effect* of making it much more difficult for low- and moderate-income households to move into that community. Indeed most residents of the state were not "able to afford one-family housing" at all.[14] Like all zoning, Mount Laurel's excluded. There was very little evidence, however, that the conscious purpose of the regulations was to keep the poor and racial minorities out of the town. If the regulations were to be challenged in a court of law, it would have to be over some issue other than exclusionary intent.

The National Association for the Advancement of Colored People (NAACP) of Southern Burlington County was concerned with the exclusionary effects of the zoning and did want to challenge them, but in order to do so it needed new grounds. It found them in the language of the enabling statute. The "public" that Mount Laurel was to serve with its zoning regulations could not be simply the current residents of the town, they argued. Each community had a duty to provide for its "fair share" of the whole region's growth and population. The NAACP claimed that Mount Laurel had an obligation to provide opportunities for all groups and income levels to join the community. In setting zoning regulation the town had a responsibility to those who might come from outside the community as well as to those actually living inside it. Its constituency must be greater than its voters and residents. When the case reached the New Jersey Supreme Court, the justices unanimously agreed. They ruled that Mount Laurel's "regulations must affirmatively afford that opportunity" to potential residents at all income levels. Mount Laurel's zoning had to accommodate its "fair share" of the whole region's growth.[15]

That decision marked a fundamental philosophical shift in the law, tilting toward a broader inclusion in the definition of the "general" welfare or the "public" to be considered in local zoning decisions. The "public" is more than just the current residents. The practical implications of the decision, however, are still limited. First, the Mount Laurel decision is only binding in New Jersey and is enforceable only via a slow and expensive case-by-case process. Second, removing a ban on high-density housing affordable by low- and moderate-income people is not the same thing as building it. Even the author of the decision conceded that it ". . . would not immediately and in itself produce low- and moderate-income housing in outlying municipalities."[16] High-quality building standards still keep the cost of new housing beyond the rent-paying ability of the poor and near poor, and thus there is still little economic incentive for *anyone* to build housing for them. Indeed eight years after the initial case was decided in 1975 so little real change had taken place in Mount Laurel that the NAACP again sued, now arguing that the obligation of the town was not merely to make affordable housing possible, but actively to promote it. Again the New Jersey Supreme Court agreed. "Affirmative governmental devices should be used to make that opportunity realistic, including lower income density bonuses and mandatory set asides."[17] Zoning regulation should not just permit, it should actively promote inclusion, and municipalities were to be judged by results in terms of low-income housing actually offered, not just by the content of their regulations. But zoning alone never *causes* housing to be built. That still depends on economics.

Rules and the Shape of Urban Space

The first type of policy intervention in housing markets, then, has been in the form of establishing rules—what kinds of structures may be built and where, for what activities they may be used, and whose interests should prevail when uses conflict. Those rules affect how housing responds to changing market forces, that is, whether apartments may and will be broken up into kitchenettes, like in the Ruby Daniels case, or whether single-room-occupancy buildings may and will be returned to single-family houses like in the Divers case. The rules themselves all have a logic and often serve legitimate ends. As with all policies, however, they may also have consequences that their authors did not foresee or intend, or they may be ill-suited to achieving the ends toward which they are aimed.

Building codes assure certain quality standards in structures but they also assure that the only source of market-provided, low-income housing will be via filtering and that it will thus be concentrated in older central cities. No profit can be made from building new, standard-quality housing to rent at prices poor people can afford. Indeed little profit can be squeezed out of well-maintained, low-income, filtered housing. The problem facing poor people is, on one level, very simple. They have insufficient resources to meet all their needs. To require by law that they buy only "high-quality" housing does not in any way increase their resources, but it does compel them to spend a high proportion of their limited funds on housing concentrated in older central-city neighborhoods.

Legitimately motivated zoning regulations in the suburbs is also slow filtering and thus contribute to the concentrations of the poor in the central cities, but their impact on the poor is indirect at best. Their effect is more to exclude people of sufficient means to afford the rents in high-density buildings that would otherwise have been built in suburbs, not the truly poor. Even widespread adoption of the inclusionary view held by the New Jersey court in the Mount Laurel decisions would likely to have little direct impact on the housing options open to the poor. George Sternlieb saw the clear flaw in the court's vision of opened-up suburbs—housing standards so high that standard-quality housing is inevitably beyond the financial reach of the poor. "They could not afford it before *Mount Laurel*. They will not be able to afford it after *Mount Laurel*."[18] If they cannot afford to live in it, no one will be able to build it for them. For the poor in suburban housing markets, reality is the inverse of the slogan from the popular movie *Field of Dreams*—"if no one builds it, they will not come."

That, of course, is the reason why "the court is virtually powerless in ordering suburbs to construct low-income housing."[19] Neither "suburbs" *per se* nor "courts" ever build housing of any kind. Housing is built by private individuals, by business firms, by nonprofit groups, and occasionally by higher levels of government, but almost never by "suburbs" or "courts." Each builder must ultimately receive sufficient revenues to cover all of the costs of construction and maintenance.

It is possible for developers motivated by good will to be consciously nonprofit in their motivation, but even they must remain *nonloss* organizations. The urban landscape is littered with buildings sponsored by socially conscious groups that failed, not because the profits were too low but because the losses were too high. No matter how altruistic, they must still pay their bills out of revenues derived from the building or from outside contributions. Governments alone can build and operate buildings that do not produce enough revenue to cover their costs over the long term, but only because they can use their tax authority to make other people provide subsidies. They still have to pay all their bills. No matter who puts them up, buildings that consume more resources than they generate slowly rot away.

The rules in effect in all American cities mean that markets cannot build new housing for the poor, and that governments can do so only if they are willing to commit to permanent subsidies to help cover the costs. Those rules have thus affected the path of America's urban development as it has been propelled ahead by the sweeping currents of technological change. Within the boundaries defined by these rules, the use and organization of space has been left to the operations of submarkets, where buildings and neighborhoods are drawn this way and that by changes in relative prices. As cities have formed, grown, and changed, American governments have also undertaken a series of policies to affect the *prices* in these different submarkets, and have thus influenced the rate and processes of the changes. It is time to examine those policies as well.

8

Housing Policies and Prices

The Price of Quality

As the Divers were rehabilitating their 100–year-old house on West Newton Street in the South End of Boston, just a few blocks away Rachel Twymon and her children were moving into a brand new apartment in a recently completed project known as Methunion Manor. The Union Methodist Church, where she was a longtime member, had undertaken this project as part of its commitment to improving the lives of neighborhood residents. In the South End affordable housing was a pressing human need and the church wanted to address it. It knew that while manna may on occasion come from heaven, urban housing most assuredly does not. Commendable motives would not be enough; they needed hard cash. Any housing they built would have to be of a high standard. Boston's building code and Union Methodist's purposes both demanded that, but Methunion Manor's target tenants would not be able to afford to pay rents high enough to cover the full cost of new, high-standard construction. The church was filled with good intentions but not with money. It could not afford to pay ongoing subsidies from its own pocket. It could provide the impetus and the vision; someone else would have to provide the money. For that it had turned to the federal government, which over the years had enacted a series of policies to provide special housing subsidies for target groups.[1]

Federal housing policies have always lacked creative names. They are known simply by the section of the law that authorizes them. Thus Methunion Manor was a "221(d)3" project in which the federal government provided a subsidy in the form of mortgage financing well below the going market rate to private, low-income developments sponsored by nonprofit organizations. The goal for both the church and the government was not just more housing, it was better lives for the urban poor. "[T]hese were not to be mere real estate deals, but havens for society's disadvantaged."[2] To qualify for the special mortgage, the church agreed to restrict tenancy to households of limited means. The lower interest rate would allow rents to be more affordable, approximately 20 percent below rents in comparable "private" buildings. The contracts were signed, the low-cost financing was arranged, and the buildings were constructed.

> Rachel was full of "great hopes" in June of 1971 as she and her children left Orchard Park and began their new life at Methunion Manor. And for a time it seemed, indeed, like a new life. The buildings' brick fronts glowed in the summer sunshine. Fresh linoleum and bright paint gleamed in the hallways. The kitchens and bathrooms shone with new enamel. Everybody was excited about the crisp, modern feel of the place. Neighbors chatted eagerly in the hallways, exchanging tales of the "pigpens" they had left behind.[3]

This was not old, filtered housing. It was new, high-quality construction, and it was being made available to poor central-city residents. Markets could not do that. Only the government subsidy made the project viable, but in the end even that was not enough to make it stable. The 20 percent rent subsidy really only made the housing affordable for the "best off" of the potential tenants. Those in more severe need began to have trouble keeping up even their reduced rent payments and the project's revenues soon fell below the church's projections. Unanticipated inflation, especially rapidly rising energy prices, pushed expenses ever higher. The church was unable to cover all the costs of operation and maintenance and so the buildings quickly deteriorated. The church's managers and the low-income tenants were quick to blame each other. The environment, both physical and social, worsened, and many of those who could afford to leave did. Those who remained behind were unable to pay rent to cover costs even with the federal subsidy. Methunion Manor fell so far behind on its mortgage payments that the bank was forced to foreclose on the mortgage and sell the building. The new owner, without the mortgage subsidy, had to raise rents, pricing the building beyond the reach of the church's original target clientele.[4] It took only two years for the project to fail completely.

Financing and Affordability

The 221(d)3 housing program had a life only slightly longer than Methunion Manor's, though of course many of the buildings constructed under its provisions are still standing. That program was only one in a series of direct federal housing policies implemented during the last sixty years. Before the Great Depression, housing was seen as an appropriate concern only for the private sector, or at most local government. However, as Franklin Roosevelt took office in 1932 he saw a nation that he described as "one third ill-housed," and as part of his New Deal housing first made its way onto the federal agenda. Building codes and zoning regulations were already addressing the issues of structural quality and conflicts in land use, and, if anything, added to the cost of housing. Roosevelt's commitment to an increased and improved stock for the whole nation could only be met via policies that explicitly targeted cost. Better structures would be built and occupied only if they were both profitable and affordable.

Affordability, then as now, is a difficult problem. Today, median family income in the United States is approximately $37,000 while the median price of a newly constructed single-family home is approximately $130,000, three and a half times median income. The price of a resold existing home is slightly less on average, $110,000, but that is still nearly three times the national median income. There are few families indeed who can pay for a house out of their cash resources.

Recall that Henry Ford, despite his success in pushing the cost of a new car ever downward, found real penetration of a mass market possible only after the introduction of widely available debt financing. Even when the price of a Model T was reduced to the equivalent of three months salary, most people found it very difficult, if not impossible, to save that much prior to a purchase. For a home costing the equivalent of three *years* income, a cash purchase for most Americans is simply unthinkable. Borrowing is a necessity, but for lenders that can be a high-risk business indeed. They may have to wait years before their funds are returned, and the ability of a borrower to pay it back many years in the future is difficult to predict. Their only security is a lien on a long-lived structure that is not under their control and that may deteriorate and lose value over time. While lenders may be willing to provide the necessary financing for some of the very "best" borrowers, they will likely do so only on very restrictive terms.

In the 1920s mortgage lenders were leery of these risks and carefully limited their loans. A conventional first mortgage typically had a term of only five years, and the amount of the loan was usually no more than half the value of the property. The borrower would pay only interest during that period, and then at the end the entire balance would come due in a single balloon payment. A new five-year mortgage might then be negotiated, but at least the lender could be assured of access to his money in five years if he needed it and he would also have a chance to reassess the risk status of both borrower and building. Similarly, the low loan-to-value ratio meant that the value of the property could fall by half and there would still be enough value left to protect the lender.

Potential home buyers, on the other hand, either needed to accumulate a 50 percent down payment before going into the market or find expensive second and third mortgages to cover their half of the cost. Their earning prospects and saving potential had to be very good indeed if the ability to repay the loan in only five years was to be realistic. Ironically, of course, the stringent conditions and high interest rates imposed by lenders in an effort to reduce their risk made home ownership more tenuous and contributed to a high default and foreclosure rate. That in turn made potential lenders even more uneasy about making mortgage loans. New homes, especially those on expensive urban land, were out of the reach of households with only modest resources and prospects. Home ownership may long have been part of the American ideal, but for most urban residents, it was not very realistic.

It was not just potential buyers of single-family homes that were affected by the scarcity and expense of real estate financing. Renters' housing costs are affected by the availability of rental units and even though *they* do not purchase the buildings outright, *someone* must. Most potential landlords, looking to acquire or build rental housing, also face capital needs in excess of current resources. They too must borrow in order to buy or build. The more prohibitive the lending terms, the higher the costs that must be covered by the rents. When financing is limited and expensive, buyers and renters alike will find housing scarce and prices high. Financing is at the heart of all housing markets when only high-quality, high-cost structures are permitted by the rules.

Government as Guarantor

If Roosevelt's goal of having more and better housing built and bought was to be realized, financing had to be brought within the reach of middle-income households, more total capital had to be made available for housing, and the risks that made lenders so uneasy needed to be reduced. Those are precisely the areas where the federal government intervened in housing markets. It moved first to create new sources of home financing. In 1932 and 1933 Congress provided legislative authority for a network of federally chartered and regulated savings and loan associations. There, small depositors were known as "shareholders" to emphasize the investment character of their participation. There they were encouraged to accumulate long-term savings that could then be used by the thrift institutions to finance longer term home mortgages. New sources of housing capital were thus created, but something also needed to be done about the terms on which it would be made available to potential borrowers.

In 1934 the National Housing Act created a new federal agency, the Federal Housing Administration (FHA) to act as a guarantor of private mortgages. If a lender made an FHA-backed loan that had to be fore-closed, the government guaranteed that it would cover any resulting losses. The lender's risk of loss was shifted to the federal government. To qualify for those guarantees, however, loans had to be made on much more liberal terms. Loan-to-value ratios went from only 50 percent to as much as 95 percent; down payments thus could be as low as 5 percent of the purchase price. The terms of FHA loans were extended from the typical five to as many as twenty-five years. As a result, monthly pay-ments were made affordable for many more households. Moreover, the affordable payments could now cover complete amortization of the prin-ciple as well as interest so that there would be no crushing balloon payments due at the end of the loan.

As the Second World War was drawing to a close, policymakers had to prepare for the return to civilian life of millions of GIs. Given the successes of FHA's liberal terms in promoting home ownership among the middle class, Congress created a similar program available to all veterans as a matter of right. Thus a whole generation of young families began forming households just as a major wave of automobile-based suburbanization was taking place. That sprawl was in part fueled by large new developments that could proudly advertise "Vets—No Money Down" housing. The federal government thus created a whole network of financial institutions to sup-port home purchases and a mechanism to protect those lenders against losses on the condition that they make financing available to a broad range of American households. Its policies reduced lenders' risks and made home ownership possible for a majority of the nation's families.

The "Mae Sisters" and Secondary Mortgage Markets

One problem still remained, however. Even though lenders were assured that they would not lose money in real estate investments, they might now have to wait up to twenty-five years to recoup it all. Their capital was safe enough, but it was very "illiquid," and lenders were reluctant to commit it for such long periods. If they could simply "call" the loan at any time, the capital would be liquid but homeowners would be under constant threat and the advantages of the liberalized terms would be lost. If there were some other way for them to turn their mortgages into cash on short notice, the last obstacle to widespread home financing would be breached. Enter the now well-known Mae sisters, Fannie and her younger sibling Ginnie. (They also have a cousin Sallie who devotes her full attention to student loans rather than mortgages.) Fannie Mae is the oldest, and though known to the industry and the press by that quaint name, her official birth certificate lists her more formally as the Federal National Mortgage Administration. First using federal funds, and later capital raised in bond markets, Fannie Mae purchases mortgages from lending institutions on the "secondary mortgage market." If ever lenders need to turn their holdings into cash they can do so without affecting the borrower's terms and payments. The loan runs for its full period and the established payment schedule is unchanged, only now the payments flow to Fannie Mae rather than the original lender. Funds from the general bond market can thus be channeled into housing markets all across the nation, and at the same time, long-term mortgages can be made highly liquid. Fannie Mae works behind the scenes, but she has played a major role in democratizing housing in America. In 1968 Fannie Mae was split in two, emerging as a much slimmer Fannie Mae and with a new sibling, the Government National Mortgage Administration, known as Ginnie Mae, a purchaser of mortgages from special government-assisted projects like Methunion Manor.

A Nation of Homeowners

As a result of its efforts in restructuring financial institutions and practices, the federal government has made more housing available and broader home ownership possible. Since FDR first evaluated the nation's condition, the proportion of the nation that is "ill-housed" has continuously fallen. Federal policies have played a role in that. In 1920, before there was much of an active role by the government, only 45 percent of American households owned their own homes. By 1950 that proportion had risen to 55 percent, by 1970 to 63 percent, and today it is approaching two thirds.[5] The proportion of home ownership in the United States is greater than that in any other industrialized nation save Australia. In some prosperous countries, such as the former West Germany, the home ownership rate is only half that of the United States. Indeed, those average statistics understate the breadth of home ownership across income classes. Many of the renter households are made up of young people, waiting to become more permanently established before taking on the responsibilities of ownership. In American households whose head is between 55 and 64, more than 80 percent own their own homes.[6] Finance policies have played a significant role in this expansion, but there are other factors as well. Policymakers have also instituted a program of direct subsidies that are active in various submarkets for shelter.

Subsidy for All. . . .

There is a humorous version of a federal income tax form that circulates by copier and fax each April. It looks like a simplified form 1040EZ, but it has only two substantive lines on it. Line 1 asks "How much did you earn from all sources last year?" Line 2 commands "Send the amount on line 1 to the IRS." Several years ago some economists began arguing for the advantages of a modified version of that joke tax form. Theirs was only slightly more complex. After listing all earned compensation, taxpayers would subtract some basic number, say $34,000 for a family of four, and then send the IRS a fixed, or "flat" share of all the rest. In their sample proposal, the total calculations would take twelve lines rather than just two but the whole form could still fit on a postcard.[7] In recent years politicians have begun to see the potential in this "flat tax" proposal. It is simple, it has universal appeal, and most of the arguments against it are too arcane to fit into sound bites and television ads. There is only one counter to the proposal that seems to erode support for it whenever it is raised—it would do away with the deductibility of mortgage interest for home owners, and that deductibility is seemingly sacred in America. Even though maintaining it would violate the whole logic of a flat tax, most politicians are willing to sacrifice the principle to preserve the support. This is not a trivial concern, for the mortgage interest deduction is by far the most expensive element of federal housing policy. It is also the most invisible and is certainly the most intractable. It is hard to defend in the abstract. It is dangerous to oppose in the concrete.

The impact of this deductibility provision is perhaps easiest to understand if it is reshaped as if it were a new policy proposal designed to encourage home ownership. In this hypothetical proposal we would make housing more affordable by lowering the total net financing costs of a mortgage. Under the liberal mortgage terms now common, the financing charges over the life of the loan may easily exceed the cost of the house. With a thirty-year mortgage at 10 percent, the total finance cost will be more than two times the purchase price of the home! The monthly payment that ultimately defines "affordability" for most people can be reduced as easily by undertaking a policy that lowers the finance costs as one that directly lowers the price of a structure. Suppose therefore that the federal government established a system of direct subsidies to help with those finance expenses. After taxes are paid on all income earned, home purchasers who submitted receipts for their mortgage interest would be sent a subsidy check to reimburse them for a portion of the cost, but different households would get different size checks. For households with annual incomes below $39,000 the government would pay 15 percent of the finance cost. For households with incomes between $39,000 and $94,000 it would reimburse 28 percent; between $94,000 and $144,000, 31 percent; between $144,000 and $256,000, 36 percent; and finally for those households with annual incomes greater than $256,000, the subsidy would be 39.6 percent.

Over the life of a long-term mortgage the cumulative subsidy would become very significant. On a $100,000 home, those in the lowest income bracket would receive a total interest subsidy of $32,000. Those in the highest group would receive subsidy checks in excess of $85,000. The subsidies could be taken anywhere in the nation—to any state, any city, any suburb. Households that chose to rent would be entitled to no such automatic federal housing subsidy. There is little question that such an incentive system should induce people to buy more housing than they otherwise would and should induce more people to become home owners. That would be the purpose of the policy, and it should indeed be effective. Somehow, though, it seems unfair to pay different rates of subsidy to different income classes, and to pay the highest subsidy to those with the highest incomes.

That policy would never get through even the most conservative Congress in that explicit form, yet that is precisely the housing policy in the United States today; it is just structured a bit differently. As a tax deduction, the subsidy comes in the form of a reduced tax liability rather than a direct check, but mathematically and financially the impact is identical to the direct subsidy outlined in the previous paragraph. The implicit tax subsidy for home ownership is far and away the most expensive but least visible federal housing subsidy. The Office of Management and Budgeting calculates that the subsidy to home owners from this single provision in the tax code was over $35 billion in 1990, more than five times the total amount of all other direct housing subsidies combined.

While the direct impact of those subsidies is felt by home buyers, tax deductibility affects all segments of the housing market. With filtering being the primary source of low-income housing, tax and finance policies that encourage and support the construction and acquisition of new housing by the wealthy and the middle class are in fact policies that also affect the price and availability of housing for the poor. When 1,000 new homes are built, several thousand households move. They obviously are not all moving in together in the new units, but as the buyers of the new structures do move in, they vacate other older housing, and the new occupants of that housing vacate still other structures. When filtering is the process, supply generated at the top and middle lead to expansions of supply at the bottom as well. Still, a more direct intervention is possible.

... Subsidies for Some

It is possible even today to see occasionally replayed on television the dramatic footage of a building demolition that took place back in 1972. After carefully placed dynamite charges are set off, a high-rise housing project shudders, seems for just a moment to pause, and then the buildings settle in on themselves in a cloud of dust and debris. The buildings being destroyed in that film were the Pruitt-Igoe public housing projects in St. Louis. Built in the 1950s with high hopes and great expectations, the American Institute of Architects granted the project a design award for its blend of aesthetics and pragmatic use of space.[8] Yet only eighteen years after they opened the buildings had become uninhabitable. They were a blight on the city that could not be saved and thus had to be destroyed. In truth, of course, the destruction did not really occur in that brief moment. The purposeful explosion was but the final act in a long tragedy of eroding structures and social environments. In popular perception, those buildings and their fate have come to symbolize the worst possible outcome of the oldest and largest low-income housing policy in America, the Public Housing Program first enacted in 1937.

Public Housing in the United States owed much of its original support to its potential for creating new construction jobs. Rather than promote more filtering, it sought new construction at the bottom, recognizing that the tenants could not pay the full cost. Under the program the federal government paid all of the construction costs so that the rents charged to the low-income tenants would only need to cover the costs of operation and maintenance. The federal government did not directly build or operate the public housing. It contracted with independent local public housing authorities that selected the sites, planned the projects, and administered the buildings.

Those design elements of the policy have had a significant effect on the organization of urban space. First and foremost, because public housing has only been built when and where requested by local governments, it is not surprising that most of it has been built in communities and neighborhoods that already had significant poverty populations. Filtering first drew most of the urban poor toward central-city housing where the lowest income submarkets then experienced shortages and strains, pushing up rents for low-quality units. The central-city communities most feeling those pressures were the communities that most often applied for public housing contracts and construction. Public housing increased the stock of standard-quality structures in cities, but it is primarily located in those neighborhoods that already had large populations of the poor. Given the prevalence of suburban zoning rules excluding high-density housing of even luxury quality, any expectation that those same communities would in significant numbers apply for new high-density developments for the poor would have been unrealistic at best.

Wherever it was built, public housing did, and still does, provide a significant subsidy to its residents, but in a different form from that provided to those in higher income submarkets. The tax and finance-assistance policies enacted to promote home ownership can be characterized as "demand" side policies. They increase the ability of buyers to participate in the market and they are "attached" to buyers in the sense that they can be taken any-where—into any suburb, any city, or any state. They are "entitlements" at the core. All who qualify may partake. There is no limit on the number of people who can take mortgage interest deductions, no limit on the location, size, or condition of houses to which they apply. Those measures increase all buyers' ability to pay; thus they increase "demand" and leave it to markets to increase the supply.

Beginning with public housing, policies targeting the poor have generally been "supply-side" policies. The government has acted to increase directly the stock of housing in that submarket and has enacted programs to price those units at below-market rents. The subsidies are attached to the buildings rather than the tenants, however. They cannot be moved. To take advantage of them a family must reside in the specially constructed, subsidized unit. If they leave, the subsidy stays behind for the next occupants. Nor are these typically broad-based entitlements, for there is only a limited number of units covered and built so that some of the poor receive a substantial housing subsidy while others, in equal fiscal distress, receive none.

The problems inherent in this form of housing subsidy became increasingly apparent over the years. During the 1970s, the rent-paying capacity of public housing tenants did not keep pace with the rise in general inflation and especially not with the rapidly escalating energy costs. Operating deficits became the norm, and the federal government was compelled to begin providing current subsidies as well. Even with those, many local housing authorities have been unable to maintain the buildings and physical deterioration has accelerated.

"Expulsionary Zoning"

The supply side emphasis concentrates the poor in specific and often isolated buildings. It creates peculiar incentives for the tenants as well as inequities among the poor. If a family's income rises above a threshold level, it must vacate its public housing, give up its subsidy, and go out into the higher priced open market. Indeed this is exclusionary zoning taken to a new level; it is "expulsionary" zoning. Instead of rules that keep out people who have the "wrong" incomes, these rules call for the expulsion of those already in if they should succeed in raising their income. For those on the cusp of success, any increase in earnings can thus lead to a reduced standard of living. Some may choose not to earn more out of fear that they may then end up with less.

Moreover, public housing projects are subject to the same problems that rapidly growing suburbs are in terms of tensions between inconsistent uses of adjoining space. On the one hand financially successful tenants may be evicted for raising their earnings while on the other it has become increasingly difficult to evict those that fall behind on their rent, who then stay on as "free riders," enjoying benefits but not helping pay the costs. Tenants in fiscal distress may double up to cover their rent, raising density and increasing wear and tear on the buildings. The losers in those cases are the households paying rent but getting reduced service. When funds available to cover maintenance of the building become inadequate, the physical quality of the building deteriorates. If drugs move in and gang activity rises, taking advantage of the cover of vacant apartments, the quality of life falls for the whole project. Many of those who have not been expelled for their success will be repelled by their conditions. Those who can move out often do, leaving only the most desperate behind as the building sinks lower into disrepair and its occupants into despair.

These are classic use conflicts, pure and simple. My life is affected by what my neighbors do with their space. Suburbs and cities have been able to establish rules to control conflicts and exclude "inconsistent" uses of space in order to preserve the quality of life for those in the community. Public housing projects for the most part have not. Indeed their rules often promote rather than prevent deterioration. In the worst of cases, the quality of life becomes so low that the high subsidies are insufficient to induce even families in dire straits to stay. Then only dynamite and demolition are left.

That is a worst case scenario of course. Most public housing has not fallen to that fate, but all of it has had serious problems. It is expensive to build, difficult to maintain, and perverse in its incentives. There is today a moratorium on new construction of more public housing by the federal government, but because of the long life of the physical structures a significant stock of public housing remains, often located in the poorest parts of our urban areas. Approximately 1.5 percent of the entire housing stock in the nation is still public housing. In some central cities that proportion is much higher, comprising as much as 5 to 10 percent of the total. The Public Housing Program, though new construction is suspended, still affects the organization of our urban space.

Give with One Hand, Take with the Other

Driving through the Hudson River Valley toward Albany, the capital of New York State, long before reaching the actual city limit one sees a series of high towers rising above the horizon, dominating the skyline. The towers dwarf any other buildings in the city. They are out of scale for an urban center that size and obviously reflect a tax-financed vision of grandeur rather than self-financed practicality. Still they are impressive. They give to the downtown area a sense of scale and wealth. If that is the seat of power, this must be a great state. Known officially as the Empire State Plaza, during its planning and construction it was sometimes called "Rockefeller's Edifice Complex" after the governor who oversaw its creation and sought to project that image of majesty for his government.

The land on which those towers sit was not, of course, vacant back when planning for the towers began. It contained much of the city's oldest and most deteriorated filtered housing. The neighborhood was a blight. In keeping with the philosophy of the day, it was deemed important to eliminate substandard housing, and so clearing the land of all those deteriorated buildings was seen as a clear benefit to the city, and in some senses it was. It also greatly reduced the city's stock of low-income housing though, but it did not, of course, reduce the number of poor people needing housing. The predictable consequence was an increase in crowding, higher rents, and a steady replacement of the low-income housing units in other parts of the city via deterioration and filtering in other neighborhoods. The slums did not disappear, they moved.

"Urban Renewal" was the official name given to the process of clearing away the worst slums and preparing the newly vacant central-city land for development before selling it to a private developer for new construction. Those whose housing was destroyed had another name for it. They called it "Negro Removal." In most of those projects, the new construction was for either commercial use or higher income housing, so that the government was reducing the stock of low-income housing without reducing the number of low-income households. Even the construction of public housing did not necessarily increase the *number* of low-income units. Public housing was, in many cases, coupled with slum clearance so that old low-income housing was often torn down to make way for new. The physical quality of the units was almost always improved, but the total number was not always increased.

As the Great Society era was dawning in politics, enthusiasm for public housing and urban renewal was fading. Disasters like Pruitt-Igoe illuminated the flawed dynamics of isolating large numbers of the poor in massive housing projects. Urban renewal's tendency to relocate rather than resolve housing problems was becoming obvious to all. If high-quality construction standards were to be maintained, different forms of low-income housing subsidies would have to be tried.

Decentralizing Housing Subsidies

The 221(d)3 program that supported Methunion Manor was the first attempt to privatize and decentralize low-income housing subsidies, but the problems that arose in that project in Boston cropped up in many others all over the nation. First, it was an expensive program for the federal government. The subsidy that the tenants received over time was in fact paid by the government all at once when it provided construction funding in a lump sum at the beginning. Second, there was no flexibility in the subsidy. If expenses rose or tenants' contributions fell, the financial responsibility all rested on project sponsors like Union Methodist. The government's contribution had already been determined and paid. Few sponsors had the resources to meet those responsibilities when times got hard. Widespread failure and foreclosure of these lower income housing projects was neither good policy nor good politics and so the subsidy programs underwent a series of modifications.

As it tried different variations, the federal government remained committed to its supply-side approach, however. It wanted to promote construction of new, high-quality units that could somehow be made affordable to the working class and the poor. It next tried long-term contracts to pay direct rent subsidies each month to sponsoring agencies acting as landlords. Below a threshold level of income, tenants' direct contributions to rent would be limited to a proportion of their income. The subsidy would be the difference between a calculated "fair market rent" and the tenants' contribution. If rising costs pushed up what would be the "fair market rent" the subsidy would be increased accordingly, taking the burden of that risk off of the sponsor. If a tenant's situation deteriorated or improved, the subsidy would be adjusted, taking the burden of that risk off of the tenant. If a household's income rose above the threshold its subsidy would melt away, but they would not have to leave their apartment as they would have had to in public housing. "Expulsionary zoning" as an element of lower income subsidies was not included in these newer programs.

The most recent versions of lower income subsidies fall under the heading of "Section 8" housing, though there are three separate programs under that single title. The first merely changes some of the details in the subsidy formulae in contracts with sponsors of newly constructed, lower income housing. The second provides direct federal support for filtering adjustments, by providing for subsidy contracts with sponsors who wish to rehabilitate older existing housing rather than constructing new. The third provision is most significant conceptually, though it remains relatively small in scale. Local housing authorities can issue federally supported vouchers to potential tenants rather than to landlords. The recipients can then search the private market for an appropriate apartment or house and use the voucher to cover a share of the full-market rent.

This "Section 8 Existing" program is the first federal lower income housing policy to separate subsidies from structures. Always before, in order to receive the subsidy a household had to live in an apartment and neighborhood the government selected. Now, tenants could choose their own. The shift in philosophy that this represents is very significant. However, the shift in resources to support it has been much less so. Section 8 vouchers, unlike food stamps and Aid for Dependent Children (AFDC), is not an entitlement program available to all households at a given income level. Through its budget process Congress has limited the number of vouchers to be funded and there are relatively few available in any given metropolitan area.

Housing Policy and Race

It undoubtedly will seem strange to many that we have come so far in this discussion of housing markets and policies without mentioning race and discrimination. Race is everything in America today. The very word "urban" in many contexts is a code word for racial and ethnic minorities. An "urban" school district to many minds is one filled with "those kinds of kids." It is not ignorance of this reality but a need to emphasize even more fundamental forces that has postponed any discussion of race and housing until now. In a world free of racial discrimination, the most a poor black or Hispanic family could hope for would be to compete on an equal footing with a poor white family, and that would not be a free ticket to a nice home in a wealthy suburb. There would be no perceptible increase in the total stock of affordable housing as a result. Poor minorities' problems would be lessened but be far from over. Indeed Derrick Bell notes that in many cases middle-class black suburbanites organize to resist the introduction of low-income housing for poor blacks in their communities, just as white suburbanites have often done.[9] If race were not an issue, class still would be.

Still, if race is not *the* fundamental issue in housing, clearly it matters. Housing policies and markets in America have not only organized neighborhoods by income class, they also display an extraordinary degree of segregation by race and ethnicity. Some of this trend toward sameness may well be the result of residents *choosing to be in* one community rather than their *being shut out* of others. Neighborhoods dominated by Hassidic Jews; Russian, Haitian, or Mexican immigrants; African Americans; or whites of Polish ancestry make perfect sense at one level and there is little cause for concern if they are truly the product of voluntary association. The culture of a community is one of the elements that defines its appeal. It is exclusion from some submarkets on account of race rather than the attraction to others that has been the focus of policy in recent decades.

Officially sanctioned racial discrimination in housing markets has been illegal for a long time. Local ordinances specifying racial neighborhoods were declared unconstitutional in 1917.[10] The restrictive covenants invented and popularized by Jesse Nichols in his vast Country Club development in Kansas City were declared unenforceable in 1948.[11] As the civil rights movement gained speed in the 1950s and 1960s, first courts and then legislatures moved from a position of neutrality with respect to private discrimination to one of active opposition. A number of states passed fair-housing legislation before Congress, in the wake of the assassination of Martin Luther King, Jr., finally passed the Fair Housing Act of 1968 making discrimination by race in the sale or rental of most housing an explicit violation of federal law.

None of these statutes and decisions has eliminated all of the obstacles that minorities face in housing markets. Individual violations are difficult to prove, but there are undoubtedly many. "Testers" made up of pairs of housing applicants matched in all respects but race regularly discover that they are given access to different submarkets by real estate agents and landlords. While discrimination may give moderate-income whites better access to whatever moderately priced housing exists in the suburbs, it does not reduce that total supply. Elimination of discrimination would not, by itself, be sufficient to increase it.

While official government policy has been moving toward a more rigorous antidiscrimination stance, there is ample evidence that government practice at all levels has often been counter to that position. In many cities the application for, and placement of, public housing, and the areas chosen for urban renewal projects, have been motivated by a desire to control the location within the city of black migrants and have been chosen specifically to keep them out of white neighborhoods. In 1976 the Chicago Housing Authority was found guilty in federal court of explicitly choosing locations for its public housing projects to contain black residents in already black communities.[12] Many other cities have followed similar policies, even to the extent of keeping separate waiting lists for what local authorities deemed to be the "white" and the "black" projects.

Finally, housing policy and race come together in the area of capital markets. Given the overwhelming significance of financing in making home ownership possible, any discrimination by lending institutions would further isolate minorities in the rental markets. The Equal Credit Opportunities Act of 1964 made discrimination in the granting of credit on the basis of race illegal, but study after study has shown a persistent statistical disparity by race in credit applications taken and approved. Recently, however, there is some evidence that a new federal policy of examining credit availability by race when deciding whether to approve bank mergers has had a significant effect on making loans available to credit-worthy minority households. Poor blacks and poor whites can still expect to be rejected, of course. Race exacerbates how housing markets respond to poor people, but the fundamental structuring of space generated by technology and broad-based policy runs deeper than discrimination.

Where We Live

When an experience affects us intensely we say that it "*gets us where we live*" or that it "*hits too close to home.*" Where we live is a crucial defining characteristic of our existence. That is true symbolically. It is true spatially. We all must live somewhere, and the location and character of our dwellings shape much of our lives. There is no question that irresistible currents reorganizing urban space and where we live within it have been set in motion by the whole chain of technological history recounted in Chapters 3–6. Industrialization with its rising incomes and growing urban populations coupled with the development of the automobile and its attendant road system were the fundamental forces beginning suburban sprawl in the twentieth century. As the wealthy and then the middle class moved outward, the poor moved in to fill the emptying structures in the central city with growing concentrations of the most disadvantaged. Technological currents moved us in that direction.

In combination, the policy interventions over this period have served to facilitate rather than resist that restructuring of urban space. The insistence on high-quality construction standards has left the poor at the mercy of the filtering process, and the locale most likely to produce low-income housing via that process is the central city with its older high-density buildings. The practice, and legal support, of land-use controls, especially in the suburbs, has reinforced, but certainly not created, the obstacles to decentralization of the poor.

The development of new sources of mortgage funds (the federal system of savings and loans) and the liberalization of mortgage terms (via FHA and

VA) have combined to finance the suburbanization of the middle class. Fannie Mae has also played a role in channeling even more capital into housing markets at favorable terms. Income tax provisions have created a hidden cash subsidy to all home buyers, again making home ownership more affordable by the middle classes and lubricating their slide to the suburbs as well. Given the reliance on filtering, all of these programs also create housing for the poor. The faster the middle class moves out of the central city, the more rapidly more of their older central-city housing will be converted to lower income units. All submarkets are connected.

The direct subsidies to the poor, however, have been attached to structures, and those are generally located in the central city. In essence the federal government has subsidized the middle class's move to the suburbs while the poor have been subsidized only if they locate in the central city. Policy did not create these trends but it clearly has supported them.

Paths Not Chosen

Could it have been otherwise? What if the government had not adopted the various pieces of the policy package? This much was inevitable—America was reorganizing into larger aggregations. Surplus agricultural population was flowing to industrial cities, immigrants from throughout the world swelled urban concentrations, and the natural growth of the total population meant more and more people were living in bigger and bigger cities, and all of them needed housing. More housing takes more capital. That much was independent of housing policy. The only policy question was how to respond.

The government could have acted, in spite of the growing demand, to reduce the flow of capital into housing, for after all, past some point, better housing is really just an unnecessary luxury. Just because people want it does not mean they should be allowed to have it. Those resources could make a greater contribution to economic growth, it might be argued, if they were devoted to the development of factories and other industrial facilities. The government could have been the sole builder of new housing, seeking to minimize the cost per unit, to avoid suburban sprawl, and to promote development in a "socially optimal" way. Housing would be in short supply, the middle class would have to stay in the central city in high-density developments, only a few of the very wealthy could acquire suburban housing. That, of course, was the policy of the Soviet Union and Eastern Europe for decades. They avoided sprawl, but few residents of, or visitors to, those cities found them to be vastly superior to those in the West. They were more likely to have a population "ill-housed" than the United States was.

When those governments became dependent on electoral support they all had to abandon that housing policy.

Perhaps instead of restricting the flow of capital into housing the government could have simply stayed on the sidelines—chartered no savings and loans, established no FHA, provided no mortgage guarantees, created no Fannie Mae. Financing for new construction would have been out of reach for most Americans, the housing stock would not have grown nearly as fast as it did. If it had not enacted the tax subsidy, home ownership would have been out of reach for a significant proportion of middle-income households and again less housing would therefore have been built. The consequences of reducing the rate of growth in the housing stock without reducing the growth in the population in need of shelter should be obvious and clear. There would have been less suburban sprawl but more and more people would have had to compete for a limited number of structures. More of the population would have had to squeeze into the old central city. Crowding would have increased vastly and the price of city housing would be much higher than it is. The poor whose meager incomes could support very little of the very expensive housing would be the most crowded and face a high risk of homelessness as very little would filter down. As with all things in short supply, the poor are likely to get the very least. That is what being poor means. Would that have been a better policy response to the technologically driven currents?

Low-income housing could have been made more affordable if governments had enacted no construction standards or zoning regulations, following the current Third World policy of allowing unrestricted shantytowns as housing for the poor. That would have made housing cheaper, but the quality would have been much lower. If that were coupled with capital restrictions just discussed we could have turned our cities inside out, keeping the middle class in the central cities while forcing the poor out to the fringes in owner-built housing. We could have gone back to the arrangement of colonial cities, but on a much larger scale.

If building standards were maintained, effective affirmative policies aimed at increasing poor people's participation in the suburbanization wave would have been hard to implement. If enough capital were made available to support the kinds of outward movement we have seen, how could the poor have been brought along? Building enough public housing for all the poor in the suburbs would have been extraordinarily expensive, politically difficult, and would have emptied central cities even further. Widespread compulsory inclusionary zoning, requiring all communities to welcome newly constructed housing for the poor would make little difference without more. Only if construction standards were abandoned could the new housing be made affordable, but at what cost in quality. If standards were maintained the housing would be legal but not affordable. Who would build it without a subsidy and what kind of subsidy would work?

Even an extensive housing voucher program available as a matter of right to all the poor might do little to affect the organization of urban space. In the 1970s the federal government funded a multiyear controlled experiment to measure the effects of a general rent subsidy on housing prices and tenants' behavior. In this Experimental Housing Allowance Program pilot studies were done in several communities using different formulae to calculate subsidy levels. When the results were tabulated the experiment's designers were surprised at how little relocation of the poor had taken place. It did not take long to uncover the cause. When given a voucher worth $50 a month toward rent most of the participants took $50 of their own money out of rent payments and spent it on other things, rather than seeking an apartment costing $50 more. The recipients turned the specific rent vouchers into a general income supplement, and apparently poor people faced with the strains of so few resources felt that more housing was not their top priority. The experimental designers had one set of priorities, the poor had another.[13]

Policies and Problems

The technologically driven reorganization of space in America has created tensions and problems of adjustment for urban residents at all income levels. Governments at all levels have responded to those problems with a variety of policy initiatives, but given the "Law of Unintended Consequences" the results of their efforts have not always been anticipated or beneficial. As they have addressed some of the problems in housing submarkets they have reinforced the trends toward isolation of the poor that technology began. For the middle class, housing policy has opened the way to home ownership, for many a major goal. For the poor, the impacts of housing policies have been less clearly beneficial. The physical quality of their housing has been systematically improved over the last fifty years, but their spatial isolation has been increased. Housing policy has not solved poverty by any stretch of the imagination, but that is perhaps inevitable. The fundamental problem for the poor is their poverty, not how housing markets respond to it. The long-run solution to their problems will have to be an increase in their incomes, not some modification of the markets in which they spend them. There is little that can be done in terms of providing housing for poor people that can overcome all of the other dimensions of their poverty.

9

Getting Around

Urban Transportation Policy

Beneath the City of Angels

In the action movie *Speed* the climactic chase scene takes place beneath the streets of Los Angeles in, and on the roof of, a high-speed subway train racing through tunnels still under construction. At the very end, the runaway train breaks through the surface of Wilshire Boulevard and comes to rest on its side in the middle of the street, creating serious obstacles to both automobile traffic and audience credulity. Only Hollywood's purveyors of the fantastic could conceive of an expensive modern subway built in the capital of the car culture. Los Angeles was built around the car. Its space is organized by and for the car. Its "central" business district has less than 8 percent of the area's total jobs. There are eighteen other "concentrated" employment centers in the metropolitan area that together account for another 10 percent. The remaining 82 percent of the jobs are widely scattered over several thousand square miles.[1] Los Angeles has been spreading and filling for half a century. It has an average population density more than twice that of New York's suburbs and nearly twice that of Chicago's.[2] People live and work *everywhere* in the Los Angeles area. Freeways criss-crossing the basin are the symbol of L.A.; fixed subways belong in old pre-auto cities like New York and Boston.

Yet it is not all fantasy. As more and more people have moved to Southern California and now attempt to drive within the metropolitan area, congestion on the freeway system has gotten worse and worse. Pressured to do something about the traffic, policymakers in Los Angeles have turned to the "high tech" solution. They have indeed begun to build a subway as part of a planned eighty-mile network combining light- and heavy-rail lines scheduled for completion by 2002. Two light-rail lines are already in operation, sharing street space with other vehicles. The first segment of the subway portion, known as the Red Line, opened for business in January of 1993. The expense has been enormous. The first 4.4 miles of subway cost an extraordinary $1.4 *billion* to construct; that works out to over $300 million per mile, $18 million per hundred yards, $60,000 per foot! For this expenditure, the Red Line now carries just over 21,000 passengers per day a maximum distance of 4.5 miles. In Los Angeles they do even small things on the grandest of scales.

The three segments of the planned subway will cover only twenty-three miles at a projected cost of $5.2 billion. The system's planners expect that by the year 2020 ridership on the line will have grown to approximately 250,000 riders daily, compared, for example, with the New York subway system's current level of 3.3 *million* riders every day. Even those optimistic estimates lead to pessimistic conclusions. First, it is unlikely that the system will ever do that well. Every other urban rail system built in the United States in the past thirty-five years has ended up costing much more than its designers estimated and attracting far fewer riders. Second, even if the Red Line were to meet its 2020 ridership goals, it would have only a minimal impact on total traffic. During the 1990s, the greater Los Angeles/Long Beach/Riverside metropolitan area population has been growing by nearly a quarter of a million people annually. Twenty-five years from now the annual ridership will at best be equal to one year's *growth* in population. The freeways will not unsnarl as a result.

Responding to the Sprawl

Since the very first wave of automobile-driven suburbs in the 1920s, America's cities have been spreading ever outward, fueled by cheaper transportation, rising incomes, and growing urban populations. As they have spread, the urban transportation problem has become much more complex for several reasons. First and most obvious, as urban space expands the distance covered by the average trip increases, but that is not all. Simple arithmetic confirms that the total area that needs to be covered by a transportation system increases much faster than the edge of development moves outward. The area increases as the *square* of the radius. Thus when the distance to the edge doubles, the total area to be served become four times greater. When the radial distance triples, the area become nine times greater. As housing policies undertaken in the last decades have served both to extend the edge and to fill in the area of virtually all American cities, the space to be served by urban transportation has multiplied.

Finally, this widely dispersed population has increasingly drawn businesses and jobs to scattered sites throughout the suburbs. There is no longer a single shared destination for the trip to work, or to shop, or to play; there is no longer a single focus to the city. The deconcentration of employment in Los Angeles is extreme but by no means unique. Moreover this relocation of work has come at a time when household labor patterns have been changing as well. Today's families are more likely than not to have two or more members working. Not only does the journey to work constitute a shrinking portion of the total trips taken in a city, the location of jobs is less centralized and for most households there is more than one journey to work. Urban travel patterns are ever more complex. Over wider and wider areas people travel in increasingly varied patterns to scattered locations, and urban transportation systems must accommodate all that. The question is how.

Elements of Transportation

If there were an extraordinarily dense residential development at MacArthur Park, housing a large number of people who worked at Union Station, Los Angeles's Red Line could provide complete commuting service to them all, but of course that is not the case. Very few of the potential riders on the new subway line either live or work at one of its end points. Most need to get from somewhere else *to* the Red Line, and *from* the Red Line to somewhere else. That subway is not a transportation system. It is only a small piece of one. Every complete transportation system has three distinct elements. First, travelers need to be gathered from more or less dispersed starting points; all trips have a *collection* phase. Second, once together, there is a *line-haul* phase. Finally, the gathered travelers disperse to scattered destinations; trips have a *distribution* phase as well.

Many forms of urban transportation fulfill only one of these functions. Cars, bicycles, and walking are the only forms that combine all three elements into a seamless whole. When distances increase and weather deteriorates only the car is left. Parked in the driveway it can travel a network of residential streets and feeder roads (collection) ultimately to join with (usually far too many) other cars on limited-access expressways (line-haul). As its destination is approached, it can leave the larger stream of traffic, follow another network of surface streets (distribution), and if lucky, park at its final destination.

All other types of urban journeys require mixing modes of travel. I could, perhaps, walk three blocks to a corner where I can catch a bus to the train station (collection), and then board the train for a ride into the city (line-haul). Once there I could take a city bus or a cab to my office (distri-bution). That method, too, would ultimately get me there but for most trips the choice of travel mode is not one of indifference. One way is better than the others. Which is best will depend upon the options that are available and the relative costs of using them.

All American cities have mixed transportation networks reflecting past, and dependent upon current, policy choices. No city has left its transporta-tion purely, or even largely, to free markets. It is government that builds and maintains streets and highways. Government licenses or operates buses and trains. It regulates taxis. It takes on responsibility for the whole. As cities have spread outward over the course of this century, governments have responded with transportation policies that did and still do affect their changing structures. First, over the long run, governments play a funda-mental role in determining what kinds of systems will be built. Then, once built, government affects the direct and indirect costs of using the various pieces of the system, influencing how and when residents travel.

Choosing Pathways

In the wilderness, travel is restricted only by weather conditions and fea-tures of the terrain. Only nature puts obstacles in the way. In cities, humans create their own obstacles to movement. The structures that we build to take advantage of proximity to others also restrict our movement. A line of skyscrapers built wall to wall creates a barrier as impenetrable as a fortress. Within cities, pathways need to be constructed so that people may move about. Without them aggregations make no sense and cannot survive, but who will decide what kinds of paths to create and where?

From the earliest colonial days, it has been government that has laid out, owned, and maintained urban streets. It has sometimes shared those spaces with private concerns. Trolleys and horse cars operated on tracks laid in the government-owned, public right-of-way. It was a conscious policy to allow that. Bus companies and taxis have often been private concerns, but their existence and operation depend on ready access to the street network built and maintained by government. To build an elevated railroad, or a mono-rail, or a subway requires, at a minimum, government approval and usually its financial support as well. What urban transportation systems there are in a city depends on explicit policy choices.

Setting Prices

Who may use these pathways, at what time, for what purpose, and at what price? Those, too, are policy choices that affect the patterns of movement with a city. It is a policy decision to reserve special lanes or roads for "high-occupancy vehicles." It is policy that places toll booths on the Massachusetts Turnpike in the Boston area while making the express roads in Phoenix all "freeways." Bus rides within Seattle's downtown district are free; in Chicago they are not. The fare on New York's old subways is $1.50. A ride on the new Red Line in Los Angeles costs just a quarter, unless you are a senior citizen or have a disability. Then it costs a dime. Those are all policy choices.

When governments set policy they are determining who will pay the costs and who will receive the benefits of a city's transportation system. With its 21,000 riders a day, the Red Line will take in less than $2 million in revenues this year, barely enough to pay 2 or 3 percent of the annual *interest* cost on $1.4 billion of construction bonds. The rest of the interest, all of the principal, and all of the operating costs will have to come from somewhere else, and that somewhere is, of course, government. To pay for itself the system would have to collect $35 to $40 from each passenger taking the four-mile trip, assuming, of course, that ticket prices that high would not discourage any of them from riding. With the current fare each subway rider receives a *very* substantial subsidy. Someone *else* is paying for them to ride. Price, access, and subsidy decisions like these are not limited to subways and they are not limited to Los Angeles. In every city in America governments determine what urban transportation modes will be available and governments directly or indirectly set the prices of using them. Through both decisions they affect cities' shape and structure.

Travelers' Choice

Once transportation options and prices are set, a city's residents must decide how and when they will travel. When too many travel at once, congestion results and all are delayed. When very few do, all can travel without delay but expensive systems go underutilized. What is it that determines when and how urban residents travel? The short answer is relative costs. There is ample evidence that urban travelers choose their routes, their modes, and their times of travel based on the cheapest overall trip. But what does "cheapest" mean in this context? The cost of travel has many different elements, some easy to measure, others difficult. Certainly any trip involves some direct money costs—buying gas for a car, or paying tolls on a bridge, or purchasing transit tickets—but for any one trip that is likely to be only a portion of the cost.

Spending time is just as much a real cost as spending money. In California, a new private, high-tech toll road has just opened along a stretch of Highway 91. Drivers who want to reduce the time lost to congestion can pay a special entrance fee of as much as $2.50 to gain access to separate express lanes running ten miles along what had been a median strip. The delay that toll booths would cause has been eliminated by the use of electronic tracking devices carried in subscribers' cars. Each time they enter the road a special credit account is charged the "appropriate" price based on the time of day and traffic conditions. If drivers are willing to spend money to save time, then the time spent in travel clearly has real value to them. Times and modes that are slower cost more even if there are no direct money charges.

Indeed, where their time is spent significantly changes its value for urban travelers. Apparently an extra fifteen minutes spent on a slower moving vehicle is not as "costly" as the same time spent on a platform waiting for trains or buses to arrive. Indeed studies indicate that travelers judge waiting time delays to be *three times* as "costly" as travel time delays.[3] That becomes important when there is uncertainty about when one will travel. The key meeting at the office may be scheduled to be over by 4:30 but it actually might last until 6:15. I may or may not have calls to return after that. A mode of transit that can whisk me home at 4:47 every day may become very "expensive" if I cannot be ready to leave when it does. The risk of those long delays becomes a cost that can be avoided by simply bringing my car to work.

Any perception or reality of increased danger is also a cost to travelers. One of the light-rail lines that travels along surface routes in Los Angeles is the Blue Line, connecting downtown with Long Beach to the south. It must of necessity travel through South Central L.A. on its way, and there was much concern that a train flying "Crip" colors would be the target of violence when it passed through "Blood" territory. Five years after its opening, the official information bulletins prepared for potential riders still emphasize the precautions made and record of relative safety.

> Although the Metro Blue Line runs through reputed gang territory in Watts and Compton, there have been no major incidents of crime and vandalism on the trains. Security on the Blue Line is provided by the MTA Transit Police. The gangs in the area are known to have a respect for the rail line, and

recognize that the trains are not part of their turf. Surveillance cameras and a station-to-central control intercom system add to the security features.[4]

Wise marketers do not usually give security such prominence in their literature if it is not already on the minds of potential riders. In many cities highways are elevated and fenced while transit systems are underground or on raised tracks, effectively isolating them from the communities through which they must pass. Rightly or wrongly, *perceived* security is also an element in the calculus of urban transportation decisions.

Finally, of course, there are comfort and convenience. Too much or too little heat adds to cost, as does excessive noise, whether from other traffic, squealing subway brakes, or loud passengers. Crowded vehicles raise costs as do dirty ones. Balancing all of this, travelers look for the route, the time, and the mode that together makes the overall costs of any journey cheapest, and then they go. Government policies cannot dictate travelers' choices, but they can and do influence them by affecting the costs of traveling by different modes or at different times. Travelers, it must be remembered, take the whole trip—collection, line haul, and distribution—and they are concerned with the total cost, not just the cost of one segment. A safe transit *segment* that ends with a long walk through a high-crime neighborhood is part of an unsafe *system*. A high-speed train that regularly arrives at the pick-up station forty-five minutes late loses much of its appeal. Punctual trains that stop only at stations far from residential areas are costly, no matter what their fare.

A Car Is Hard to Beat

As soon as Henry Ford's innovative production techniques drove down the price of automobiles, their relative cost advantage for urban travel became clear. With a car there is no "expensive" wait time spent shifting between modes. There is no time lost to picking up and delivering other passengers. Door to door, all segments of the trip are combined in one. Completely flexible, the driver can go whenever he or she wishes, varying the departure each day and modifying the route in infinite variation. A car can accommodate side trips to the day-care center, the cleaner, the grocer, and the garden center, any time, any day. Its passengers are relatively safe from assault. Both climate and music are under the driver's control. In a car one need not accommodate anyone else's route or schedule. In combination all these factors give automobiles a distinct cost advantage, and urban travelers have made their choices accordingly. In most American cities the car dominates all other modes. There are only seven cities where even a quarter of the journeys to work involve *any* form of public transportation (mostly buses), and all of those are older, high-density cities.

Contagious Congestion

More cars result, of course, in more congestion, and it was fear of impending freeway paralysis that motivated Los Angeles to invest in its subway. It is important to understand the peculiar phenomenon of congestion. On the one hand it is always contagious; it spreads over both space and time. Once begun it is most difficult to contain. On the other hand, efforts to reduce it are always at least partially self-defeating.

When congestion raises the cost of travel at any one time or on any one route, at least some travelers will divert to less congested times, or routes, or modes, taking some of the congestion with them. When the traffic helicopter pilot tells the radio audience that traffic is backed up on one road and urges drivers to "seek alternate routes," he is urging them to spread the congestion. When traffic into town becomes intolerable during the 8 to 9 A.M. "rush hour," increasing numbers of commuters will start leaving at 7, expanding the rush "hour" into two, or three, or four. When a new freeway opens, it will attract not only drivers taking "new" trips but also drivers from older, more congested freeways for whom this becomes one of those "alternate routes." The new freeway will finally lose its "cost" advantage only when congestion on all routes becomes equalized. Until then more drivers will choose it, bringing more congestion with them. There may be less congestion overall, but what there is will spread everywhere. It cannot be contained in a single route or period.

Any policy that is effective in reducing congestion is also an invitation for more drivers to take to the road. If a new expressway is built more people start driving and existing drivers take more trips. If the Red Line succeeds in taking large numbers of cars off of L.A.'s freeways and reducing travel times for those remaining, that alone would be enough to induce more Angelenos to start driving to work. Whatever governments choose to do about urban transportation policies, it is individual travelers' choices that cumulatively decide how and when people will move about within a city. Their policies inevitably affect urban transportation but they never completely control it.

Cycles of Construction

For the last seventy years, policymakers have overwhelmingly chosen to develop pathways for cars, usually offered free of direct charge to all comers. Anything else has been an afterthought. Cities began building streets with cars in mind almost as soon as the first automobiles appeared. The first special "expressway" for cars was built in New York even before the First World War. The federal government began funding intercity highways in 1921, and by the 1950s work on the vast national Interstate Highway System had begun.

Through all this two things have become clear: building highways creates a need for more highways and not building highways creates a need for more highways. Over the past seventy-five years the urban population of the United States has quadrupled. One hundred and fifty million more people are living in and around our cities and they all must reside somewhere. There was no feasible way to pack four times as many people onto the land area of already crowded World War I–era cities. Urban development was going to push outward no matter what policies governments adopted. As peripheral communities grew, traffic increased and congestion developed. Government has generally responded to that congestion by adding greater highway capacity. That is, of course, a policy that is always its own undoing. Each new highway makes some additional portion of a region more accessible, making it a superior choice for development, raising the number of trips ending and originating there. Indeed, it remains a superior location until added travel raises the level of congestion enough to undo its advantage. Reductions in congestion attract more development and travel. Increases in development recreate congestion.

Quadrupling the population in urban aggregations meant that more people were trying to move about in close quarters. Preventing outward expansion while trying to put four times the trips onto a fixed transit system and an unchanged highway network would have given the concept of congestion a wholly new dimension. The only thing worse than the congestion on an ever-expanding highway system would have been the congestion on a nonexpanding highway system.

It is important to remember, however, that cars did not create congestion and they certainly did not create suburbs. Nineteenth-century urban streets often became impassable as waves of pedestrians, horses, and wagons all tried to move through high-density neighborhoods to even higher density central locations. It was not cars but the development of early transit systems—first omnibuses and horse cars, and then trolleys and commuter railroads—that began the shift of the middle class to the suburbs. Cars came later, and as mass production technology made them affordable they accelerated suburbanization but they did not invent it. After the 1930s, housing policies providing accessible mortgages and tax-subsidized homes accommodated the outward push of the automobile, and of course the outward expansion of housing also increased reliance on the automobile. As urban development spread cities, cars became the obvious choice for many more intraurban trips. Only paralyzing congestion could destroy their overall cost advantage, and governments could not realistically tolerate transport paralysis. As with housing, they had to respond to the problems that developed. In urban transportation that meant accommodating the automobile. They might have done so less completely or less enthusiastically, but they could not have prevented its outward impetus toward sprawl.

Social Costs of Cars

It is not even clear that significant resistance to the car would have resulted in a "better" outcome for central cities. They are the areas most damaged by sprawl, but it is likely that failure to respond to population growth and traffic congestion with more road construction would have worsened, not improved, their fate. Once inexpensive cars existed and peripheral low-density housing became affordable and accessible, congestion began to reduce suburbanites' automobile access to the old centers. That congestion had two possible consequences—not just one. Modern critics of sprawl often argue that the middle class would have been induced to live closer to central-city jobs and businesses, preserving the tax base of the city, if only highways had not been built. It is equally likely that central-city jobs and businesses would have moved more rapidly outward toward the population, accelerating urban decline. Recall that it was the *downtown* Los Angeles merchants who were the impetus behind the construction of California's first freeway. Population moved outward first. Then merchants tried to recapture business by making it easier for outlying residents to reach them. If the people could not get back into the city to shop, business would likely move out. Congested city streets are as likely to choke central cities to death as to trap the middle class within them.

Still, housing policy and highway construction have combined in ways that have doubly damaged low-income urban neighborhoods. This was not the intent, but as with all policies there were unintended consequences. Cities always build from the center outward, and so the oldest, densest housing will always be in neighborhoods surrounding the center. If growing suburbs were to be connected to the business core, the new highways had to pass through old neighborhoods. Land that had been used for housing had to be given over to highways. There was no other way in. Thus the construction of expressway networks, especially in the pre-auto cities of the North and East, decreased the stock of lower income housing, disrupting those communities and pushing housing costs higher for the poor who were not reduced in number but were more restricted in housing options. Indeed, to keep the costs of new highways as low as possible, planners often routed them through the most deteriorated neighborhoods, directly reducing the stock of housing available to the worst-off city residents. The fact that those people were the least able to mount political resistance undoubtedly reinforced the economic incentives.

Similarly the profusion of automobiles has had a negative effect on air quality, particularly in certain cities, and the reliance on the car makes urban transportation systems vulnerable to disruptions in oil supplies. While clean-air policies have reduced pollution levels, smog remains a threat to health in most major American cities. The long gas lines and high prices that resulted from a combination of Organization of Petroleum Exporting Countries (OPEC) restrictions and U.S. energy policies are gone for now but stand as reminders of the risks of dependency. Cars have not been an unmitigated blessing for cities. It is easy to understand the motives behind attempts to use policy to free urban transportation systems from such heavy reliance on them.

Central cities have been especially concerned about changes wrought by the automobile, and rightly so. When businesses and residents move outward, they leave in the center poor people, a high need for services, and a limited tax base to support them. The management problems of cities can then become overwhelming. If the car was behind all of this, then creating a modern alternative to the car, designed to recentralize people and jobs, might save the cities, but what realistic alternative could there be? It is too late to undo the car. Commuter rail systems and subways were the solution to the urban transportation problem in high-density, pre-automobile cities. They moved large numbers of people along fixed paths through cities, using special corridors separated from other traffic. Until cars came along they had worked wonders, but no city had ever tried to introduce a *new* rail system on top of a spatial development that had already been structured by the car. American cities that had rail systems built them in high-density, pre-automobile spaces. Only later did autos come along and add sprawl. Still a few cities are trying, somehow, to turn back the clock and return to an older logic of location.

BART and the Birth of Modern Rail

By the 1950s the automobile was dramatically reshaping all of America's urban aggregations, including the San Francisco Bay Area. Suburban housing development was spreading south down the peninsula. The construction of the Bay and Golden Gate Bridges in the 1930s had made it much easier to get to downtown San Francisco from points east and north, but they also were making it easier to move out of the city in search of more space and cheaper housing. Sprawl was creating more commuter traffic, resulting in more congestion on the bridges and highways, and an incentive for many businesses seeking ready access to consumers to follow their customers out to the suburbs. The core of the city was in danger of becoming inaccessible and irrelevant. Only a conscious policy of redesigning the urban transportation system could save the downtown, or so thought the city fathers (and probably mothers as well). How can people commute long distances in safety and comfort if they are not in cars? The answer seemed clear. The way they did before there were cars, on rails.

Thus was born the first modern experiment in retrofitting a rail system onto an urban structure that had been built up around the automobile. Always before, in New York, Boston, and Philadelphia, to say nothing of London, Paris, and Tokyo, cars had been late additions to nineteenth-century rail systems. Now in San Francisco they were proposing to add rails to an already developed auto-based system. Could they alter the spatial course of history? Could they contain sprawl? Could they change its form and direction? They certainly set out to try.

If anyone could succeed at this, it should be San Francisco. Built on the tip of a peninsula, the city is surrounded by water on three sides. There were few close-in suburbs from which employees could easily commute or to which employment could disperse. People either lived in the city or a long distance from it. The average commute into San Francisco was more than twice Chicago's and nearly four times Philadelphia's.[5] A rail system speeding passengers into the city would seem ideal. The new system known as Bay Area Rapid Transit (BART) began with some basic design assumptions and tradeoffs. First they had to decide what kind of system to build. Urban rail systems can perform two functions. They can be designed as networks to move people around within an urban center like the "Tube" does in London, or they can be commuter rail systems designed to bring shoppers and workers from outlying areas into a central location like the Long Island Railroad. The city of San Francisco itself was a living transportation museum. It had the only cable car system still operating in an American city. It had both electric and diesel buses. It had operating ferries, commuter trains, and the landmark bridges. Movement within the city was not the problem. It was access from the suburbs. So BART was designed to be a commuter rail system to bring people to a few key points in the city from the suburbs and then leave them to find other ways to get around the city once there.

To be effective BART would have to entice significant numbers of commuters out of their cars and onto the high-speed rails. What would motivate travelers to do that? Clearly the relative costs of commuting by car and rail but, as we have seen, travel costs are not determined only by out-of-pocket expense. Commuters also value their time, comfort, convenience, and safety. BART would have to win on a broad front to succeed. The system's designers began with a fundamental assumption.

> We are convinced that the interurban traveler, facing the choice between using his private automobile or using mass transportation, will be influenced in his choice more by the speed and frequency of interurban transit service than by the distance he must travel in his own car or by local transit to reach the nearest rapid transit station.[6]

Unfortunately, research since then has shown this assumption to be wrong. What commuters hate most of all is the inconvenience and delay in the collection and distribution phases of the journey.

Nevertheless BART was built on that premise. Trips on buses take so long in large part because they stop every block or two to pick up or drop off passengers. Thus BART stations were placed an average of nearly three miles apart to minimize the time *trains* would spend in stations. Commuters, unfortunately, care more about the time *they* will have to spend in getting to the train. Given the spacing of stations, nearly all passengers have to drive or take a local collector bus to BART before they can take advantage of its high line-haul speed.[7]

The next major decision was where to put the dispersed stations. When the old commuter rail systems were built in the nineteenth century, dense suburbs grew up around the rail lines because of their special accessibility to the city. In the Bay Area, suburbs based on the automobile had already been built, sprawling through every valley. Building rail lines through the middle of those densely developed areas would make BART accessible to more people, but it would have been very disruptive and *very* expensive. The system would have had to buy up vast tracts of highly developed land containing some of the most expensive homes in the nation. The right-of-way would have cut right through established communities and commercial centers, creating barriers to local travel and bringing noise and disruption to residential neighborhoods. The only practical solution was to place the routes and stations along the edges of suburban development, but that of course meant that walking to the station was impossible for all but a handful of potential riders. Thus stations had to be designed with extensive parking surrounding them, making them poor candidates for commercial or retail development. They were far away from suburban subcenters, making them less attractive for residential development.

When BART finally opened in 1972, ridership was far below planners' projections. Their emphasis on the line-haul segment meant that the system had little advantage over other modes in terms of the total trip. Indeed half the initial ridership on the transbay portion of the system was made up of commuters who previously had used buses to get to work.[8]

> Paradoxically, because so many commuters switched from buses to BART, the number of buses in the bridge traffic stream was reduced, thus creating more space for cars. Contrary to plan, even if only to that extent, BART has made it easier to commute by car.[9]

The hoped-for shift from automobile to mass transit still to this day has not met the planners' expectations. Ridership has grown substantially since the 1970s, but BART has not dramatically restructured urban space in the Bay Area. Sprawl is still the norm. The car is still king. BART's riders love it, and well they might. It is fast, safe, and, for some, convenient. It is more comfortable than the commuter buses many of them would be riding otherwise, and it is relatively cheap—for the passengers. The system cost about $23 million per mile to build, back in the 1960s. Its operating costs even in the best years are more than twice its operating revenues. Thus BART passengers each pay only about 30 percent of the total costs of their trip and get a subsidy equal to approximately 70 percent.[10] Moreover, much of the tax subsidy is collected from a regional sales tax that is regressive in its impact while most of the regular long-distance commuters are well above average in income. What BART does in part then, is to tax lower income people to pay for subsidies to higher income people, allowing them to live farther away from the central city.[11]

BART is clean, fast, "cosmopolitan," and impressive. It just is not very efficient. It has had some impact on congestion, but far less than its original supporters projected, for whenever congestion has eased more cars have been attracted to the freeways. It has done little to contain or redefine sprawl. Indeed some feel that its subsidized fares from the most distant and wealthiest suburbs have encouraged rather than contained further spread.

Past as Prologue

BART fell far short of attaining its stated goals, but as an experiment it provided useful information about the effects of adding a rail system to an automobile-age city. The currents carrying cities toward sprawl have been too strong to reverse with a few trains, no matter how fancy. Still BART *looked* so modern and seemed so *correct*. Cars are so *selfish* and *wasteful*.

Buses are so *unglamorous*. Modern rail transit seems so *progressive*. Thus other American cities have come forward with their own plans and systems. The second retrofitted rail system was built a few years later in Washington, D.C., where the "Metro" today carries passengers on a network system that combines line-haul with central distribution. On the Metro people can get around within the District, not just to it. It is clean, fast, and convenient. That helps to make it an appealing choice for many trips. It, too, is also relatively inexpensive—for riders. Like BART, the Metro was *very* expensive to build and it remains *very* expensive to operate. Construction costs were approximately $67 million per mile, and fares cover only a fraction of its operating costs. Like BART, the Metro provides high subsidies to all its riders, and like BART it has not really affected the overall shape of the metropolitan area. It is an expensive add-on to an automobile-age–shaped aggregation, not an investment that is redefining the logic of location and urban space.

Atlanta also has a rail system now, known as MARTA, that it proudly showcased during its time in the international spotlight as the host of the 1996 Summer Olympics. MARTA, too, is modern, fast, and showy, and like the others, its fares cover only a quarter of its annual operating costs.[12] Its riders like it, in part because someone else is paying for their rides. A few other cities are on the same track, including, of course, Los Angeles with its *$300 million per mile* construction cost for the heavy-rail segment. More than thirty American cities are now operating or seriously considering some form of rail, though most are focusing on light-rail "trolley" systems rather than much more expensive, special right-of-way, heavy rail like BART. In very few of these indeed could the system be termed a success by any measure. In none of them does the system come even close to covering even its own operating costs.[13]

Retrofitted rail systems are not going to be the answer to urban sprawl. They are much too expensive to build and operate, and since American cities have already spread so widely, the area they would have to cover to be comprehensive systems is vast. They are only cost effective when tens of thousands of riders per hour are all going from point A to point B, making them sensible only for very heavily traveled line-haul corridors. American cities simply do not have those anymore. Scattered locations, made possible by cars, have already created the need for an areawide transportation web. Most potential riders would have to travel long distances to get to point A and then long distances from point B to get to their final destinations. They would have to incur the much-hated cost of time lost in switching modes at each end. There is little to recommend that choice to most travelers.

The Path Not Traveled

Could different transportation policies have effectively resisted the currents that caused American cities to sprawl? Did we miss an opportunity to avoid this? With better foresight could we have created a different structuring of our space? Not without completely abandoning a market economy and democratic government. Certainly no change in transportation policies alone could have done so. An economy organized on free-market principles meant that cars *would* become widely available and that homes *would* be built how and wherever developers saw potential profit. Americans wanted cars and homes; markets responded. Prevention of that would have required redefining the whole economic and political system. To be sure, government supported these trends by building roads and lowering obstacles to home finance and ownership, but as long as the government was democratically elected it had to respond to the problems that the voters cared about. They wanted less congestion and more housing. A powerful central government unconstrained by elections and willing to take central control over the economy could, perhaps, have stopped sprawl, but little short of that would have been enough.

That has been tried, of course, just not in America. The old Soviet Union severely limited national production of private automobiles. Potential buyers had to put their names on waiting lists for periods of up to ten years. When their names finally came up, they would have to take whatever was available at the time. There was no picking a favorite model, or color, or package of factory-installed options. When there were no cars available, travelers "chose" public transportation in high numbers. The state also produced all urban housing, limiting the total resources that went into it, and dictating the location and style of all that was built. They rationed by administrative authority and people "chose" to be tenants in crowded, bland, central-city apartments in high numbers. There was no other option.

Those Soviet cities did prevent the sprawl that has come to characterize Western cities, but few indeed who have experienced both found living in that kind of spatial organization clearly superior. Certainly it did not materially improve the quality of life for the nation's poor. For the most part they could not live in cities at all because there was no housing for them. Filtering could not provide it because the middle class was prevented from moving up. No buildings could be transformed into Chicago-style "kitchenettes" for the poor. The state did not really provide it. It was too busy building poor quality housing for the middle class who were allowed to live in the cities, but as if they were poor.

Bumps in the Path Ahead

Until a superior new technology of urban transportation is developed cars *will* remain the foundation of cities' systems. Intraurban rail was a nineteenth-century solution that will never fit well the wide webs that are late twentieth-century cities. Adding new rail lines can make marginal contributions to congestion relief, but only at a very high cost per passenger, supported by endless taxpayer subsidies. The transportation that we see in cities today is largely what we are going to have. Automobiles generate real problems, of course, and those need to be addressed, but for better or worse we will continue both to curse them and rely on them for the foreseeable future. There is no other policy option possible.

Some of the problems are receiving attention. Congestion is a terrible waste, and cities are using policies to discourage driving alone, especially during peak usage hours. High-occupancy vehicle lanes reward carpoolers for taking the extra vehicles off the road. Free parking at "Park and Ride" suburban bus stops creates a significant cost saving over expensive downtown parking. Stop lights on freeway ramps make the last cars to get on bear the congestion delays all at once.

Gasoline engines in private vehicles are a major source of air pollution. Policies will more likely affect the power source than the character of the vehicles. There have already been partial technological solutions. Others are on the way. Lead additives have been removed from fuel. Catalytic converters have reduced the level of harmful emissions. There are ongoing experiments with both natural gas and electric powered vehicles. New zero emission gas engines are expected to be available within the next two years. Improvement of cars rather than their replacement is the likely future for cities.

One of the main problems of auto-based webs, however, is not being meaningfully addressed. Increasingly isolated in central-city neighborhoods while jobs are continually spreading throughout the suburbs, America's urban poor are being *spatially* separated from employment opportunities. Lack of education, skills, and experience have always been problems for the poor. More and more, physical distance is as well. Access to a dependable car is a precondition to participation in urban labor markets. The rail systems that do exist or are being added are poorly suited to suburban job search and reverse commuting. They typically join suburban *residential* areas to central-city *business* districts, not inner residential neighborhoods to suburban industrial parks. The poor need a separate collection mode to get them to the central-city transit terminals and another to distribute them to scattered edge jobs. BART, for example, provides no service at all to low-income residential neighborhoods in San Francisco. It provides no distribution to scattered job sites in the outer ring. New rail lines could not solve that problem, for by definition they are only viable when there is a concentrated end point to which all travelers are going. In the suburban job market there is no such shared destination.

Only a dependable car can provide easy transportation throughout the whole of the modern urban web, but owning one is beyond the reach of most inner-city poor first setting out in search of work. That is the basic "Catch 22" of urban transportation for the poor. If they only had a decent paying job they could afford the costs of transportation to look for employment. If they do not have one, they cannot. Where you are in space affects where you are in life. How well you can get around affects how well you can get by.

10

Governing Sprawl

Ford to City: Drop Dead

In the fall of 1975 the city of New York ran out of money. Its current receipts were not enough to cover all of its bills and so it tried to borrow enough money to carry it over. Required by law to operate within a balanced budget, it could only legally borrow to finance long-term capital projects, or short-term ones in anticipation of tax receipts coming due within the year. For several years tax collections had never been quite enough to cover all of its expenses and the city had been using "creative accounting" to shift current expenses onto capital budgets and in "anticipation" of tax payments it had no real expectation of ever collecting. The big New York banks had cooperated in this method of finance, and by 1975 they held several billion dollars worth of New York City bonds. By the fall of that year they were becoming uneasy about the city's ability to carry so much debt, and they began to sell off their holdings just as the city tried to sell a major new issue to cover its 1975 shortfall. There simply were not enough buyers for all the bonds, and some of the new issue went unsold. New York ran out of money. With bills to be paid but its bank accounts empty, the city turned to the federal government for aid, only to be rebuffed. The New York *Daily News* graphically characterized the federal response in a front page headline—"Ford to City: Drop Dead!"

How could this happen? The New York Metropolitan Area was, and is, one of the wealthiest in the world. The average per capita income for the whole sprawling area is higher than in almost any other urban aggregation in America. This is the Big Apple—New York, New York. Yet despite all that wealth the city could not make ends meet. Perhaps Frank Sinatra should sing instead, "if we can't make it there, we can't make it anywhere." Indeed in recent decades city after city in the United States has found itself on, or over, the brink of financial disaster. Why does this happen time and time again? Does the evolving organization of space play a role in these recurring financial difficulties? Do the recurrent financial difficulties affect how the logic of location evolves?

Politics and Sprawl

There is, in the United States, an official Census of Governments. That is really remarkable when you think about it. Every few years we have to count up the total number of governments, and the numbers are truly staggering. The 1987 census found over 83,000 different governments within the borders of the United States. There were, of course, the one federal government and the fifty separate states. In addition there were over 3,000 counties, over 19,000 municipalities, over 16,000 townships, nearly 15,000 independent school districts, and nearly 30,000 other "special" government units created to deal with issues such as waste disposal, water supply, transportation coordination, and environmental protection. As overwhelming as these numbers are, they represent in fact a significant decline from earlier years. At the close of the Second World War there were nearly twice as many governments in the United States.

As with all species, governments are the progeny of other governments. It was the state governments that joined to form a new federal government under the U.S. Constitution in 1787. It is state governments that create counties and charter municipalities. It is they who create the special districts. They grant to lower levels of government "jurisdiction" over particular matters in defined territories. The word *jurisdiction* derives from the Latin and means literally the authority to "speak the law." In modern usage it has geographic dimensions defining who may speak the law within a particular space. In creating different units with differing, though occasionally overlapping jurisdictions, governments create a distinct *political* organization of space within the ever changing urban aggregations. They define who will make policy decisions, have access to what resources, and be responsible for what problems.

Urban aggregations continuously change their boundaries and their shapes. There is no central design to the process. They evolve organically. The political organization of space is more conscious and more rigid than the economic, but is not wholly fixed. It remains fixed until there is a conscious legislative decision to alter it and that, of course, is a process that is cumbersome, slow, and uncertain. A change in political boundaries always generates winners and losers, and those fearing loss often have means to slow or stop change. That is not true in the *economic* restructuring of space. That is automatic. It happens impersonally and diffusely, leaving no clear target or route for those wishing to prevent or forestall change.

Over the last seventy-five years the dominant spatial change in America has been the growth and spread of America's cities. Governments have facilitated that change by building highways and adopting liberal housing policies but they were merely riding the tide. They did not cause it. It was an unplanned tide that could not easily have been stopped or turned. What governments have not done is to reorganize the political space to match the changes in cities' structure. City limits, for the most part, have stayed in place while populations have not. Old boundaries established long ago remain fixed so that cities and their multiple suburbs are separate *political* jurisdictions even though economically they are an inseparable whole.

Cities and Services

This might not be an issue of concern if local governments were not called upon to provide so many of the services necessary for sustainable urban living. The transportation pathways through cities must be maintained. If people and goods cannot move within cities, they slowly strangle. Water must be provided to densely packed residents. Garbage, sewage, and waste must be removed. Cities suffered deadly epidemics before this was done. Order must be maintained. Fire must be prevented, and failing that it must be contained and extinguished. Chicago, Boston, and Seattle all burned to the ground before their building codes and fire departments were established. Both logic and history tell us that without those kinds of services unnatural human aggregations cannot long survive. It is local governments that organize, administer, and fund those activities. Their ability to do so effectively depends on the match between their needs and their resources. What they *must* do and what they *can* do need to balance if local governments are effectively to fulfill their necessary role.

The balance between needs and resources within any jurisdiction is not, of course, fixed and given. The continual processes of urban reorganization cause both needs and resources to change over time, following dynamic paths leading perhaps to plenty, or to adequacy, or to insufficiency. How they balance now is no guarantee of how they will balance in the future. The fragmentation of urban areas into separate political jurisdictions means that different governments make decisions about, and provide different services for, different subsections of the urban whole. The balance in some parts of an aggregation may tilt toward plenty while in other parts of the same metropolitan area it may be clearly inadequate. Over it all, however, some elements of local finance are always the same.

The Tendency for Local Governments' Costs to Rise . . .

Local governments tend to provide "labor intensive" services—activities undertaken for people by other people. They do not manufacture much, they do not ship products, underwrite insurance, grow wheat, or mine coal. They provide services to their residents, and thus labor costs are their largest single category of expense. Fire protection, garbage collection, street repair, and police services require lots of people to do lots of tasks. American cities have, for well over a century now, also provided education to the children who live within their boundaries. In most cases that is the largest single expense undertaken by local governments. Like the other elements of local budgets, education too is primarily a service. What school districts buy more than anything else is the time and effort of their employees. Well over half of the total operating budgets of local governments in the United States goes directly to wages, salaries, and employee benefits.

All of these services tend also to be fairly "low-tech." No one has designed a computer that can collect garbage, a robot that can police the streets (despite *Robocop* of fictional fame), or an assembly line that can fix potholes in streets. All of these things are still done on-site by real people in much the same manner as they have been done for decades. In one sense city governments benefit from this technological stability. It means that they must hire lots of employees and, for politicians, control over jobs is a political treasure. It also means, however, that cities inevitably face higher and higher costs for providing a given level of services, and that ultimately has political costs. What is it about local public services that makes it so difficult to contain their costs? There are two elements to the answer. The first is technical; the second is political.

When Henry Ford suddenly began paying his production line workers $5 a day at his new assembly plants his total labor costs doubled, but the cost of the labor in each car actually fell. The output per worker on his new assembly lines more than doubled, so it took less than half the labor hours to produce each car. Cars sold for half as much, workers earned twice as much, and Ford's profits increased—a neat trick made possible by a simple economic principle. Wage increases matched by productivity increases have no inflationary effect at all.

Labor productivity increases have been hard to come by in American cities. Local governments still produce their services much as they have in generations past. Teachers still teach with blackboard and chalk. Indeed when technological change comes to the classroom it is as likely to increase as reduce labor costs. Installing computers in schools usually means hiring extra computer aids and computer repair technicians rather than replacing teachers. Curricular innovation is likely to add extra layers of administration that cost more money but educate no more children. Fire fighters still drive trucks to fires and handle high-powered hoses and axes once there. Streets are paved by work crews pretty much as they have been for several generations. Crews of sanitation workers still gather trash left out on curbs and in alleys and load it onto trucks bound for landfills.

Technology, and hence productivity, has changed very little in these activities. Productivity increases in public services are hard to generate and sometimes difficult to accept. Eli Whitney introduced the American system of manufactures by standardizing all the parts and building precision machines to produce them. Henry Ford increased the productivity of his workers by standardizing the tasks they performed and controlling all phases of the process. Each Model T was indistinguishable from any other. But no two children in need of an education are exactly alike. No two fires raging in urban buildings are identical. No two breaks in water mains occur under the same conditions. What local governments do varies from moment to moment and case to case. Engineered increases in productivity come from designing machines and processes to do anticipated and repetitive tasks. We are, so far, incapable of designing machines that can diagnose infinitely variable situations and then undertake infinitely variable responses. People are still required for that. While much of what local employees do is "routine" it remains too variable for any machine process designed to date.

In addition there is less incentive to seek labor saving techniques in these areas than there is in the private sector. At least in the short run decision makers in local governments probably gain more from having more jobs to offer than they would from reducing the costs of the services they provide. Since the 1960s there has been a trend toward unionization of local government employees and the establishment of rigid work rules that restrict any gains to be made from reorganization of effort. Thus technology and politics combine to limit growth in labor productivity in local government. That alone is not sufficient to explain the tendency for local government's costs to rise. If wages simply stayed fixed, costs should stay the same even if productivity did not increase. That is enough to explain why costs do not fall, but not why they persistently rise. That requires the next step—an understanding of how wages for public employees are determined.

Public sector wages are not, of course, simply set by measuring productivity and paying workers accordingly. Politics and market forces both play important roles as well. Thus the wages paid to private sector employees become a standard against which to measure the fairness and adequacy of public sector pay. If an increase in pay for workers like Henry Ford's $5 a day men causes local governments to have to pay their workers more in order to "keep up," then the real costs of local services will rise because *their* wage increase is unmatched by a productivity gain. Governments and taxpayers will pay more for the same level of services. While workers in both areas receive the same wage increase, the labor cost of the Model T will fall while the labor cost of government will rise.

William Baumol several years ago recognized the consequences for local government of uneven growth in productivity. Private industry has, year after year, mechanized, standardized, computerized, and organized with an eye toward improved efficiency. New techniques have led to steady improvements in labor productivity and, appropriately, to steady increases in the wages paid to workers in those industries. Higher wages without any increase in costs is the result—but it is the productivity gains that are the magic elixir. The rising wages in the private sector inevitably put pressure on public sector wages as well, but without generating corresponding increases in productivity. Fairness, not efficiency, becomes the question. Are not the people who teach our children as important to society as the people who assemble our motorcycles? If the latter are earning $30,000 per year how can we justify paying a high school calculus teacher $25,000? If plumbers earn $15 an hour to respond to drain pipe crises, should not trauma center nurses who respond to human life crises earn at least as much? The inevitable political, and probably ethical, answer to those questions is a resounding "yes." Thus public sector wages tend to keep pace with private sector ones, even if productivity increases do not. That is only fair. It is just. And it causes the real costs of providing public services to rise year after year. It takes more and more money just to provide a constant level of public service.[1] Alternatively, a constant level of expenditure is sustainable only if service levels are reduced.

This is true, of course, for all the various political segments of the urban whole, city and suburb alike, but for central cities this problem, like so many others, may be worse. There the buildings are older, taller, and more densely packed. Fire fighting is more complicated, more dangerous, and likely more expensive. Central-city streets are older, more heavily used, and more often in need of repair. They cover a larger proportion of the total land area than do the streets in suburbs. Moreover, they are traveled on by city residents and suburban commuters alike, much more than suburban streets are traveled on by central-city residents. Their water systems are older and more in need of repair; their sewers are more primitive and more costly to maintain. Crime is more prevalent and police services more strained. Central-city schools are more likely to be filled with children of the poor need-ing extra services—before and after school sanctuary programs, hot meals for poor children, protection from violence, and health services. Their schools are more likely to be in older buildings, constantly in need of repair. Central cities are concentrations of older buildings, older infrastructure, and especially poorer people. Like Alice in Wonderland running faster and faster but always staying in the same place, local governments, and espe-cially central-city ones, pay more and more but provide no increase in services, and taxpayers understandably wonder why.

... While Revenues Do Not

Cities can provide no services at all if they have no resources at their command. If they are to maintain their services, the resources needed by local governments rise year after year, but where does their funding come from? The need forever more would not be so limiting for local govern-ments if they had a source of revenues that grew apace, but given the *political* ordering of space in the United States that is an unlikely outcome indeed. Local governments are characterized by small geographic areas. They typically cover a fairly arbitrary piece of a metropolitan whole, delim-ited more by historical accident than by any coherent logic. Still each juris-diction is responsible for making local decisions and for providing local services. If they are to be able to do so they must have a revenue source that is truly their own and that they can maintain over time. If services are not sold directly to users they must be funded by taxes, but local taxation is a complicated issue.

Taxes may be as inevitable as death, but they are qualitatively very different. One either is or is not dead but tax liabilities can always be greater or less. Death comes to each of us but once; tax bills are recurring shocks. Death is often beyond our control, but there are distinct ways in which we can influence the size of our tax payments and what we get for them. Indeed politics is largely a contest over taxes and public services. How much of the service pie can I get allocated to me? How much of the tax burden can I shift onto others? Can I get someone else to pay for them so that I may ride free? That is much of what politics is about at any level. It is certainly true in the case of taxes.

There are two stages to the game of taxation—the political and the reactive. The first occurs when government defines its tax instruments. There lobbyists lobby, constituents complain, hearings are held, and profes-sionals profess. Governments, recognizing the second stage, seek to shape their tax instruments in ways that prevent escape, for potential taxpayers always have a strong incentive to find ways to avoid the burdens they impose. When potential taxpayers reorder their affairs in ways that minimize their tax liabilities the "game" is in its second phase. Governments can punish those who evade taxes illegally. They can only mourn the loss of revenues from those who avoid them legally.

Personal Tax Rebellions

The fragmented structure of local government increases the potential to avoid local taxation. It creates a geographic "appeals" process. If I do not like the package of benefits and taxes in one subdivision of the city I can always get a different package by moving into another. High-quality services attract businesses and residents. Many a suburb stakes its appeal on the perceived superiority of its schools. Families moving in get a better educational package than those living on the other side of arbitrary political boundaries, and their willingness to pay for that package is reflected in higher property values within the district. Higher tax burdens unmatched by superior services have the opposite effect of course. By moving away, businesses and residents can escape the burden of taxes without really losing benefits. Changing nations is a difficult adjustment. Changing suburbs is not.

Tax Possibilities

This potential for flight from taxation places practical limits on the kinds of tax instruments local jurisdictions can use. The easier it is to relocate what is being taxed, the easier it is legally to escape the tax burden and the less suited a tax is for local government use. Thus there is not really much that a local government can effectively tax for long. Income taxes will not work on a local level. If one local jurisdiction imposes taxes on the incomes of its residents or on incomes earned within its limits, the tax is easily escaped. Neither live nor work in that jurisdiction and the tax disappears. Employers who move their operations to another location could pay their workers less and the employees would still take home more money. Residents with jobs outside the jurisdiction could raise their disposable incomes by moving to a different fragment of the urban whole.

Sales taxes are similarly avoidable. The smaller the jurisdiction that imposes a sales tax, the more easily it is avoided. Massachusetts, for example, does not charge sales tax on clothing purchases costing more than $50, while neighboring Connecticut does. Connecticut residents living near the state line can get a 6 percent discount simply by crossing an invisible boundary. With the rise of mail order catalogs in recent years, states are now losing a significant share of "their" sales tax revenues to purchases made by local customers going "out of state" to buy without ever leaving their homes. If states cannot protect their taxed sales transactions from leaving their jurisdictions, what hope do the fragmented pieces of cities have? Businesses could move to the next jurisdiction and offer an automatic discount to their customers. Consumers could shop in the next fragment and give an automatic discount to themselves. There is little financial advantage for a government in creating incentives for viable businesses to move out of its jurisdiction.

For cities to have a viable tax base they must find something within their borders that is both valuable, practically taxable, and *very* hard to move away. What of value do cities have that is difficult to take away? People and transactions can and do leave easily and regularly, but land and buildings are permanent. Real estate is geographically captured. Land is immovable and buildings are firmly rooted to the ground. Taxes on real property cannot be easily avoided by picking up the land and buildings and moving them to another low-tax jurisdiction—or so it would seem. It is because of this spatial fixity that local governments are largely limited to property taxes. Across the nation, property taxes account for two thirds of the total tax revenues of local governments. In many states the proportion is well over 90 percent.[2] What other option do they have?

Dynamics of the Property Tax

On the surface a property tax is a fairly simple instrument. Unlike the federal income tax there is no need for volume after volume of regulations and interpretations to define it. Simply calculate the market value of the property and then send a tax bill equal to some fixed percentage of that amount. Though easier to administer than other taxes, a property tax has its own special problems, however.

First it creates an obvious disincentive to improve property. If I invest my funds in a new addition to my home my property tax liability will rise as a result. Then I will have both the cost of the addition and the cost of the new taxes to contend with. Moreover I may not be able to get back the full cost of my new addition when I sell the property, for any sophisticated buyer will know that he or she is "buying" the tax liability along with the house. Buyers will not pay as much for a house located within a high-tax jurisdiction as they would for the same building in a low-tax one. Perhaps, then, I should just invest that money elsewhere. There is a disincentive to improve property.

Then there is the problem of "shifting" the tax. There is within economics a complex debate over the "incidence" of the property tax (i.e., over who really pays it). Certainly, if the federal government collects from oil companies a twenty cents a gallon tax on gasoline, it is not clear that the companies will really be paying it. They are the ones who deliver the money to the government, but whose money will they deliver? If they can pass the tax on to motorists in the form of higher prices, then it is consumers who bear the burden, not the oil companies. If they can pass on only some of the tax, then consumers and oil companies share the burden. Assessing the final "incidence" of any tax is one of the more complex puzzles that occupy economists' time. Property taxes are no exception. It is clear that the legal owner of a piece of land and its buildings is the one required to transmit funds to the local government. It is less clear that the final burden remains there. If a landlord can raise rents in response, the burden will be shifted to his or her tenants. If the tax changes the value of the land or the buildings on it, that may affect other investors in real estate or even other assets.

Buildings are investments; they are physical embodiments of wealth. They are long-lived, but they are not permanent. Slowly but surely they succumb to age and depreciation. Weather and wear combine to use them up so that, unless maintenance capital is added year by year, they do in fact diminish, both physically and financially. In the short run, the value contained in real property is captive wherever the buildings stand. In the long run that capital can be withdrawn through depreciation. The funds necessary to maintain buildings can be redirected to other locations or other uses that are not subject to taxation. Property taxes generate capital flight from taxing jurisdictions. Jurisdictions with higher tax rates will experience greater withdrawal of capital.

On this all sides in the incidence controversies agree. Their debate is whether the primary result of the capital flight is an increase in rents over time or a reduction in the returns to all investment as the capital driven from real property floods other investment areas. In either case, capital is driven out of jurisdictions imposing property taxes so that over time high tax rates eat away at the tax base. To be sure this is only the tax half of the fiscal equation. If the higher tax rates support clearly superior services, then there is an attraction to balance the repulsion. But if increasing tax rates do not provide improved services, then the net effect of the increase is always to push capital away.

What then are the financial options for local governments? Baumol's Principle implies that they will be faced with ever rising costs of providing fixed levels of public services and the dynamics of property taxation implies that they must rely on a source of revenues that cannot be expected to keep pace. Then a Hobson's choice ensues. Raise tax rates to garner a short-term increase in revenues and raise simultaneously the incentives for taxpayers and their wealth to leave the jurisdiction. Maintain current tax rates and balance the budget by reducing service levels and again the government creates incentives for those able to escape its jurisdiction to do so, and to take their wealth with them.

All local governments face this dilemma, but as with other urban ills it is central cities that feel it most. It is they who have the highest costs for services, populations with the greatest needs, and the oldest structures most in need of maintenance capital. Transportation technology and housing policy have combined to carry much of the middle and upper classes out to the suburbs. Central-city properties have deteriorated and in places whole blocks have been abandoned. Compared to their suburbs, central cities invariably have a lower base of taxable property per person. They inevitably have the highest tax rates among the many jurisdictions within the urban whole. Decade after decade the ratio of taxable property per person in central cities to that in suburbs has constantly eroded. For the largest cities, in all sections of the country save in the West where post-automobile organization predominates, the central-city base per person is less than 75 percent of that in the suburbs. In the worst areas of the nation that ratio is barely half.[3] Central cities invariably need more and inevitably have less. All local governments have felt the fiscal squeeze, but central cities have felt it most. Any response they make to their fiscal imbalance can only accelerate the relocation of taxpayers and their property.

Help from Above

There is really no way for a local government to solve this fundamental dilemma. The political and economic divisions in our urban areas just do not match. There are only two ways in which a local government could assuredly meet its revenue needs over time. The first would be for a central city continuously to extend its jurisdiction to cover the whole metropolitan aggregation, but of course cities cannot do this for themselves. Any annexation of suburban communities, indeed any reordering of local political boundaries, requires an explicit action by the state legislature. In the very earliest days of the nation, legislatures were reluctant to grant municipal charters to cities because those outside feared that the city would become too wealthy and powerful. Today state legislators, responding to the fears of suburban constituents, are reluctant to pass annexation measures. The fear now is that the cities have become too weak and needy. They would eventually drain the ring of its resources, and if Baumol's Principle holds, they would do so without really solving the problems of the city.

The second possible solution to local governments' fiscal imbalance would be to find a way to utilize "better" tax instruments, especially ones whose revenue streams would be more likely to keep pace with rising expenses. An income tax would be ideal, but that is an impractical instrument for a local government; in a small, open space it is too easily avoided by moving away. The next best thing might be for an income tax to be imposed at a higher level of government but for the revenues to be passed down for local use. Obviously, this is not an original idea. Intergovernmental fiscal grants have been part of the financial landscape in America for decades, though they have changed form from time to time.

The first such transfers were earmarked for specific purposes, as in the 1920s when the federal government first made grants to states and localities to help pay for the creation of a highway system. By the 1960s budget analysts were projecting federal surpluses far into the future while the growing pressure on local budgets was becoming increasingly apparent. Thus a program of general "revenue sharing" was enacted whereby federal income tax receipts were to be transferred to state and local governments— no strings attached. Those surpluses at the federal level never really materialized, however. Instead as entitlement programs swelled surpluses were soon replaced by large and growing deficits, and it became clear that there were limits to what the federal government could and would provide. General revenue sharing was replaced by a system of block grants that gave the national government both more budgetary control over how much it would contribute in total and more control over how the funds would be spent.

Not only was the amount of federal aid being reduced, its distribution among cities was being altered to reflect changing political realities. During the late 1960s and early 1970s new distribution formulae for federal aid shifted funds away from older northeastern cities toward the "Sunbelt" states that had provided the main base of support for the Nixon administration. Indeed it was that restructuring of federal aid that finally pushed New York City to its abrupt crisis in 1975. Baumol's Principle was the underlying cause. Nixon's revenge was the precipitating event.

Today America's cities continue to face unremitting fiscal pressures. They can, on their own initiative, draw only on property tax receipts, but that is an instrument ill-suited to serving their needs as cities continue to reorganize and sprawl. Neither the federal government nor the states are likely to provide sufficient aid. With higher levels of government facing budgetary difficulties of their own, cities will be fortunate if aid levels do not fall. Flat funding for aid is the most optimistic future they can reasonably hope for. They will be dependent on the property tax with all its shortcomings for the foreseeable future, but at least control over the property tax is theirs—or is it?

Taxpayer Rebellions

Howard Jarvis was born in Utah just as the twentieth century was beginning and thus he was a personal witness to the reordering of space in America during the age of the automobile. He began his professional life as a publisher of newspapers, but in mid-career he sold them all and moved to California where he made his living as an inventor and manufacturer until his retirement. Then a particular conjunction of time (the 1970s), location (California), and personality (Howard Jarvis) created just the right conditions for a social and political reaction to the forces that were pushing the cost of local public services ever upward.

The 1970s had been a period of rising prices throughout the United States. The cost of virtually everything rose steadily from year to year, and, of course, the cost of local public services rose too, partly because of the general inflation and partly because of Baumol's Principle. Nowhere was this more apparent than in California. Experiencing a real estate boom along with the general inflation, property values in the state exploded and property tax bills, calculated as a fixed proportion of property values, rose year after year. Property tax increases are typically collected in a lump sum once or twice a year. The impact of increases cannot be diffused or hidden in slight changes in regular withholding. They are right there to see and feel. In California they were felt and they hurt. Services were not improving while taxes were constantly rising.

The California constitution added another element to the special conjunction of circumstance. It provides for an initiative process for the direct enactment of laws, independent of the legislature. Anyone can propose a law in California, and if enough signatories to a petition supporting the proposed statute can be found, the proposition will appear on the ballot for approval or rejection by the electorate at large. If approved it becomes law. Howard Jarvis decided to take advantage of that opportunity, and he made a populist tax revolt his mission in retirement. He drafted a proposed rollback in tax rates to reduce total revenues by $7 billion a year and to limit annual increases from that base to a minimal level. He publicized his proposal and organized a successful petition drive. In June of 1978, California's voters went to the polls and approved Proposition 13 by a 2 to 1 margin. America's property tax revolt had begun.

Very shortly at least a dozen other states were facing populist attacks on property taxes. Idaho and Nevada copied California's proposition, almost verbatim. Massachusetts voters approved their own Proposition 2 1/2 that immediately reduced local government revenues by over 11 percent. Legislatures in several other states tried to forestall populist attacks by undertaking tax rollbacks on their own. In the two years after Proposition 13, legislatures in thirty-seven states enacted measures of some type reducing local property tax burdens.[4]

It is easy to see the logic behind voters' anger. They were being asked to pay more and more each year but were not getting anything more in return. Why should the cost of services keep rising if the level of services was constant? It had to be mismanagement and widespread "waste, fraud, and abuse." Indeed in polls taken at the time over three fourths of those who voted for the California measure believed that the tax rollback would not result in *any* reduction in local services. If only government were called to task residents should be able to get the same services for a lower price, or so they thought.[5]

At the time, California's state government was running a surplus and so the effects of Proposition 13 were not immediately felt. Increased state aid covered much of the reduction in local revenues, but eventually the state, too, ran out of excess funds and then harsh reality set in. Significantly reduced service levels were the result.

All across the country voters opted, *de facto,* for stable total costs with lower levels of service. They did not necessarily expect that to be the outcome, but it ultimately was. They believed that the explanation for rising costs lay in mismanagement rather than in the dynamics of uneven productivity growth in the public and private sectors. There was little explicit consideration of Baumol's Principle. Certainly there is mismanagement aplenty and cost saving can be squeezed from some local government activities by reorganization, but the fundamental problem cannot be changed by a mere political vote any more than gravity can be reduced by one. The tax revolt wished for, but did not provide, a solution to the need for resources felt by America's cities. Instead it merely intensified the pressures on local governments.

Tragedy without Triumph

In the theater the tension that drives a dramatic tragedy builds as a network of events, forces, and conditions that set the central character on a path leading inevitably and inexorably toward disaster. Unlike modern action films where the question is how the hero will ultimately overcome, in a true tragedy the question is only how and when the hero will finally succumb.

Caught in an unfolding dilemma from which there is no real escape, his or her actions determine only which bad outcome will result. There is no way out. In that lies the tragedy. American cities are playing out a drama of their own, and like the actors in a classic tragedy, they may choose how to approach their destiny, but there seems no way to avoid it.

Automobiles and roads have fed pervasive sprawl, carrying the middle class outward beyond the political reach of central cities. Housing policies and land-use controls have also contributed to this reorganization, drawing wealth outward while drawing poverty into the center. Those forces have been irresistible. People, the need for public services, and tax capacity have all moved freely around the urban landscape, unimpeded by arbitrary political boundaries established long ago. They all organize themselves spatially without regard to the fragmented jurisdictions of local government.

Providing labor intensive services in an economy where persistent private sector productivity growth is the norm, local governments feel the inevitable pressure of Baumol's Principle—it takes more dollars each year to provide a constant level of services. Dependent on the property tax for their revenues, cities face the hard choices that that imperfect instrument offers them. They can raise tax rates and, in the short run, their revenues will rise but the higher rates inevitably lead to a flight of capital and of the middle class, leading finally to an erosion in the tax base itself. Individual tax rebellions break out as people "vote with their feet." Today's solution becomes tomorrow's problem. And there is always another Howard Jarvis in the wings. Increasing taxes without improving services will eventually trigger taxpayer resentment. Those that do not leave may well raise their voices in protest and compel a rollback in rates. Collective tax rebellions lead to sharp cutbacks in services and further incentives for those who can leave to do so.

If cities instead respond to the pressures of Baumol's Principle by cutting services at the start, the deterioration of urban environments also leads to flights of taxpayers and their wealth from low-service jurisdictions. Tax rates do not rise. Instead public services fall. Poor schools inevitably lead to poor communities as those with the resources to relocate to better quality districts do so—and of course the flight of the tax base means that the schools will stay poor. Neither people nor capital are fixed in urban space. Only political boundaries are.

Of course, suburbs are not exempt from these pressures. They too face competitions over tax rates and public services. They too must worry about rising costs and rising needs. If they limit development in order to ease the pressures on their financial resources, they become like Mount Laurel, excluding those of modest means. If they welcome unlimited development they undermine their own fiscal stability and can easily fall into a downward spiral of tax increases and flight from taxes. Suburbs have their own problems and fears and they resist attempts by cities to annex them. State legislators seldom challenge that resistance, understanding that suburban residents do not wish to be responsible for the fiscal plight of central cities as well as their own. Moreover, an annexation of today's suburbs is not likely to be a permanent solution. If close-in suburbs are annexed, their taxes will rise and their services will fall as revenues are redistributed toward the needier core. There is then an incentive for the tax base to move farther out to still another, more distant, jurisdiction. Annexation may merely motivate more sprawl, pushing people and jobs to farther edge communities. In America's urban aggregations only governments are fixed in space. Everything else can relocate at will. Local governments are always at the mercy of migrations.

11

Mapping Explored Space

Knowing Where You've Been

When Meriwether Lewis and William Clark returned to St. Louis in September of 1806 they had spent almost two and half years exploring the vast territory of the northwestern United States. The most valuable cargo they brought back with them was their extensive collection of field notes. In volume after volume they had recorded all that they had seen and done as they crossed that unexplored expanse. When they reached St. Louis the worst of the physical dangers and hardships were past, but perhaps the most challenging part of their endeavor still lay ahead. They had been commissioned by President Jefferson not merely to traverse the land but to comprehend its character and significance. They had now to turn their notes and observations into a comprehensive vision of where they had been, a vision that they both believed to be accurate, and one that they could share with others. They had to see for themselves where they had been and to share that understanding with the world. "[W]hat he [Lewis] and Clark had recorded in their journals, papers, and maps, was invaluable—but of no value at all unless it was disseminated."[1]

Somehow it was that last part of the endeavor that paralyzed Lewis. He just could not bring himself to undertake the rigors and dangers of hard analysis. Three years after finishing their exploration he still had made virtually no effort to prepare his journals for publication. In 1809 Thomas Jefferson wrote, chastising him for the delay.

> I am very often applied to know when your work will begin to appear; and I have so long promised copies to my literary correspondents in France, that I am almost bankrupt in their eyes. I shall be very happy to receive from

yourself information of your expectations on this subject. Everybody is impatient for it.[2]

Two months later, suffering from deep depression, in financial distress, unsuccessful at love, and unable to meet his obligation to publish what he had found, Meriwether Lewis took his own life. As his journals lay in the corner of the room he shot himself. He never did complete the task of working through what he had seen on his exploration.

It has not taken us quite as long to explore urban space in America today. At no time during the expedition has our task put us in mortal danger or caused us to suffer serious physical deprivation. Any discomfort we have had to endure has been mental, not physical. However, like Lewis and Clark's journey, it will all have been in vain if we cannot put together a comprehensive map of where we have been and what we have found. The real value of their trip, and of ours, is in what it can teach future travelers through the same space. What can they expect, what must they accept, what is inevitable, and what is avoidable?

Throughout our exploration of cities the only sure constant has been perpetual change. What *is* differs in significant fashion from what *was* in the past, and most importantly, from what *will be* in the future. We cannot return to the past. We cannot forever preserve the present. We must be prepared for the future. Only that much is certain. Still we have uncovered in our exploration a few key conclusions about the logic of location and the resulting organization of urban space. They are worth emphasizing here.

1. *Cities in America are the product of human culture, not nature.* What we see before us is our own doing. It is the result of human endeavors and institutions. There is nothing in nature that says we must live in cities, and certainly nothing that says our cities must look as they do. Indeed there is much in nature that dictates against urban living at all. No other organism gathers in massive permanent concentrations far from crucial supplies of food and energy, relying on social institutions to induce others to bring the necessities of life to them. Cities are fundamentally unnatural. Indeed without extraordinary advances in technology and the invention of important social institutions large, permanent cities would be impossible. For most of human history they were unknown. When they did finally appear, it was not because of alterations in our DNA sequences. We did not somehow mutate into mammal versions of the eusocial insects whose aggregations and interactions are dictated by genetics and natural selection. There is in nature no counterpart to a modern, industrial city. The aggregations we increasingly live in are unnatural indeed. Cities are what we have made them.

Thomas Jefferson's hope was for a nation of yeoman farmers spreading across the continent, leaving cities on the margins of American life. We have seen how very wrong his vision was. It did not fit with the logic of location. Technological change has created ever greater agricultural surpluses, has narrowed the chasm of distance, and has created new products and processes giving cities a broad economic purpose. America could not have prevented those changes and still have been American. Other societies in other times have fought against "progress." Americans have always embraced it. The first known ribbon loom was built in Danzig in 1579, but it did not feed a growing industrialization movement. Its inventor was drowned by order of the city council.[3] When William Lee invented a knitting frame in 1589 he was driven from England as an outcast.[4] The first power loom was not built by Edmund Cartwright in the eighteenth century though he is remembered for that accomplishment. The first one was built in Poland some centuries before, and its inventor was hung for his efforts. A society that offers wealth to inventors of new techniques is likely to experience more rapid technological change than one that offers them a hangman's noose.

To tinker, to invent, to improve have always been valued activities here. Doers have been more honored, and certainly more rewarded, than thinkers. Cyrus McCormick and John Deere were responsible for creating an oversupply of farmers that eventually drove many off of the land yet they were rewarded as champions of farmers' interests, not punished as threats to their survival. Robert Fulton was the winner in a nationwide competition to adapt steam power to water travel. When he succeeded he was glorified and rewarded, not hung. When Henry Ford devised ways to replace workers with machines he was a national hero and became one of the richest men in the nation. In America the attitude has always been that if it is conceivable, it must be doable, and if it is doable, it should be done.

Technological change has shaped our cities as have other cultural institutions. In America, a social commitment to open markets has provided fertile ground for rapid adjustment to the changing logic of location. It is expected of all that they will seek the best price, the best product, and the best place. Private property and the right to use it or sell it at will have always been fundamental. Those with new products, techniques, or services have always been free to test them in an open market, and if they proved superior to other alternatives in the eyes of those who buy, the reward has been wealth, often of extraordinary scale. Markets like skyscrapers are human inventions. Jointly they dominate our urban skyline.

There has, over the life span of the United States, been a massive shift from farm to city, from agriculture to manufacturing, from dispersion to aggregation. The cities themselves have grown immeasurably in size and have turned inside out. The nation's poor are increasingly concentrated in the center of these cities while the middle class and the wealthy are increasingly spread farther and farther out from the edges. It is human activity that has done all this. There is nowhere to look for an explanation of our cities and their problems other than to us. We have made them and they are ours. After all, they are wholly human.

2. *Though dependent upon human values and endeavors, cities in America are not the product of conscious design. They are an outcome rather than an intention.* Our urban aggregations have *evolved* over time and will continue to do so. They are the product of technological change and policy initiatives, culturally supported and combined into a flow of history far beyond anyone's control. They reflect the whole totality of culture and technology and as such they are beyond design. Humans do not consciously design or choose their culture. We inherit it, we live within it, we individually and collectively modify it in countless ways, and we pass it on to our progeny. There is no process or point in time in which cultureless people can gather to create their culture by design. Culture evolves. It is not consciously created. So it is with the organization of space. Jesse Hawley had no conception of how his design for the Erie Canal would affect economic development in twentieth-century Baltimore, but it certainly has. Eli Whitney had no intention of promoting sectionalism between the North and South when he devised his cotton gin and his American system of manufactures, but he certainly did. Henry Bessemer only wanted to build a stronger canon. He gave no thought to buildings rising hundreds of feet above central-city streets, but he made them possible.

The nineteenth-century reformers who fought for building codes to ameliorate the horrid conditions of the crowded tenements had no intention of creating policies that would concentrate the poor in central cities, but their high construction standards have had that effect. The sponsors of government-guaranteed mortgages for people of modest means did not intend to subsidize the flight of the middle class from cities, but their policies have done so. The proponents of expensive new mass transit systems in American cities did not plan to transfer income from low-income tax payers to higher income commuters, but their systems generally do so.

The forces shaping our space are too complex, too big, too intertwined, and too long-lived for anyone to foresee or to control them. The roots of our situation go too deeply into the past. The effects of our actions go too distantly into the future. The currents we are on are too strong to control or contain. Space *will* continue to evolve into new shapes and organizations, and we are powerless to design the future to fit our wishes. What we do, we often do not intend. What we intend, we often cannot do. Part of the American culture is a belief that we can do anything we set our minds to—put a man on the moon, conquer polio, or save the whales. Designing the future of technology and space is, unfortunately, beyond our capabilities. We can willfully affect it but we cannot control it. After all, we are only human.

3. *The urban aggregations created by human culture are interdependent "systems." All of their various elements are connected one to another in a seamless web. They cannot be separated.* There are two reasons we cannot design and control urban space. One is that we cannot know what technological changes will come with the future and how people will react to them. We cannot anticipate what we cannot know. The other is that we cannot isolate the various elements of urban aggregations and affect them just one at a time. They comprise a system, complex and interconnected in so many ways that it is not humanly possible even to predict all the effects of our actions, let alone control them. We can care about them one at a time, but we cannot affect them that way. Nowhere is the Law of Unintended Consequences more apparent than in the space we have been exploring. Each part of the whole is connected to every other part. There is no way we can do just one thing and leave all of the rest of the system unaffected.

If we were to decide that no one in a just society should ever have to live in "substandard" housing, we could not just legislate better buildings. Increasing standards without subsidizing the inevitably higher costs will lead to greater central concentrations of poverty drawn together through the filtering process. More central-city poor would then alter the need for public services and increase the pressures on local governments' budgets. The resulting increases in tax rates or reductions in service levels would cause the relocation of both tax bases and taxpayers. The redistribution of people would affect the logical location for stores, medical offices, and factories that serve their needs. Building standards always affect far more than just buildings.

In a system as complex as a city it is never possible to regulate just housing standards without setting into motion a full chain of other, unintended consequences. Housing standards are inexorably tied to land-use controls, issues of community home rule, tax rates and service levels, households' location choices, work incentives, distributional equity, transportation systems, and more. It is never possible just to build a road, construct a subway, protect a wetland from development, enact a new curriculum, or raise a property tax rate. In urban aggregations all those are part of a system. Each is connected to everything else. We can only do one thing at a time, yet we can never do just one thing.

4. *In these urban aggregation systems that humans have created but have not designed, government policies are, of necessity, largely marginal*

and reactive. Governments are not gods. They are just structured organizations made up of some of us all-too-frail human beings. They have no way of knowing the future any more accurately than the rest of us, and professionally they are likely to care about the distant future less. Politicians by necessity have very short time horizons, typically from now until the next election. They cannot be visionaries, and in that we are as much to blame as they. We only elect people who we believe can address our current problems, not ones who can best anticipate the next generation's. Politicians that forsake concern with the next election in order to focus on some distant future assuredly will soon be able to add the word "former" to their title—as in "former" Senator or "former" Congressman. Those who, like Henry Clay, would truly "rather be right than president" almost always get their wish. We do not elect visionaries for the future. We elect doers for today. We do not elect people to do the right thing. We elect them to solve *our* problems.

When citizens perceive home ownership as too expensive for the "common man," governments can respond with mortgage guarantees and tax deductions. When residents of a community fear falling employment opportunities, government can respond with tax credits for firms that create jobs. When commuters complain of congestion, government can add capacity to a highway, providing at least short-term relief. When parents complain of deteriorating educational standards, governments can impose mandatory curricula and testing. All these are concrete issues of the small. They are addressable by specific policy measures and the responses are all announceable at a press conference or on the evening news. Policies are made up of little pieces, small adjustments from the past. That is all that governments can reasonably do, twisting occasional knobs here and there in large and complex systems that are beyond their comprehension or control, establishing small policies that affect specific urban problems while inevitably generating unintended consequences in the process.

But what if the "problem" I am concerned with is not too many potholes, but an "unjust" organization of space where millions of households and businesses, in making their own "best" choices about where to live and work, have created a system that is "wrong." *And* the technology of transportation has evolved in the "wrong" way and people have responded "unwisely" and "selfishly" to it. *And* voters have taken too narrow a view of the need for public services and have "wrongly" resisted paying for their own and others'. *And* finally, the political-economic system as a whole has created a distribution of income that is "unjustly inequitable" and the spatial organization that this has supported is therefore "unjust and inequitable" too. What exactly is the specific action that a government could undertake to reshape the entire spatial legacy of the past into a future that "solves" all of these problems and that its populace would accept? Those are problems of the whole and government policy decisions are really only effective for the small. There has never been a government anywhere on earth that has been both smart enough and powerful enough to do all that well.

Some have tried. Occasionally governments have been powerful enough to shape the spatial organization of their nations, but few who have looked at the results of their efforts have judged those results to be either wise or desirable. For decades the old Soviet Union shaped its cities by severely restricting the production of automobiles, limiting the construction of urban housing, allocating what existed by state decree, and controlling all internal migration into cities. They successfully dictated the organization of space, but perfect cities were not the result. The Khmer Rouge under Pol Pot successfully deurbanized Cambodia by marching city residents to rural re-education camps at gunpoint. The cities were depopulated, the size of aggregations was reduced, congestion was eliminated, and class segregation in neighborhoods was abolished. "Antisocial urban values" were eliminated by killing all who held them. They consciously reversed history, explicitly choosing dispersed rural poverty over the logic of urban industrialization. A "wrong" spatial structure was made to match an "ideal." Millions lost their lives and all lost their freedom, but the pattern of space was brought under the tight control of the government.

Democratically elected governments have fewer options. They lack the power to coerce spatial reorganization into a mold unwanted by the population, and they certainly lack the wisdom to design perfect ones. They must adapt their policies to fit what their people want. Both by their actions and statements Americans have made clear that they share certain core values and they expect their governments to support those. They want to be able to own their own homes and be free to relocate wherever and whenever they wish, to travel freely and easily around their communities, to open and operate businesses wherever they choose, and to have some say in the education of their children and the public services they will receive. That core of freedoms has resulted in the organization of space we now have and the attendant problems we now experience. We will allow government to respond to those problems, however, only in the small and only on the periphery. We will tolerate no interference at the core, and that is probably for the best since government is ill-suited to design our spaces for us and to do so wisely and effectively.

Americans believe strongly that government should do things *for* us, not *to* us. We have little patience with politicians who try to force us to do things against our will, even if it is "for our own good" or the "betterment of society." Even if it might in some sense have been socially desirable to limit suburban sprawl in the postwar period, a candidate who ran on a platform of keeping home ownership limited, expensive, and available only to the rich would have had a hard sell indeed. There are not enough "spin doctors" around to patch that one up. It is clear that American governments may dabble only on the periphery. The values at the core are off limits, yet it is those values that define our space. We look to government only to ameliorate the specific problems that our spatial organization generates. We will not, indeed we dare not, tolerate attempts to redesign that space for us. Policy will be marginal and reactive.

5. If our unnatural urban aggregations are complex, integrated systems that no one has designed and no one controls and that government cannot fully redesign, then our urban problems cannot simply be blamed on the misdeeds of bad people. Nor can the solutions be as easy having the good people prevail over evil ones. In the last year African-American families trying to move into an all-white, largely Italian neighborhood in Philadelphia were driven out by harassment and threats of violence. Racist hatred is one of the clear evils of our day. That cannot be stated too strongly. Yet in the preface to this book I stated that in a literal sense, when it comes to the organization of space, issues like race are "superficial." If "bad acts" were the fundamental cause of urban problems they would be much easier to address effectively than they are. "Bad acts" are not inconsequential, but they are surface phenomena played out in a spatial context that derives from forces more fundamental than racism, and certainly less easy to condemn. If somehow America could tomorrow be made a truly "colorblind" society, the basic organization of space would be little changed. There would be some alterations in the skin color of the persons living at different locations within the urban arrangement, but central cities would still be places where low-income residents lived in high-density housing while suffering a shortage of employment opportunities and an insufficiency of tax resources to meet public-sector needs. Those aspects of urban life are not primarily the product of evil people and evil deeds. They would be much easier to address if they were. Too often they result from our attempts to do good.

If racist acts like those in Philadelphia are not primarily responsible for the organization of space that we experience, what is? Much of that responsibility must rest with Henry Ford and his vision of inexpensive cars available to all Americans, with the Chicago builder who devised the balloon-frame construction technique that made separated houses affordable, with the inventor of the mechanical cotton picker first tested on the Hopson plantation back in 1944, and with Eli Whitney whose American system of manufacture allowed workers with modest skills to produce large volumes of high-quality goods. It must rest with all the others like them who have contributed to and have been carried along by, the basic currents of technological change that flow throughout our history. It must rest with those of us who have shared in the national commitment to private property and free markets. Technological change and markets' adaptation to it together have defined a particular logic for the organization of space that cannot be denied. The good and bad acts that we see are most visible to us because they occur on the surface. The most impact comes from the powerful currents that lie below.

Evil acts are easy to see, easy to abhor, easy to blame. We can march against them, protest their occurrence, and sue their perpetrators. Attacking them will not, however, fundamentally change the spatial systems we experience. There was a real sense of moral satisfaction when the "Ratlord" was sentenced to live in the squalor of his own buildings. He was a wealthy man who seemed to display a callous disregard for the quality of the lives of the people from whom he collected rent month after month. He, it appears, was motivated by greed and devoid of compassion. Wealthy and powerful, he did not solve the housing problems of his poor tenants and that was "bad." But then neither did the "good" congregants who first sponsored Methunion Manor in Boston. They undertook their project with the very best of intentions and highest of motives. There was no desire for material gain in their hearts, no greed or callousness, only a genuine desire to do good for people in need, but in the end their tenants fared no better than did the "Ratlord's." Bad hearts are not the primary cause of concentrations of deteriorated housing. Good intentions alone are clearly not a solution. Ironically good intentions are sometimes a contributing cause to bad results.

Over 200 years ago Adam Smith offered his fundamental insight about political-economic systems. Social interactions, he argued, are not the simple sum of their parts. Institutional arrangements and social processes can sever connections between intentions and effects so that any of us can be ". . . led by an invisible hand to promote an end which was not part of . . . [our] intention." As we experience the effects of our spatial structure in America, what matters really are the outcomes, not the intentions. If good intentions can worsen serious problems, better intentions will not necessarily help. If bad intentions can lead to good outcomes, why should we care about the motivations? If we persist in seeing the organization of physical space as the result of a simple struggle between good and evil, we will be like Columbus, convinced that we are where we are not, and never really understanding where we are.

Our predilection for seeking the bad persons to blame is strong. For Lewis Mumford "highway engineers and city planners have helped to destroy the living tissue of the city."[5] They are villains indeed. In his book about newly developing subcities at the edge of old centers, Joel Garreau confesses that he began his inquiry by mapping a moral framework onto physical space. He had the "notion that if I could find out who was 'doing this to us,' it might be possible to get the SOBs indicted." Yet in the end he, like we, ended up finding the root causes of urban change much closer to home—"summed up in the wisdom of Pogo. I have met the enemy. And he is us."[6]

He is us because we are no different from government when we participate in complex systems. We cannot do just one thing and certainly we can not do nothing. We undertake actions, as we must, and in complex systems those actions have consequences, often unanticipated, unseen, and unintended. Ironically many of our most persistent urban problems are rooted in conflicts between good and good, rather than good and evil. If we believe that hard-working families of modest means should have an opportunity for the social and financial security that comes from owning their own homes, we are not pursuing an "evil" end. If we enact policies that support that commendable end, say FHA guarantees and Fannie Mae support, we encourage sprawl and finance the flight of the middle class from central cities. Our good acts have negative consequences.

When the Stanford Environmental Law Society became concerned over the environmental damage caused by rapid development of open spaces and green areas, they were on the side of "good." Yet as they encouraged litigation to stall economic development of outlying communities they restricted the development of new housing, slowed the filtering process, and increased crowding and the cost of housing in central cities just as surely as if that had been their primary purpose. They wanted exclusionary zoning to promote good ends. They are as responsible for the conditions in Los Angeles' slums as is the infamous "Ratlord," but they were trying only to do good.

Promoters of the landmark civil rights legislation of the 1960s that opened new housing, employment, and educational opportunities to African Americans were unquestionably on the "side of the angels." As African-American families have taken advantage of those opportunities to achieve new levels of economic success, many have moved outward from the cores of poverty that mark our central cities. They have sought nothing more than the white families who left before them—quality education for their children, safety for their families, and more living space. The increased isolation of what William Julius Wilson has termed the "truly disadvantaged" left behind is no different than if a sadistic delight in abandonment had been their purpose. We can never do just one thing, no matter how commendable that thing may be. The problems of our cities are so intractable because reorganizing them would require not only stopping "bad" acts but also preventing so many "good" ones. We have met the enemy. And he is us, not because we wish to do harm but because in complex systems there are so many "invisible hands" that lead us to promote ends that are no part of our original intention.

Because our urban aggregations are such large and complex systems it is not clear that any of us acting alone can do much to further "good" outcomes, even if we wish to. If I stay in a city with deteriorating schools, my presence will have no noticeable impact, and the schools will continue to decline. I can sacrifice my children's education and still not change the overall situation. If I leave the city my departure will have no noticeable impact, and the schools will continue to decline. I can improve my children's education and still not affect the overall situation. Individually my decision to stay does no good. Individually my decision to depart does no harm. In the face of that reality, can we say that choosing to leave is "wrong" or that those making it are "evil." Yet when many of us make those individual choices, the cumulative impact of our staying is to stabilize the schools and the cumulative impact of our leaving is hasten the decline. Collectively we matter; individually we act.

Can we then act collectively? That of course would require us to agree on an understanding of the system and the consequences of our actions. That much might conceivably be achieved. It would also require us to agree on which "good" is the most important one—environmental protection, quality housing, good schools, or freedom to live wherever we choose. I do not see consensus on moral priorities ever emerging, not because we are bad but because we are different. We often fall short in the pursuit of one good end, not because we have "chosen evil" over it but because we have chosen to pursue a different "good" instead. We cannot isolate even good things from unintended consequences.

The problems in our cities are not the result of some overriding conspiracy of evil that we good people can somehow uncover and defeat, making them all just go away. If this exploration of space has uncovered anything at all it is that we *have* met the enemy and he *is* us. When *we* do good things, bad consequences often result. When *we* individually make logical choices, they too often cumulate into negative outcomes. When *we* seek to collectively define the *most good* we inevitably fail. The "good guys" are as responsible for the organization of our space as are the "bad."

Surviving in the Wilderness

Where, then, does all this leave us? Several hundred pages ago we set out to explore cities with a fresh eye, anticipating perhaps that we would be traveling through civilized territory under human control. We likely expected that we could comprehend it, map it, and then reshape it as we wished. Yet we find ourselves instead amidst a wilderness shaped by vast, powerful, and changeable forces that we barely comprehend, much less control. We are far more controlled by our spatial environment than we control it. As humans we affect our space but we do not design it. As individuals we undertake small actions; collectively we experience the cumulative consequences. We cannot choose social outcomes but we must live with them. As the organization of our space evolves we find ourselves following a path leading to places no one really anticipated, selected largely by accident in a time long past. We find ourselves in a present with much to recommend it, but also much that we do not like. We find ourselves facing a future we have not chosen and may not wholly want, but cannot really avoid. That is not what we wanted to find. We undoubtedly had hoped that the solution to all of our urban and social ills lay simply with a better understanding of their root causes. In that we have been disappointed but that is the reality we have found. It would be folly, however, to fail to see what is there.

It is the evolution of the whole system over the nation's history that has resulted in the growing concentrations of the poor in old central cities, physically separated from employment opportunities and subject to high taxes and inferior public services. The root causes of America's urban problems cannot be found in "irresponsible decisions" made by welfare mothers or in abandonment of "family values." Nor can they be found in "pervasive racism" and "conspiracies of oppression." All of those matter, but none of them is at the ultimate core. If we are to find answers to our urban ills we will have to go beyond workfare adjustments and compulsory multicultural curricula. Significant improvements will come only from anticipating and adjusting to inevitable changes in our space.

Too often we have reacted to change by seeking a return to the past, but the currents propelling spatial systems through time travel only one way. There is no going back. Failure to see that leads to failure of policy. During the 1950s and 1960s Urban Renewal projects cleared central-city land of deteriorated buildings on the presumption that there would then be a rush to claim inner-city land for commercial and industrial use or for higher quality residential structures. After all, at the turn of the century that land had had enormous appeal. The thing that was keeping economic activity out of central cities must only have been deteriorated structures. Remove those ugly buildings and central cities would revive. We could go back to the way things used to be, or so the planners thought. But of course downtown theaters and stores were becoming obsolete because of the development of suburban malls and multiplexes miles away, not because of slums close at hand.

"Urban Enterprise Zones," or in their most recent incarnation, "Empowerment Zones," are based on a belief that we can somehow bring back to central cities large numbers of low-skill, high-wage jobs, that somehow we can go back and make cities like they were fifty years ago. Two or three generations ago the ticket to middle-class status for low-skilled workers was a factory job in the manufacturing sector. Starting with Henry Ford's $5 a day men and continuing through the high wages brought about by unionization, workers with minimal education could earn a reasonable living, stepping onto the assembly line, hoping for enough overtime to cover the boat payments. The extraordinary migration of African Americans from the rural South to the urban North was driven by the wide availability of those jobs in industrial cities. To be sure, manufacturing jobs have moved out of central cities, but it is not so much the location of jobs as their number and their character. Manufacturing is a much smaller share of the total economy. The jobs there are fewer in number and different in character. Those that still exist demand more skills and education, characteristics least likely to be produced in central-city schools. Charlie Chaplin's *Modern Times* mindless automaton in service to his machine is less accurate as a depiction of factory work in truly modern times. A different economy will have a different logic for the organization of its space. Tax breaks will not alter that fundamental fact.

We all tend to see our own experience as the "real" or "normal" one. Others who have not shared that experience do not understand how it really is. The generation that lived through the Depression saw that as "reality" and worried that their children did not understand how insecure things always are. Those who lived through the Second World War saw that as the defining moment in modern history. Those who came after and experienced only Vietnam "didn't really understand what it was all about." They had had it too soft. Those who came of age during the Vietnam War era knew that government could not be trusted. It was their parents who did not understand reality.

We perceive cities in much the same way. The organization that we have experienced is the "norm," the "natural," the "real." When it changes, we perceive it as a deviation from the norm. We expect it to return. We try to make it do so. In his book about edge cities, Joel Garreau notes that we have built cities with strong central business districts dominated by tall buildings and surrounded by light industry only in the last hundred years. Before then cities did not look like that, and yet we tend to see that construct as what a "normal" or "real" city should always look like. Ask a modern American to draw a picture of a city and that is the image that will appear. That is what we have known. We expect somehow to preserve and maintain that kind of city for the future. But if its time is past then policy efforts aimed at reestablishing that kind of city are really attempts to paddle upstream against dominating currents. If fundamental changes come, as eventually they always do, it would be better perhaps to find ways to facilitate the transition rather than to resist it.

IV

Prospects for the Future

12

Looking Ahead

Changing Jobs

The first automobile assembly lines installed in Henry Ford's massive River Rouge plant in 1913 were based on a simple design principle—each individual task had to be one that, in Ford's words, "the most stupid man can learn in two days."[1] For the next decade and a half those lines operated almost nonstop, producing millions of copies of an unchanging product, all assembled by workers repeating the simplest of tasks over and over and over again. Their job satisfaction was undoubtedly low, but their earnings were unprecedentedly high.

By the time the Motorola Company began to set up production facilities to assemble equipment for its new cellular telephone business in the mid-1980s there had been fundamental changes even in assembly line work. William Wiggenhorn, Motorola's executive vice president for training and education (a position conspicuously absent from Ford's original plant) characterized the new industrial reality.

> [Y]ears ago we hired people to perform set tasks and didn't ask them to do a lot of thinking. . . . Then all the rules of manufacturing and competition changed. . . . We learned that line workers had to actually understand their work and their equipment. . . . At Motorola we require three things of our manufacturing employees. They must have communication and computation skills at the seventh grade level, soon going up to eighth and ninth. They must be able to do basic problem solving—not only as individuals but also as members of a team. And they must accept our definition of work and the workweek: the time it takes to ship perfect product to the customer who's ordered it.[2]

Into that environment they cannot hire just anyone. They cannot replace any one worker with any other. Increasingly, even assembly line work requires multiple skills, not just physical but intellectual and social as well. Wiggenhorn notes that in one instance they had to screen *forty-seven* applicants before they could find *one* who was both drug-free and could meet the minimum mathematical skills requirements for the line task. There is no place for "the most stupid man" in that assembly plant.[3] There is no job that can be learned in two days and then be done unchanged for decades at a time. Clearly times have changed since Ford's day, and they are changing still. We are heading into a future far different from our past.

Changing Times

If there is one conclusion that derives from the exploration and analysis that fills this book it is that there is a logic to the organization of our space, a logic that rests on a material foundation. What it is that sustains us and how we provide it together dictate where and how we will live. Societies that subsist by raising sheep do not organize that activity around central-city skyscrapers; it would make no sense to do so. Societies that build wide body commercial jets do not organize that activity around a pattern of dispersed subsistence farms; it would make no sense to do that either. There is *always* a logic to the social organization of space. We have seen that in our examination of the past. We will experience it in our future. It is change in that logic, not some central design, that dictates how we all, collectively and cumulatively, live and work in space. There is no escaping that fact.

Throughout this book I have emphasized the special significance for cities of three different aspects of material culture. The first is the ability of a society to produce a significant agricultural surplus. How many households other than its own can a farming family feed? Unless that number is significant, large urban centers are simply not possible. The second is the production possibilities and technology available to those who do not engage in agriculture. What can they do to earn a living? What can they produce to trade for food and other necessities? How do they produce these things? Finally, how well can people overcome the "friction of space," moving themselves and their things from one place to another? Each of these elements has both technical and social dimensions, reflecting what people know how to do and what their social institutions will allow them to do. As change has occurred in each of these over the last two centuries, the logic of location in America has been redefined. As change continues in the future, that logic will continue to adapt.

None of us, of course, knows in advance exactly what those changes will be. There is no crystal ball that can foretell the future. At the time of the

1893 Chicago World's Fair a newspaper syndicate asked dozens of the most prominent Americans to predict what life would be like in 1993. Not too surprisingly, they were mostly wrong and nowhere more so than in their failure to recognize the significance of the internal combustion engine that had been patented a decade before.[4] We cannot predict with any more surety than they could what the most significant developments of the next century are going to be, but we know with certainty that there will be some. There always are. If we look carefully, however, we may be able to see the beginnings of some trends that will surely help to define how the organization of space will change in the future.

Down on the Future Farm

The great transformations in agriculture are likely past. The movement of the population from the farm to the city is the story of the last century and a half, not of the next. Today scarcely 3 percent of the nation's population is directly engaged in agriculture, down from 95 percent at the time of the American Revolution. If dramatic improvements in farm labor productivity should occur in the future, reducing the need for workers by even half or more, the impact on the organization of our space will be only minimal. If the farm population were to fall to a mere 1.5 percent of the U.S. total, the number of those "released" to the cities would be too small appreciably to alter the urban landscape. If instead technological setbacks should lower agricultural productivity so that we would need 50 percent more labor to grow the same amount of food, that would require the "reverse" migration of only a tiny fraction of the population. The great waves of migrants that marked both of the post-world war eras in America are done. There are not enough people left on farms to fuel any more significant movements in the future. We are today an industrial nation serviced by agriculture, no longer an agricultural one serviced by industry. That transition is done and is surely irreversible. The big changes in the logic of our space in the next century will likely come from developments in the other two areas, industrial production and transportation.

The First Industrial Revolution

The last great reorganization of space in America came about because of the Industrial Revolution. Mass production replaced craft industry. Economies of scale in the manufacture of standardized products drove companies and factories to grow ever larger. New power sources, first water and then electricity, provided the energy to run the new machines and facilities. Steam engines, and later internal combustion engines, allowed people and goods to move to and from these factories and mills with unprecedented ease.

That production technology was based on using large amounts of low-skill labor working at the pace of the machines, subservient to the needs of the line. Eli Whitney produced his muskets for the federal government in unprecedented numbers by using precision machines to turn out interchangeable parts. The work from the hands of any one worker automatically fit the work flowing from the hands of any other. The need for skill moved from the manufacture of muskets to the manufacture of machines. In Whitney's scheme it was the precision of the machinery that ". . . fashion[ed] the work and g[a]ve to every part its just proportion."[5] Compared to the gunsmiths who had preceded them, the factory workers needed very little skill.

A century later Henry Ford simply extended the same principle to assembly. Those who built his cars needed no understanding of how the final product worked or even the purpose of the part they added to the whole. They needed only to know that the bolts delivered to their station were always to be inserted into the same holes on each chassis that moved past them. They needed only to know where their particular part belonged. They did not need to know why. The final result was the assembly of precise, interchangeable parts into complex products, but the skills needed by the average worker were few indeed. Wages could be high because the machines and the system raised labor productivity, not because the individual worker was intrinsically skilled.

Frederick Taylor and the "Deskilling" of Work

Ford was an open and explicit disciple of the principles of "scientific management" proposed and popularized by Frederick Taylor. Taylor believed that production could be increased and efficiency improved by transferring skill, power, and control to management specialists. Time and motion studies could uncover the "best," or "most scientific" way of doing anything. Workers could then be trained, step by step, in that "best" process, and often the less they knew when they started, the less retraining would be required. Scientific managers would think. Unthinking workers would do.

> . . . the workman who is best suited to actually doing the work is incapable of fully understanding this science, without the guidance and help of those who are working with him or over him.[6]
>
> Thus all of the planning which under the old system was done by the workman, as a result of his personal experience, must of necessity under the new system be done by the management in accordance with the laws of the science.[7]

Management and control became synonymous. Workers' obedience was more important than workers' skill.

> It is only through *enforced* standardization of methods, *enforced* adoption of the best implements and working conditions, and *enforced* cooperation that this faster work can be assured. . . . Thus it will be seen that it is the assumption by the management of new duties and new kinds of work never done by employers in the past that makes this great improvement possible and that, without this new help from the management, the workman even with full knowledge of the new methods and with the best of intentions could not attain these startling results.[8] (Emphasis in the original)

So it was during the period of our greatest industrialization and urbanization. Low skill requirements were no bar to employment. A willingness to submit to managers' authority in the production of standardized products by unvarying methods was all that was needed for working people to improve their material living standards. The steady expansion of jobs like that in America's urban factories meant that waves of migrants and immigrants could be absorbed into the industrial system. It meant that factories would be concentrated in large urban settings connected to national and international markets by transportation networks. It meant that the location of production depended often on access to key inputs or to final markets. It meant that workers would move to the work. That was the logic of the time.

A Second Revolution

Ford's and Taylor's thinking characterized the productive technology of the past and has left its mark on the present, but it is Motorola's thinking that characterizes the future. Indeed there are those who see the developed world today in the early stages of a *second* industrial revolution as significant as the first. The initial shift to industrial production was characterized by the development of machines that could duplicate and magnify *muscle* power. A worker operating a backhoe with only the pressure of his fingers on hydraulic levers can do the work of many strong backs. In this new industrial revolution change will come from the development of technology that multiplies *brain* power. The "scientific" knowledge of Taylor's "experts" is increasingly embodied in computerized systems made directly available to line workers, but to take advantage of it they must have fundamental cognitive skills. They have to know what questions to ask of the system and what to do with the answers. They have to recognize and understand problems as soon as they arise, and they must be able to help solve them.

The kind of production system established by Motorola could not survive using workers whose only real "talent" was a willingness to be controlled by authority. Its success depended on finding and then continuing to develop "people with basic skills who were quick to learn—and quick to teach."[9] Motorola today spends $120 million per year to train and educate its work force, *$120 million every year.* Henry Ford and Frederick Taylor must be spinning in their respective graves. Today, and tomorrow, skill and education are a worker's ticket to success. "The most stupid man" and the least educated will find it hard-going indeed in the modern manufacturing economy.

Changing Products

One of Henry Ford's most quoted remarks was his promise to give consumers any color car they wanted "as long as it was black." His product was standardized and unvarying. Each one was exactly like all the others, and workers on the line never needed to vary their efforts. How times have changed. Masahiko Aoki, studying Japanese car manufacturers, was struck by the extraordinary variation in their products and thus their manufacturing process.

> On the final assembly line, wagons, two-door hatchbacks, and four-door sedans with red, beige, and white bodies; with left-hand (for export) and right-hand (for domestic) steering wheels; with a variety of transmissions, engines, and options; are rolled over seemingly at random. . . .
> The firm . . . produces about 20,000 kinds of cars, distinguished by the ways various features are combined, and about 50 percent of the total cars sold are produced at the rate of fewer than fifty vehicles per kind per month.[10]

It is hard to imagine how Taylor's "superintendent and clerks" could ever control every motion on that kind of an assembly line. Firms producing complex and varying products have to rely on the adaptability, judgment, and flexibility of the line workers to make the manufacturing process work.

Ford's Model T was manufactured with only minimal changes for over fifteen years. Today new products are introduced and revised many times over in that span of time. Existing products change their characteristics and production processes again and again. In the same span of time that Ford produced his black-only Model T, personal computers went from being completely unknown to being ubiquitous, evolving through multiple generations, some lasting only a matter of months. The plant where Motorola began its cellular phone production had been producing radios. The employees of that plant had to be able to adapt quickly to new jobs, new processes, and changing products. Like the personal computers, the cellular phones that they produce have undergone technological changes and redesign over and over again. An educated, literate work force is essential to producing products like these.

Changing Processes

Facing heightened competition, both at home and abroad, many American firms have altered their production processes in ways directly counter to Taylor's principles. The Japanese were the first to adopt a process known as the *kanban* or "just in time" system. American firms soon followed. In this system firms try to minimize the costs of carrying large inventories of parts by scheduling deliveries so that parts arrive "just in time" to be added to the assembled product. In some cases parts deliveries take place several times a day. This reduces overhead costs and frees up more building space for actual assembly, rather than unproductive storage. It also uncovers problems with parts much sooner since the ones just manufactured are used right away. There can be no accumulated stocks of parts whose deficiencies will be discovered only after they have all been made.

Responsibility for solving quality problems has increasingly shifted from after-the-fact inspectors to on-the-spot production workers. In years past there were separate workers whose job it was to correct defects in product coming off the line. Line workers were supposed to keep going no matter what and let others fix things later. Today in many factories each employee has both the authority and the duty to stop the line whenever quality problems arise. Each employee is responsible for finding solutions as quickly as possible.

> [Before] if a machine went down, workers raised their hands, and a trouble-shooter came to fix it. . . . Today we expect workers to know their equipment and begin any troubleshooting themselves. If they do need an expert, they must be able to describe the malfunction in detail. In other words, they have to be able to analyze problems and then communicate them.[11]

The flip side of this increased responsibility for workers is a generally "flattening" of hierarchies. When line workers have more and more responsibility, there is less of a role for Taylor's "superintendent and clerks" to supervise them. Layer after layer of middle management is being eliminated in many manufacturing companies. When Motorola set up its cellular phone plant it ". . . wanted to leave no more than two or three levels between the plant manager and the greenest entry-level hire."[12] Line employees have to make more decisions and have to have access to more relevant data. In the early 1980s Motorola increased the number of computer terminals available to its work force from 5,000 to over 55,000 but that would have been of no value whatsoever if its employees could not input data correctly and interpret output effectively. One of the oldest principles in computing is known as the GIGO principle. GIGO of course stands for "garbage in, garbage out." Neither Motorola's hardware nor their software can produce useful results if high-quality data is not entered into the system correctly and promptly at every level.

Line workers are increasingly viewed as part of production teams. It is they who will see problems first and often see solutions most easily. They must understand their role in a larger process and be able to communicate effectively and persuasively with other members of the team. This is the story of the modern age. Even assembly employees need to be articulate, perceptive, and "quick to learn." They need to be flexible. They need to understand their jobs, and they must be able to find ways to increase their own productivity. It is not just at Motorola that this is true. One of the legends of successful management in America over recent decades is a company called Emerson Electric. In an industry marked by harsh competition its rate of return on equity has consistently been 30 percent to 70 percent higher than the average for the Standard & Poor's 500. Its success can be attributed to its persistent drive to cut costs and improve productivity year after year, but the employees who find the cost savings are not Taylor's experts but the line workers themselves. Top management sets cost reduction objectives each year and then *each* employee is required to identify measures to achieve those objectives. Each employee is also required, as a condition of employment, to understand the economics of his or her particular job. Frederick Taylor's "scientific" principles have no place today at Emerson Electric, or at Intel, or at the most successful firms supplying auto parts to Ford, or most other manufacturers. There are, of course, still Taylorized plants in America but they are remnants of the past, not indicators of the future.

The Shrinking Globe

American manufacturing firms are not abandoning Taylor's "scientific" approach because they have been persuaded that it was too "inhumane" or "immoral." They are doing so because they find the new processes to be more efficient, and they face relentless pressure to improve their efficiency year after year. Domestic competitors push harder today than they once did, and new competitors arrive each day from foreign shores. In the years after the Second World War, executives at Ford worried only about General Motors and Chrysler; they gave little thought indeed to Honda or Toyota. Those days are gone forever. "Global economy" is the main buzz word in both corporate and academic halls these days, but it is more than just the latest buzz word. It is an accurate description of a modern world. National boundaries have little to do with defining markets any longer. No firm can afford to ignore the forces of foreign competition. Lower costs, cheaper products, higher quality standards—all must be a part of the modern working environment. Taylor will increasingly be relegated to the past because the rapidly changing products and processes that are to be found in the shrinking global economy today will increasingly require an educated, thinking work force. Jobs like those available to Ford's $5 a day men reflect the needs of yesterday's manufacturing technology, not tomorrow's. *Education and skill will continue to increase in importance as the character of manufacturing jobs continues to change. Multiple, high-wage opportunities for large numbers of unskilled and uneducated workers were a characteristic of past labor markets, not future ones.*

The Shrinking Manufacturing Job Pool

In addition to the changing character of manufacturing work, there is a fundamental reordering in the composition of output taking place in the American economy. That will continue for the foreseeable future. As average income rises, people seem to shift their priorities away from more goods and toward more services. Employment patterns inevitably reflect that. The Department of Labor regularly projects future employment by industry. Between now and 2005 it expects the economy to generate 16.8 million new wage and salary jobs—98 percent of which will be in the service sector. Manufacturing output, as a share of the total value of goods and services produced each year, will not decline, but because of increases in productivity, it will take fewer and fewer workers to produce it. Manufacturing employment is expected to fall between 5 and 10 percent over the coming decade.[13] *The American labor force will increasingly be engaged in providing services rather than producing products. Urban employment will continue to shift from manufacturing toward service industries.*

The shift to services, in itself, is neither good nor bad. It is likely inevitable, however, and it will have consequences for how our space will be reorganized. The growth in services is often bemoaned in popular discussion because people perceive a service-based economy as somehow inherently inferior to one based more on manufacturing. Some worry that the U.S. economy will be producing fluff while the rest of the world takes over all the "real" work. Some believe that because service jobs do not result in tangible "stuff" they are not really productive. A service economy somehow is not "real." Others believe that service jobs are all low pay and dead-end, the "McJobs" of popular conversation. A service economy is to be avoided because it "demeans and stifles workers." There may well be important consequences to an increased emphasis on services, but none of those concerns is among them.

The shift to service-based economies is not limited to the United States. It is a characteristic of all advanced industrial nations. We are not producing more services while *they* are manufacturing for us. Their economies are shifting to services as well—because services are what both our population and theirs want most to buy more of. Nor is that necessarily any indication of declining economic strength. There is no clear social advantage to producing more stuff as opposed to providing more services or vice versa. The social value of both goods and services is their ability to improve the quality of life of the members of that society. There is nothing intrinsically superior about manufacturing as a social activity compared to services. People who mold plastic lawn flamingos hold manufacturing jobs. They produce "stuff." Scientists seeking more effective treatments for AIDS work in the service sector. They provide "only" a service. Is there any rationale that would support a conclusion that more lawn decorations are clearly of greater social value than more medical knowledge, simply because the former have physical dimensions while the latter do not? I can see none. Are more dashboard dice, that arise from manufacturing jobs, of greater benefit to society than more symphony performances, produced by service jobs, just because one can be held in your hand and the other cannot? The social contribution of any job depends on the worth of what it does for other people. If people living at the material standard typical in the United States feel that they benefit more from additional services than from additional "stuff" that is not evidence of a "weakening" or "artificial" economy. It is probably more indicative of a wealthy one.

Nor do most "service" jobs entail flipping burgers in a fast-food restaurant. According to the Department of Labor's projections, 2.5 million new service jobs will be created over the next decade in education, most of them for teachers. Jobs classified as "professional specialty" will experience the greatest number of opportunities. Health services will provide nearly 3.5 million new jobs, involving everyone from physicians to home health aides. Registered nursing will be one of the most rapidly growing occupations. To be sure there will also be large increases in jobs for cashiers and retail salespersons whose wages are historically low, but a growing service sector does not, by itself, mean that good paying jobs are a thing of the past.[14]

It may mean, however, that they are a thing of the past for the least skilled and least educated. McJobs *will* be the service sector jobs available to the uneducated and that augurs ill for *their* economic status. It is not the consequences of a service economy for the nation as a whole that are distressing, but the implications for those least well adapted to the coming changes. The Census Bureau recently published a study of income inequality in the United States covering the period from the end of World War II to the present. It found that inequality declined until about 1968 and that since then it has been increasing, and it presented several reasons why. The changing composition and character of employment were the first.

> The long-run increase in income inequality is related to changes in the Nation's labor market and its household composition. The wage distribution has become considerably more unequal with more highly skilled, trained and educated workers at the top experiencing real wage gains and those at the bottom real wage losses. One factor is the shift in employment from those goods-producing industries that have disproportionately provided high-wage opportunities for low-skilled workers towards services that disproportionately employ college graduates, and toward low wage sectors such as retail trade. But within-industry shifts in labor demand away from less educated workers are perhaps a more important explanation of eroding wages than the shift out of manufacturing.[15]

The nation's productive efforts will be focused in different directions and utilized in different processes. Successful enlistment in the second industrial revolution will depend on education and skills. In the future there will be ample opportunities for those with both, but there will be fewer high-wage opportunities for workers with neither.

Commuting Work—Stationary Workers

When Boeing designed the 777, its newest generation passenger jet, many of the most important innovations did not involve aeronautical engineering at all. They involved new techniques for organizing and coordinating the efforts of the thousands of people joined in purpose but separated in space. No *one,* after all, can design and build a modern jetliner. That would be an impossible task. A jetliner is far too complex a machine for any single mind even to begin to comprehend. It is of necessity the joined work of thousands. Indeed the people at Boeing often spoke of their new craft as "four million parts all moving in close formation."[16] What individual people can do is design individual parts. The trick is getting all of the pieces to fit together and function as an integrated whole—to stay in that close formation. If some of the parts should break ranks, the gravity of the situation would immediately become apparent to all on board.

Overcoming the obstacles to effective coordination was more of a challenge for Boeing than the more technical problems of calculating lift forces and payloads. How could the efforts of 10,000 people involved in the design and manufacture of a complex machine be effectively coordinated? Somehow Boeing had to bring together people with different responsibilities for the same component, along with those who had responsibility for different but interrelated components, on a regular and recurring basis. Yet Boeing's employees literally covered the globe.

Years ago, when the first generations of commercial aircraft were being designed and built, the task of coordination was easier. Everyone was in the same physical location. All of Boeing's employees worked in the same facility, and the friction of space was not an element in their coordination.

> [T]he factory was on the bottom floor, and Engineering was on the upper floor. Both Manufacturing and Engineering went back and forth. When there was a problem in the factory the engineer went down and looked at it and said "Well, you'd better do this." The entire Design Department was within fifty feet of each other.[17]

By the late 1980s, when the design of the 777 began, that kind of spatial arrangement was no longer possible, and newly designed communication channels had to take the place of physical proximity. Phil Condit, the president of Boeing, described it as follows.

> I would love to have a building in which the entire organization was within fifty feet of each other. With ten thousand people, that turns out to be really hard. So you start devising other tools to allow you to achieve that—the design-build team. You break the airplane down and bring Manufacturing, Tooling, Planning, Engineering, Finance and Materiel all together in that little group. And they are effectively doing what those old design organizations did on their bit of the airplane.[18]

What is most significant about this is that Boeing did not bring all of those people together physically. It only brought them together organizationally by requiring regular communication at all stages among everyone who would play a part in designing, producing, installing, and paying for each individual component system. In each Design-Build Team (DBT) the designers had to consider how their vision would affect manufacturing processes and costs. Manufacturing personnel had to understand the design trade-offs. Both groups had to consult with others about the availability and cost of competing materials. There were over 250 such teams, and each team had to understand how its components would relate to those of all the other teams. Two components could not occupy the same space. Revisions in one system had implications for others. Somehow the work of thousands of different people in all parts of the world had to be brought together, and each participant had to be kept up-to-date on the daily activities of all the others. Here was a communication and transportation problem of vast proportions that could not be solved simply by having the engineers go downstairs to the factory. They could not relocate all of the people into one central place so that they could meet face to face every day. Should they, at great expense, periodically transport everyone to some central location for regular team meetings? Should they leave people where they are and physically move drawings and data sequentially to all other team members on a regular basis? Or should they completely abandon physical transportation and move all of the information electronically? Obviously only the latter could be done efficiently and in a timely fashion.

Using sophisticated design software the work product of each member of a DBT was linked to that of every other team member, and all of the various components were assembled into a complete, three-dimensional virtual "airplane" in a central computer linked to all work sites. Every change in a component by any member of a DBT was immediately built into the shared model and was thus available to all other team members and to all other teams. The computer checked each modification for "interferences" (for example, two parts trying to occupy the same space) and highlighted for all groups to see any that it found. The people never moved to a central location in order to combine and coordinate their ideas, but their work product "commuted" daily to the "central office." The people stayed put and the work moved.

People working in the same place regularly got together, as in the old days, but when face-to-face conversations between people separated by distance were necessary, Boeing set up a series of teleconference rooms so that people at any facility could "meet" with people at any of the others and no one would have to leave home. Words, voices, and images moved around the world with lightning speed, but human bodies stayed put. It is the closest thing to the science fiction fantasy of "beaming up" to a new location yet achieved.

This is a transportation innovation as significant, perhaps, as many of those that came before. There is less need for continual physical proximity in carrying out work in conjunction with other people. Documents and data can move as quickly coast to coast as from one desk in an office to the next. Virtual face-to-face meetings can take place between people continents apart. Technical companies do not have to entice all of their employees to move to wherever the home office is. They can set up satellite facilities and move the work to where the highly skilled employees already are. Publishing companies can work as effectively with editors several states away as they can with those just down the hall. The work can move while the workers stay put. Telecommuting and network links will not, of course, replace all direct human interactions. They will not change the location of work for everyone, or even most of the work force, but they will have an increasingly large effect on where some businesses choose to locate and where their work will actually be done. Transportation technology always has played and always will play a key role in shaping our cities. These innovations too will affect the future organization of space.

The Logic of Location and Central-City Advantage

A location attracts people and activities only when it offers some advantage over other alternatives. People were originally drawn to Boston and New York because they offered easier access to the sea than other locations. Later they were drawn to Chicago because it offered superior rail connections to the nation. Businesses were drawn to the Buffalo region in the 1820s because it was the terminus of the Erie Canal and in the 1890s because huge new generators driven by nearby Niagara Falls offered cheap electric power. People were then drawn to Buffalo because that is where jobs were. Vast numbers of African Americans were drawn to the industrial cities of the North in the decades following each of the world wars because they saw there better economic opportunities. The new suburbanites of the mid-twentieth century moved to the edges of cities because the land there was both much cheaper and, with the automobile, still easily accessible. People, businesses, jobs, and social activities will go where it makes sense for them to go, not where planners or social critics may think they belong.

Between the Great War and the Great Society the logic of location drew people and their activities first into cities and then spread them outward, suburbanizing vast metropolitan areas. At first the suburbs were primarily residential bedroom communities occupied by commuters who traveled daily to the thriving central business districts in the core cities. Over much of this century central cities and downtown business districts enjoyed special locational advantages that drew much of the regional activity into them.

1. Central cities offered the best access to the dominant transportation system of the day. Harbors and rail networks were the focus of central cities. The port and the union train station were always downtown.

2. Central cities offered direct access to the largest pool of labor that matched the needs of growing industrial concerns. Industrial employment under the Taylor system needed a steady supply of workers within easy

reach of large-scale factories and mills. The workers needed few skills and little education. Housing markets and policies combined to concentrate that labor pool in high-density neighborhoods in central cities. Thus factories, too, were drawn in.

3. Central business districts developed because commercial, managerial, and legal professionals needed proximity to the others with whom they had to transact on a regular basis. The one place that all could get to with ease, given the commuter rail systems of an earlier day, was the center of the main city. If that is where most other people do business, then that is where my business should be.

4. Central cities also provided the single most accessible point for retail trade. No other location was as easy to reach from any other point in the whole aggregation. Intracity transportation systems that were designed to bring employees into central business districts were well suited to also bringing in shoppers.

It was the conjunction of those four elements that fueled central-cities growth, decade after decade, drawing both residents and business activity into themselves. No one planned it that way. No one designed it. No one consciously made it all happen. That was simply the spatial logic of the day. That day may now be past.

The New Logic of Life on the Edge

Today *none* of those four advantages to central-city location really holds. Over the future they are likely to weaken further. Goods are shipped by truck and by air more than by rail and ship. Information is moved by electronic impulse, not by paper. An office gains more advantage from proximity to an airport, inevitably on the edge of development, than from proximity to a train station at the old center. A factory is likely to gain greater advantage from proximity to an interchange on the interstate highway system than from proximity to a harbor. That will not change in the foreseeable future.

The labor force needed by industry in the future is less likely to be found in central cities. Better educated employees are in greater abundance in suburban areas. Housing markets and policies have served to concentrate less educated, less skilled, lower income people in central cities, and that is not the labor pool from which most businesses will draw. Even assembly work will need fewer but better educated people. There is little central cities can offer most businesses in the form of a location advantage. Indeed they often present disadvantages. Given the dynamics of public finance in a system of fragmented jurisdictions, central cities often promise higher taxes and fewer public services along with less access to the labor pool they most need. Much of the growing service sector, too, needs an educated work force, and all services need to be located in places accessible to their clientele—and population is inexorably moving outward from central cities. As the buyers of health care and education and financial services move further outward, the providers of those services will follow.

Even central business districts are losing their special attraction as locations and that trend, too, will likely continue. The character of suburban communities has changed. They are no longer simply bedrooms for the city's work force. In many cases they have become complete cities in themselves, located near, but no longer dependent on, the older core. As population moves outward and travel by car throughout the metropolitan area becomes the norm, the pool of educated labor increasingly needed by business and industry is to be found in suburban locations, not central ones. Then as some offices begin to locate on the edge to tap this pool, the face-to-face advantages of a central business district location diminish. No longer is all business being conducted downtown. At some point in this dynamic a critical mass is reached and the concentrated business district at the edge location has its own draw. It becomes a new "downtown" but it is not located downtown. If that is where most people *now* do business, then *that* is where my business should be. When both residences *and* jobs are in new suburban communities then the best location for stores and the health centers and the schools and services will be there too. Central-city locations are increasingly *isolated* from growing markets rather than at their core. Today and for the foreseeable future the logic of space says to employers and retailers as well as households, move out, not in.

Few of us yet perceive the real scope and significance of this change. We still see "normal" cities as the ones of our youth or of our parents' stories, marked by huge office towers in a central business district staffed by suburban commuters. But those are more yesterday's cities than tomorrow's. Joel Garreau is one of the few to see the real change that is taking place. He calls the new structures *edge cities* as opposed to suburbs. They are increasingly not subservient to the core but stand on their own. To be an edge city in his scheme a location must display several distinct characteristics.[19]

1. It contains at least 5 million square feet of leasable office space.
2. It has at least 600,000 square feet of leasable retail space.
3. Its population *increases* during the working day, that is, it is not a bedroom community but an employment one.
4. It is perceived as a singular place (e.g., Tyson's Corner, Galleria, etc.).
5. It has been transformed from a pure bedroom community or from farmland in the last twenty-five or thirty years.

By that definition, Garreau identified over 200 new edge cities in America in 1990, with dozens of others in early stages of formation. In a few places, such as Boston, Houston, and Dallas, almost three quarters of the office space in the whole metropolitan area is *already outside* the central city. In Denver, Baltimore, Kansas City, and Miami nearly two thirds is.[20] The "Galleria area west of downtown Houston . . . is bigger than downtown Minneapolis."[21] Walnut Creek, California, east of the San Francisco Bay, has more white-collar jobs than does downtown Oakland.[22] A downtown location is essential for a business based on white-collar employment only if most of the other firms with which it will have to transact are there. If most of the other offices are *not* in the central city, there is much less reason to go there. Today, increasingly, in America's cities, even most white-collar employment is no longer downtown. That trend will continue. *Economic activity of all kinds, including white-collar employment, will continue to decentralize, moving to cheaper and more accessible locations on the periphery of the older central cities. Urban areas will continue to develop as multicentered economic networks rather than as "wheels" focused around a single hub.*

Future Logic and the Core

Two things, then, seem certain about America's future. First, the character of employment will continue to change. The skills necessary for manufacturing jobs will continue to increase while the number of such jobs declines. Most of the growth in employment will come in the service sector where education will bring high wages and lack of education will bring low. Second, the location of employment will continue to decentralize. There is little advantage to a central-city location for most businesses. Peripheral sites and new business centers in edge communities will continue to provide more and more of the nation's jobs. As a result central-cities' special economic advantages as locations in which to live or work will likely continue to diminish in the future. A majority of urban jobs of *all* types are already on the edge and that relocation will continue. Retail shops, entertainment centers, financial service centers, and medical centers will continue to follow population and jobs outward. More and more professional sports teams are playing in stadiums that are not even within the boundaries of the cities from which they take their names. There is no National Football League team listed as the "New Jersey Meadowlands Giants," but truth in advertising would dictate that there should be. With the loss of population, jobs, and economic activity, central-city tax burdens will continue to be higher and their service levels lower than in the less dense, newer, and more affluent communities on the edge. That, too, pushes businesses and households outward. That is the path we are on.

There are no transportation innovations on the horizon that could revitalize older downtowns. Despite expensive experiments like the new Red Line subway in Los Angeles, independent vehicles will still predominate. Nothing else can effectively serve the multicentered urban areas we have by now created. There may be changes in fuel sources and technology, but no form of mass transit can match the automobile in the kinds of cities we are going to live in for the foreseeable future. Our cities have spread too wide and refocused too completely. New rail lines may provide a convenient mode of travel for some trips and may take the edge off of congestion on some routes, but only if they are heavily subsidized. There is no way that they can ever put cities back the way they were in the past. Humpty Dumpty is already off of that wall.

Central cities will be just one of several economic centers in larger metropolitan economies. They will never again be *the* location for business. They will never again be the site of ever expanding jobs for people with minimal skills and education. Those days are past. Above all else we must adjust our perceptions of cities and space to that reality. That does not mean that central cities will have no locational advantages for anyone, that they will not fit at all into the logic of space in the future. First, of course, they remain the only logical place for most of the nation's poor to seek housing, even though by doing so they are being increasingly isolated from job opportunities. Our housing markets and policies really leave them with few other options. Without major changes in policy, that will continue to be true for the foreseeable future. Housing the poor is a function for central cities but it is not much of a future for them or their residents.

In addition, central cities will continue to have a unique potential in the form of their pasts. They contain old buildings with historical value and unreproducible charm. They offer access to scenic waterfronts. They contain transportation relics of the past that can be fun to ride even if they are ill-suited for modern commuting. Many of the redevelopment successes of recent years have involved turning historical neighborhoods into entertainment districts and tourists attractions. In Cleveland, private investors have turned old warehouses in The Flats along the river into a thriving district of clubs and restaurants. In Boston, Quincy Market has drawn millions of tourist dollars back into one of the oldest historic districts in the city. The Waterfront area in Baltimore with its aquarium, shops, and restaurants draws large crowds on a regular basis. The Riverwalk in San Antonio is featured in all of its tourist literature as an essential part of a visit to that Texas city. The ambiance that makes each of those areas so appealing cannot be reproduced in a new office- and mall-based edge city. It is uniquely part of the central city.

Other economic activity may well stay anchored in the central city by tradition, politics, or civic pride. As long as the New York Stock Exchange physically remains on Wall Street (and financial investors do not like big changes) brokerage houses will continue to maintain offices in the financial district. "Back room" support and research services may, however, relocate virtually anywhere and still be immediately accessible to traders. As long as courts stay in the core of cities, so too will the offices of the litigators who practice there. As long as nonprofit museums stay committed to the core, their buildings will stay there as well. As long as opera, theater, and ballet companies believe they need to stay "on Broadway," those activities will stay in central cities. However, if enough patrons stop coming in, even they may be forced to consider relocation out.

Despite their historical focus, most successful redevelopment efforts in central cities reflect the future, they do not recreate the past. None of these successes rebuilds the old employment bases. None brings a resurgence of the higher wage, lower skill factory jobs that marked cities in the past. The jobs they do create draw from a different labor pool than did the assembly lines of Ford's early factories. The currents of change do not flow backward. Low-skill manufacturing was central cities' past. It will not be their future. There will continue to be a growing mismatch between the people who live in central cities and the jobs that exist there.

That does not mean that individual cities and neighborhoods should "go gentle into that good night." Some may be able to buck the trends for awhile and forestall the consequences. They should fight for all the manufacturing jobs they can hold in order to ease the transitions that are taking place, but they dare not stake their whole futures on such a strategy. Economic development plans based on building a local manufacturing base can help individual neighborhoods for awhile, but they will not in the long run provide the solution for America's cities. If they are going to "rage" effectively against the trends they must first see where the organization of space is going. The fundamental question is not how we can *stop* these trends for the fundamental answer is that we cannot. The issue to be faced is what we will do in response to them.

This may not be the future we would chose, but the choice of the future is not really ours to make. It may not be a reality we like, but that is no grounds for denying it. Failure to perceive where we are and where we are going is not just intellectually dishonest. It can paralyze our efforts to respond effectively. When we try to help we may harm instead. There are many critics of automobiles' impacts on central cities who would like to "save" cities by banning cars within them. They propose pricing automobiles out of use by quadrupling the price of gasoline and eliminating most downtown parking. They presume, apparently, that people *have* to work downtown and this policy will force them to live in dense communities served by mass transit. Given the erosion in central-city location advantages, that policy would as likely destroy downtowns as force commuters to mass transit. Increasingly downtowns need jobs more than businesses need downtowns. If it becomes too expensive or inconvenient to commute in, the jobs will likely just move out that much faster. Unless we can see clearly where we are and where we are heading, we will be completely helpless in the journey.

If we see the logic that shapes our cities as fixed we will forever look backward, facing upstream as we travel down, certain to be caught by surprise time and again. Cities today are not as they were. They will not always be as they are. Changes *will come* in the organization of our space. They are inevitable and we do not control the fundamental currents. What is in our power, and in our responsibility, is how we will respond to them, and particularly how we respond to the dilemmas raised for those least able to adapt to the demands of the new logic. For most of us the new structural arrangements work out better than the old. We prefer them or we would choose to live as we once did. For others, the changes create whirlpools and eddies threatening to entrap them in conditions from which there is little chance for escape.

The direction of flow of the current redefining of our space is increasingly clear, and we will not be able to stop it or reverse its flow in any significant way. Acceptance of that fact is the first step in arriving at a successful survival strategy, but there is more than one channel in the broad riverbed that lies ahead. Precise application of policy may allow us to pass through one rather than another, but we have no means at all that can propel us back upstream to perfect the cities of the past. We will have to figure out how we are going to live in the cities of the future, and that is not yet at all clear.

13

Two Tales of a City

The Current Destination

In Charles Dickens's classic tale, *A Christmas Carol,* Ebenezer Scrooge is visited by three spirits. The first takes him back into his past, the second offers him a new perspective on his present, and the third shows him the "shadows of things that have not happened, but will happen in the time before us."[1] Like Scrooge, we, too, have now explored the past and present, but of cities. And we, too, can now see the "shadows" of things that "will happen in the time before us." Like Scrooge we may rightly be fearful of what we see there.

The "Spirit of Christmas Yet to Come" never spoke directly to Scrooge. It merely led him from place to place, pointing here and there with a "steady hand," directing Scrooge's attention to the conditions surrounding him until he came to see with his own eyes where his path was leading. Forced to look carefully, he came to see clearly what lay ahead. A careful look should also be enough for us as well. The path we are on leads inexorably to a relocation of economic activity ever outward leaving older central cities economically diminished, perhaps even irrelevant. Without special advantages to central location, the logic of location will draw less and less economic activity into the central core. However, because central cities are still surrounded by growing, vital aggregations, and because they are already the site of so much permanent infrastructure, they are not likely to be fully abandoned by all. Their residents, however, will be ever more isolated from the most vital aspects of this future society. We are on a path in which edge communities are destined to grow and thrive, while central cores are poised to wither further. Those left in the old centers will stay there while the main currents of progress move ahead, unmindful.

On Course to the Future

Guided by a "Spirit of Cities Future," let us visit American cities as they are likely to be a few decades from now. Like Scrooge's Ghost, our spirit simply directs our attention to the salient features and leaves us to draw the inevitable conclusions for ourselves. The cities that we see before us are wider and flatter still than those of our own time. They are networks of suburban clusters, organized as complex webs rather than single-hub wheels. The logic of location in the decades *before* our time dictated extraordinarily dense concentrations of people, packed tightly around cities' commercial and manufacturing centers, but that was an artifact of the technology of that time. Populations were compressed onto as little land as possible, in structures rising ever higher as we approached the core, but that logic was not permanent. In these future cities the forces of compression have been greatly reduced, and urban populations have continued to spread outward as the forces holding them in have diminished with changes first in transportation and then communication. As they have flowed outward they have drawn most commerce and industry outward in their wake. Urban populations compress only as much as is necessary. They always spread in space as much as possible, and now much more spread is possible. Dispersal, after all, is more "natural" than aggregation. With less need to draw inward, urban populations have expanded outward.

In these future cities the centuries-long process of turning residential patterns inside out is largely completed. Relative to colonial cities, the poor and the wealthy have almost completely changed places. We now find the middle and upper classes almost entirely in suburban communities; the poor have been drawn into the central-city vacuum created by their departure. Except in a few special enclaves there are very few residents of even modest means left in central cities for there is little indeed to draw or hold them there.

Housing in the suburbs is still newer, more spacious, and of better quality. The farther out one goes, the cheaper that housing becomes. The special transport and production advantages of central cities that once focused urban space inward are long since lost. Economic activity is to be found primarily in the new *noncentral* business districts of the suburban ring. Thus the special accessibility to job markets that central-city residence once offered has been lost completely. For most of the metropolitan work force, a suburban residence is closer to the workplace than living downtown would be. For most employers a suburban workplace is closer to the labor force than a central location would be. Neither employer nor employee derives much benefit from a connection with the old central city. What began in our time was simply precursor to this future.

The Shadows of Rails and Cars

When the Spirit points toward the transportation systems in these multi-centered aggregations it is obvious that the systems surviving are those that match the structures. While a few cities followed the late twentieth-century examples of San Francisco, Atlanta, Washington, and Los Angeles and invested heavily in expensive rail systems designed to provide suburban access to the central city, it is finally apparent in this future that rails cannot match the new spatial realities. The rail systems are wonderful for those few who still follow a suburb-to-city commuting pattern, but, of course, that was the norm for the last century, not the current one. Ridership levels have never reached designers' projections and all of the systems operate at substantial deficits, requiring taxpayers to provide large and endless subsidies. Rail systems always need very dense and heavily traveled corridors to be efficient, and these future cities simply are not organized in dense corridor patterns. Rails can never effectively serve multicentered webs. Automobiles have of course evolved technologically, but it is far too late to substitute any form of mass transit for individual vehicles as the dominant form of urban transportation.

Shadows of Housing

When the Spirit's steady hand points toward the housing in this future America it is clear that the preference for home ownership and space is as strong as ever. Nothing has altered a cultural icon so long held and firmly entrenched. For over two thirds of the nation's households, the homes they own *are* their castles, as well as the largest single investment of their lives, and for many of those only the federal income tax breaks have made their homes affordable. Congress has made no move to eliminate the tax benefits of home ownership. Voters simply will not stand for it. Proposing their elimination is still a sure path to electoral defeat. In American politics housing subsidies for the middle class still constitute a fundamental right.

Americans still hold firmly to their belief in the wisdom of requiring high-quality construction and of regulating land use. In a nation so rich there is no tolerance for poorly designed and built housing. We can afford quality structures and we demand them. In a nation so advanced there is no tolerance for inconsistent land uses. Americans still defend the sanctity and value of their "castles." The widespread limits on growth and the enforcement of strict building codes have pushed new construction farther and farther outward from even the newer edge centers. The ability of local communities to protect their character is a fundamental right.

As in our day, high standards leave only the filtering process as the provider of housing for the vast majority of the poor, and as in our day, most of that filtered housing is in the older core or in the oldest suburbs closest in to the central city. It is still impossible to build new "affordable" housing for the poor under the pervasive restrictions on quality and land use. The federal government, constrained by political resistance to new taxes and the twentieth-century legacy of high debt, has been unwilling and unable to take on any major new social initiatives. It has not stepped forward to overcome housing markets' isolation of the poor in the older core. Local governments are ill-suited to the task and, even more than in our own time, are suffering the dynamic consequences of their fundamental fiscal imbalance. Dispersed, affordable housing for all is a still unattainable. Concentrated, filtered housing for the poor is still the reality.

Shadows of Public Sector Decay

The Spirit points next toward local governments where we can immediately see that conditions within central cities have worsened in a steady downward spiral ever since the late twentieth century. Metropolitan areas are still made up of multiple smaller governments, each with its own separate jurisdiction, its own separate menu of services, and its own separate tax revenues derived from a tax on real property. Indeed as fiscal conditions worsened for local governments, more and more communities followed the path taken by the San Fernando Valley in the 1990s, seeking legally to separate themselves from the neediest parts of their jurisdictions. Faced with the responsibility for funding the ever growing needs and rising costs of providing services to central-city residents, many enclaves turned inward and sought to protect their castles from decay by constructing new protective barriers in the form of new political boundaries. Unable to really solve the problems of central cities, more have sought to separate from any fiscal responsibility. Not all attempts at separation succeeded, but enough have so that American cities are even more fragmented than they were in our day. Given the realities of Baumol's Principle and the sluggishness of the property tax as a revenue provider, they could not have saved central cities and by staying joined to them they risked being dragged down as well. Often individual households have left central cities. Occasionally whole communities have.

The fiscal pressures on old central cities are still too great for a local solution. When cities tried to relieve those pressures in the latter part of the twentieth century they merely accelerated their own long-term decline. With falling population and fewer jobs, with the need for social services ever greater, and with their physical infrastructure aging and in decline, the pressure on local budgets grew year after year. It took the same number of firefighters to protect central-city buildings even though fewer people occupied them, and given Baumol's Principle, that fixed level of fire protection cost more year by year. In central cities the costs became ever higher and the taxpayers became ever fewer.

American cities had only two possible paths to follow and both led toward decline. Some tried to fill the jobs vacuum left behind by departing private employers. They become the employer of last resort, a provider of jobs rather than a producer of services. As early as the 1980s some cities had already begun to follow that route. Between 1980 and 1992 New York City increased the number of its employees by 30 percent and ended the period with the ratio of public employees to residents one and a half times the average for American cities of the day. Washington, D.C., increased its employment by 10 percent over the same period and ended with a ratio *twice* the national average. By the early 1990s one of every *seven* workers in the District was employed by city government. By increasing their own hiring these cities helped to slow the total decline in central-city employment for awhile, but their ability to maintain that role was limited. The consequences of such high levels of public employment soon became obvious. More and more employees meant a need for ever higher taxes without necessarily improving services, resulting in ever greater incentives for still more residents and businesses to leave. Not surprisingly, when they were leading the nation in the ratio of employees to residents Washington and New York also had the highest per capita local taxes of all the cities in the country.[2]

That policy proved unsustainable over the long run. Inevitably the rising costs overtook the shrinking resources available. Eventually those cities, too, had to succumb to the inexorable budget pressures and bring their expenditures in line with their tax revenues. Given the labor intensity of local public services, that meant only one thing—layoffs. While New York and Washington were expanding employment during the 1980s, other cities were already beating a hasty retreat from that position. Boston reduced its public employment by 15 percent while Baltimore and New Orleans cut theirs by nearly a third. St. Louis reduced the number of its employees by half and Newark, perhaps the most distressed American city of the time, cut two thirds of the employees from its public payroll.[3] Ultimately the policy of expanded local public employment in central cities was doomed to failure. The high taxes required simply accelerated the flight from the central city and contributed to its own undoing. Even New York and Washington have by now had to come face to face with that harsh reality.

The cities that adopted austerity programs early on have been no more successful in halting fiscal decline. The drastic reductions in service levels, coupled with the deterioration of unmaintained infrastructure, made them much less pleasant places in which to live and work. Further decay in the schools made them unappealing places to raise families, and the public-sector layoffs added directly to rising job loss and unemployment rates with all of the attendant social ills. Central-city governments throughout this future nation have become as impoverished as the citizens they must serve.

Shadows of Work

As the Spirit's finger scans across the urban horizon there is a dramatic change apparent as it passes from edge communities to the core. In the former most adults are firmly attached to the world of work. In the latter most are not. There they are physically, educationally, and culturally isolated from mainstream employment. In every sense of the word, they live in a different place. The ring bustles with economic activity while the center decays.

The education and skill requirements for manufacturing jobs have continued to rise ever higher even as the number of those jobs has decreased. Those that remain are located in suburban industrial parks rather than central-city factories. Service employment dominates the economy even more than it did in our day, and well paid service jobs require education and skill. Most of those, too, have long since left the central core for there is little to hold them there. As urban aggregations have spread, employment has followed. Edge communities now thrive while central business districts struggle to stay alive.

There are still jobs in the core, but far too few of them to employ all that live there, and most of the jobs are not really available to the residents. There remain some highly paid professional jobs, most related in some way to government activity. There is little reason for banks, insurance companies, and advertising agencies to be downtown any longer. Most of their clients long ago left for edge locations and they have followed. Most urban law is practiced outside the core. Still some government activities, located via the logic of policy rather than of profit, remain. Courts and legislatures still operate in the old centers, and lawyers and lobbyists needing ready access work there as well. Social service professionals are needed in central cities because that is where much of their clientele is. The teachers and school administrators of central-city districts work there because that is where their students remain. These are jobs that are still within central cities but they remain out of reach of the low-income population, isolated by education rather than space.

There remains some retail trade within the city, servicing the residents and the remaining central business district employees, and providing some employment, but the shopping patterns of the early nineteenth century are reversed, a trend well evident by the late twentieth century. Most central-city residents who want to shop in large, well-stocked stores offering a large variety of goods have to travel out to the suburbs to find them. The best retail jobs have gone outward to the malls.

The newly developed tourist areas in the core, along waterfronts and in the historic districts, provide some service employment, but entry-level jobs provide minimal pay and offer little prospect for advancement. Many require skills and characteristics uncommon in the poorest of communities. The revitalization projects have done much more for neighborhoods than they have for the people who once lived in them. They do provide more tax revenues and kindle a sense of life in previously depressed areas in central cities, but they do not provide anywhere near enough jobs to affect high unemployment.

Finally there are public-sector jobs providing fire and police protection, as well as infrastructure maintenance. But cities' fiscal realities have forced them to operate with austerity-level forces, keeping public employment to bare minimum levels. Without more private jobs to generate more tax revenues, cities have been unable to maintain, let alone expand, their own job base. In all, inner-city potential workers far outnumber the jobs remaining within the core, and the jobs that do exist pay limited wages at best and offer little security and few prospects for advancement. Unemployment, underemployment, and discouraged withdrawal from the labor force are vastly more pervasive here than in the edge communities.

Back in the 1990s William Julius Wilson, among others, warned of the connections between the social pathology of poverty and the absence of work in America's central cities. He saw grave social danger in the growing loss of central-city employment.[4] When legitimate work disappears, people turn to illegitimate activities to survive. Growing crime rates spread violence through the community, keeping people off of the streets and out of positive social activities. Social institutions decay, families disintegrate, and the people left living there are pulled ever downward into a permanent underclass. The Spirit of Cities Future shows us through countless inner-city communities in which Wilson's worst vision has become standard reality. There has been no change in the logic of location since the 1990s that has either brought more work into cities or has dispersed the poor outward from them. The forces have all worked to draw employment out while holding the poor in.

Place versus Race

When we look outward toward the growing edge communities it is apparent that they are increasingly culturally, racially, and ethnically diverse. The patterns of the 1980s and 1990s have continued. Middle-class households of *all* racial and ethnic groups have suburbanized at rates at least comparable to those of white households. The long-noted predictions of a rising proportion of the *nation's* population made up of minority groups has been realized. The proportion of the nation's *suburban* population made up of members of those groups has risen even more. The logic of location does not change with skin color or ethnic background. Good jobs, quality housing, better schools, greater safety, and more efficient transportation are all more easily gained on the edge. As even today a majority of black, Latino, and Asian households are *not* poor. As even today the majority of those groups do *not* live in concentrated, inner-city poverty neighborhoods. As even today a majority of the nation's poor are white. Still the population left within America's central cities is disproportionately poor and disproportionately made up of members of minority groups, but they account for only a minority of those minorities. Indeed what may be most significant for the life chances of children born to the urban poor in these future cities is not their skin color but their physical location. *They are more handicapped by place than they are by race.*

The currents of changing employment opportunities, of residential segregation of the poor, and of decaying public services in the core all meet within these central cities. In the main channel the combined currents of change propel the population forward. On the fringes of society, which is what central cities have become, they join to form powerful whirlpools, capturing those within their draw, pulling them ever downward, offering little chance for escape into the mainstream. Escape requires meaningful employment. Meaningful employment requires education and skill. Yet it is residence in the central city that makes education so difficult to attain and employment so hard to find. Round and round the currents flow.

Shadows of Schools

Failure to go far, and to do well, in school leads to ever more greatly reduced economic opportunities over a child's lifetime, and in these future cities it is now more clear than ever that a child's *physical place* within the structure of urban space has an impact on his or her prospects for success in school. Even back in the 1990s one of the issues most thoroughly studied by social scientists was the identification of the factors that most contribute to a child's success in school. It is by now clear that the organization of space has affected educational opportunities in a variety of ways.

First, of course, there is the obvious impact of funding schools via local property taxes, especially when central cities are suffering ever-worsening fiscal distress. Tax capacity is not evenly distributed across metropolitan areas, and thus the time-honored practice of fragmenting urban areas into smaller, independent jurisdictions, each responsible for its own educational system assures uneven expenditures on schools from one neighborhood to the next. The continued restructuring of space in the early decades of the twenty-first century has only made this unevenness worse, and central cities have suffered the most from it. Jobs and tax capacity have left central cities. There is little wealth left in them to support central-city schools.

It seems obvious to most people that deteriorated buildings, underpaid teachers, and a lack of books and equipment must all combine to make learning harder, and now, even more than before, it is the children of the inner-city poor who receive the fewest dollars. While that is somehow fundamentally unfair, it is not the most important consequence of the spatial structure. There is very little evidence that simply adding money to those school districts would, by itself, materially alter the school performance of the children in them.[5] It is not hard, of course, to find social critics who think that unequal money is the most important thing. It would be nice if it were, for then all the problems in urban education could be solved simply by moving money from one school to another. Of all the things in urban space, dollars are the easiest to relocate. However, if the damage done to educational opportunity from the organization of space is a result of other aspects of the spatial structure—residential patterns, the quality of the housing stock, or the location of employment—then a simple reallocation of funds between schools will do little to equalize opportunities and outcomes. Unfortunately, there is a great deal of evidence that indicates that a relocation of education dollars alone will not do much to change the life chances of inner-city children.

In fact, careful reading of even one of the most damning critiques of inequality in our public schools undoes its own premise regarding the relationship between the gross amount of money spent and educational results. Jonathan Kozol's book *Savage Inequalities* written back in 1991, rightly condemned the inadequacies and unequal conditions found in most inner-city schools in the 1980s. In our future cities the inequality has only gotten worse. His implicit thesis, however, was that money differences resulted in educational differences, else why would they matter so? He noted, for example, that the inner-city schools in New York City spent scarcely $6,000 per pupil per year in the late 1980s, while in Great Neck, New York, schools were spending nearly twice that amount. How could anyone expect to educate children adequately with such obviously inadequate funding? At only $6,000 per year, it was obvious to Kozol, the inner-city children were being deprived.

A few pages later Kozol described the excellent, well-funded public schools in Cherry Hill, New Jersey, and in Grosse Point, Michigan. They achieved quality education by spending approximately $6,000 per pupil, just what was being spent on the "deprived" students in inner-city New York.[6] Cherry Hill and Grosse Point were spending twice as much per pupil as the schools in central Detroit but no more than in New York City. Alternatively, the New York City schools were spending twice as much as the Detroit schools, but there was not much difference in Kozol's evaluations of their products. Resource inequalities were unfair. They were unjust. But they were not the sole cause of unequal opportunity. There must have been more to the equation than simply the number of dollars. What else affects educational outcomes?

Schools and Space

By the mid-1990s there was a growing body of research that tried to measure not only the effects of schools' resources and characteristics but also the effects of peers and places. Laurence Steinberg, Bradford Brown, and Sanford Dornbusch had by then completed an extensive study of student performance in American high schools. What they found was not really surprising, but in these cities of the future it has become frightful in its consequences. What happens in schools, they concluded, is less significant in affecting student achievement than what happens outside of them. Student performance is most strongly affected by what students do outside of school and with whom they do it.

Family characteristics of course matter. "[N]ot surprisingly students do better in school when their parents are wealthier, more educated, employed in prestigious jobs and married."[7] Those are characteristics almost completely the opposite of those likely to bring families to live within the central areas of these future cities. In these Cities Yet to Be we have, even more than in the 1990s, concentrated the poor, the uneducated, the unemployed, and the single-parent households all in central cities, and we have assigned their children to the worst-funded schools in the nation.

It is not just funds and families that have mattered, however. The increased *concentration* of disadvantaged households has had a devastating cumulative negative impact on students' academic achievement. *Neighborhoods themselves affect school performance, even holding students' own home environment constant.* Adolescents from homes with equally effective parenting styles, strong parental involvement in education, and adequate family incomes do worse when they live in neighborhoods where those characteristics are not the norm. Students without those home advantages do better than similarly situated students when they live in a neighborhood where their *peers* enjoy those supports even if they, themselves, do not.[8]

All of this undoubtedly stems from the finding that academic success is most greatly affected by peer-group behavior and values.

> [P]eers were far more influential than parents in influencing teenagers' achievement, especially when it comes to day to day matters such as doing homework, concentrating in class or taking their studies seriously.[9]

By the late 1990s adolescent peer culture throughout the United States had become anti-intellectual for all groups of students and had become overtly hostile to academic success for many in America's minority populations.

> The adolescent peer culture in contemporary America demeans academic success and scorns students who try to do well in school. Schools are fighting a losing battle against a peer culture that disparages academic success.[10]

Particularly in black and Latino youth cultures academic success became scorned. To do well in school was to try to be "better" than one's peers, to disrespect the culture of the street.

> [S]omething in Black students' lives undermines the positive effects of parental involvement and authoritativeness. . . . According to our study this "something" is the peer group.[11]
> [S]tudents who tried to do well in school were teased and openly ostracized by their peers for "acting white." . . . Many Black students in particular are forced to choose between doing well in school and having friends.[12]

The pressures that black and Latino students feel to *avoid* academic success have not been unique to their subcultures, but they have been more pronounced. Poor black and Latino children are most likely to come from homes without the family markers for academic success, to attend the worst-funded schools in the metropolitan area, to be concentrated in neighborhoods where group effects are likely to lead them to disengage from school and where peers shun them if they succeed academically. This mutually reinforcing confluence of obstacles comes together locationally in the central cities of this future America where its poorest citizens are concentrated, and it occurs at a time in history when economic security has become ever more dependent upon educational achievement. Most of the children born into that confluence come through it ill-suited to effective participation in the labor markets of these future cities. They have emerged primarily qualified to continue in, and perpetuate, their poverty for another generation.

Caught in the Confluence of Currents

The loss of work in central cities, the fiscal impoverishment of their governments and their people, the erosion of public services, and the cumulative social and psychological effects of so much concentrated poverty all feed on each other, creating the powerful whirlpools from which escape is so very difficult. We can see that most of the students in these future inner cities come from homes with minimal educational advantages and go to school with other students who suffer the same handicaps. The schools they attend are the ones most sorely stressed for resources. They are surrounded by peers who, and live in neighborhoods that, collectively reinforce rather than counter the pervasive disadvantages of their home environments. So powerful are the forces of the place that inner-city parents who try hard to support their children's educations and futures too often see their efforts go for naught as the combined effects of neighborhood concentration overwhelm them.

Those few who do successfully overcome those obstacles flee from the inner city as soon as possible. Because they, of all people, know the risks of life there, few are willing to risk sacrificing their children to the streets if they can find ways to separate them from their threats and dangers. Youth who grow up in these cities see few examples indeed of economic success around them. Those who succeed on society's terms quickly disappear from their world. Few are left in their communities who hold secure, satisfying, and rewarding jobs. With no employment payoff to education visible before them most of these students see their own journey through school as meaningless, and in a perverse way, their resultant unemployability serves to validate their early perceptions of hopelessness. Disengaged from school and work, facing the bleak prospect of a limited future, residents in these central cities both commit and suffer crime at extraordinary levels.

City governments lack the resources and ability to address the underlying social forces fueling this crime, and unable simply to ignore it, they respond in the only way left to them, with repressive police measures attempting, at least, to contain it. To fund the police in these cities of the future they have to bleed resources from other needs, including education, thus further straining their budgets and worsening their fiscal distress. Fearful that the growing crime will drive remaining taxpayers out of the city, local governments try to contain the crime within the poorest neighborhoods, lest it spill over into tourist or central business districts, eroding further the already decayed job base.

The magnitude of the problems concentrated in central cities, combined with the paucity of resources there to address them, result in explosive tensions between poor communities and local governments. The police are seen as repressive and the government's disproportionate concern for tourists' safety seems unconscionable to poor central-city residents whose own safety is always in jeopardy. Few cities indeed escape recurring civil disturbances fueled by all of the unrelieved frustration and a pervasive sense of injustice. The ever present threat of crisis scares more and more employers away, leading to still more erosion of the local economic base. This social decay in America's central cities feeds on itself. What they need most is more good jobs, but what about these communities is now attractive to employers? Their high crime rates? Their fiscal packages of high taxes and inadequate services? Their ill-educated and inexperienced labor force? Their physical isolation from markets? Their decaying infrastructure? What? The obvious answer is not much at all. Central cities' primary remaining function is to contain those people who do not "fit" well within the labor markets of this future, and yet when they are concentrated there they become isolated even further—socially, educationally, and physically—from the world of work.

Meanwhile, many edge communities are riding on the crests of the waves of change, though their local governments, too, suffer degrees of fiscal distress arising from the imbalance between service costs and property tax revenues. To the extent that they and their residents are aware of the human tragedy unfolding in old city cores, they are largely unable to respond in any meaningful way. The first rule of lifesaving, of course, is not to let the victim drag you down, turning one tragedy into two. Money alone will not undo this great confluence of forces and even if it could, no suburban community has the resources to fund a real revitalization of the ancestral core. An attempt to do so would but sink the boat they are riding in without really pulling the central-city residents from the whirlpool's waters. Firms or households attempting rescue by relocating into that maelstrom would likely just accompany others on their downward spiral rather than extract them from it. Perhaps unwilling to pay the costs, but even more unable to stop the whirlpools, the edge communities that benefit from the currents of change mostly just move on with them. The crises in the core are not really theirs.

The vanguard of this caste of inner-city poor was apparent well before the twenty-first century. Social scientists and policymakers debated much about terminology—were they best described as a "permanent underclass," as the "truly disadvantaged," or as the "most oppressed?" Political agendas dictated the choice of terminology more than analysis did. The heated academic debates did more to fix fault and blame for the past than they did to alter the fundamental logic of location and the consequences for those inner-city poor in this future. Economic activity in these future cities has largely left behind the high-density structures and centrally focused organization of the past and moved to a new pattern of webs, connecting lower density arrangements on the edge. Income and wealth are being generated at unprecedented rates in the larger urban aggregations, but there is little to draw those activities within cities' cores. The reorganization of space has increased the divisions, in every sense of the word, between those who participate effectively in the economic life of America and those who do not. Indeed the ongoing spatial reorganization has propelled most Americans outward and forward, leaving behind a few trapped within the inner cities, keeping this "permanent underclass" in its place, literally as well as figuratively. That is a frightening future, but it is the one toward which the Spirit of Cities Yet to Be now silently points with a steady hand.

14

Two Tales of a City

The Way to a Different End

When Scrooge was shown his future he became fearful of what he saw there. Before he could bear even to approach a gravestone shown to him by the Spirit, fearing that it might be his own, he pleaded,

> Before I draw nearer . . . answer me one question. Are these the shadows of the things that Will be, or are they shadows of the things that May be, only? . . . Men's courses foreshadow certain ends, to which if persevered in, they must lead. . . . But if the courses be departed from, the ends will change. Say it is thus with what you show me![1]

Is the future that we have just visited what "*Will* be" or only what "*May* be?" In Dickens's tale it was not the Spirit but later events that finally answered Scrooge's question. The Spirit would not respond to the question. Scrooge had to change course in *his* present to discover whether he could alter *his* future. So too it may be for us. The shadows we have just seen of America's Cities Yet to Be represent strong probabilities, but not certainties, for our cities' future is not yet set in stone. It is clear that our current course, if persevered in, will lead us to these frightening ends, but if it "be departed from" we can perhaps in some measure change "the ends" awaiting us. It should be clear by now, however, that we cannot shape those ends wholly as we might like. We cannot undo the major forces driving the continual reorganization of space. They are inescapable. We can choose only how we will adapt to them. If we adapt wisely we can *perhaps* move the nation and its cities toward a future less awful than the one we have just seen. But, faced with all this, what could we possibly do?

Scrooge succeeded in changing his course only after he came to see clearly where he was and where he was going. Changes in his perception had to precede changes in his actions. If we are successfully to alter our "ends," our actions too must reflect the clearer perception of urban structures that has arisen from this lengthy exploration of urban space. We should now see that any attempt to change our course will be ineffective if we persist in seeing the organization of space as static, as if there is some shape for cities that is permanently "normal," some "correct" shape to which we can and should always return. Instead we now recognize that the logic of location will inevitably change over time. We cannot go back to centrally focused cities, based on compact commerce and abundant manufacturing jobs, willingly occupied by all income classes living in proximity. That is no more likely to be the logic of the future than is a return to the colonial "norm" of subsistence farms surrounding small, low, compact seaport cities serving the sailing trade with Europe. Those were both patterns of the past. Neither will be the pattern of the future.

We now know that attempts to change our course will be ineffective if we perceive the fundamental logic of location as something we can choose, something that is within our conscious control. The social organization of space evolves. It is not designed. It is, and always will be, the cumulative result of multiple forces, past and present. Urban planners cannot make cities entirely to their liking. When they fail to recognize that, they are like King Canute, standing on the shore commanding the tides not to flow—arrogant and ignorant, irrelevant and ineffective.

We now know that attempts to change course will be ineffective if we look at the elements of urban places as a mere collection of independent pieces that we can adjust one by one, expecting the other aspects to be unaffected. Successful adaptation is possible only when we recognize that the multiple elements comprise a system, joined, interrelated, and connected on multiple levels in ways that are always partially unknown.

We now know that attempts to change course will be ineffective if we continue to look at the problems of cities as primarily the result of "bad" people prevailing over the will of "good" people. We stand a chance of changing our "ends" only if we recognize that cities' structures are shaped at the base by powerful, impersonal, and largely amoral forces. To be sure, there are in America today ample supplies of evil deeds, harmful policies, and immoral acts, but these play out on the surface of deeper currents. Many of our urban problems arise when "good" people pursue "good" ends that nevertheless have unintended, "bad" consequences elsewhere in the interconnected system. Persistence in seeing everything in terms of a conflict between "good" and "evil" threatens to paralyze efforts to affect change.

In short this exploration has enabled us to see where we are going and why. We know where we have been and we also know that we cannot move into a better future by struggling always to go backward, yet time and again that is how we have sought solutions to the problems of cities. The "Urban Renewal" programs of the 1950s and 1960s operated on the presumption that if central-city land were simply cleared of deteriorated buildings, the attractions of central location would be sufficient to draw commercial activity and housing back into the core. Fifty years earlier that might have been true, but by the time the policy was tried, the opportunity was past. The logic of location had long since changed. The modern renaissance of interest in commuter rail systems added to auto-age cities, starting with BART and running through a dozen other cities, still sees "good" *future* cities as looking like *past* cities, that is, dominant central business districts surrounded by bedroom suburbs. Web networks of edge cities are seen as aberrations to be undone rather than inevitabilities to be accommodated. Urban "Enterprise," or "Empowerment," Zones see the solution to central-city unemployment in recreating enclaves of low-skill, high-wage manufacturing jobs in central cities. That policy seeks to adapt *current* labor markets to residential patterns arising from a logic of location that is now long *past*. These policies and others like them have all tried to overcome urban problems by returning pieces of cities to the way they once were. The frightful future we visited in the previous chapter cannot be avoided by standing still or going back. Our only hope is to face forward and move ahead wisely. How can we do that?

A Future That Works

We will not attain a future that is perfect, but we might attain one that is better. There will *always* be disadvantaged people in America (as in all nations) and there will always be social pathologies. However, if only we will, we can take steps to *diminish* their numbers and stop accepting spatial structures that serve to *magnify* them. Unfortunately, the issues that currently occupy center stage in political debate in America are often of minor significance for the real problems ahead. Those who think that they are addressing America's urban poverty ills simply by putting time limits on the receipt of AFDC benefits either have no comprehension of the scope of the problems or no genuine interest in solving them. None. Period. Likewise, those who think they can revitalize cities by requiring multicultural curricula in all schools have just as little understanding of root causes.

The crisis facing our cities is not at base an "ism" issue—too much racism or too little moralism. Those are rightly matters of concern, but to divert the future of America from the one we have just visited there is a *material* foundation below those observable attitudes that must be seen and addressed. Success at that means attacking head-on both the unemployability and the isolation of the poor. They, too, must be effectively connected to the urban "web" structure that is evolving. In short we must both revolutionize education and reduce the spatial concentrations of poverty. There is room for controversy over the details of policies necessary to accomplish these, but the necessity for real changes in both areas is really indisputable. We cannot succeed at either without also succeeding at the other. We cannot just do some of this. We cannot do any of it partially. Failure to undertake coordinated and significant initiatives in both areas means that the stark future to which the Spirit's hand pointed will, in fact, be our future.

First and foremost, the terrible waste of human potential we observed in those future cities came about because large sections of core cities became *economically irrelevant.* The resulting absence of work in those communities served to undermine all other social institutions. *If the most frightful elements of that future are to be avoided, the residents of those communities must be reconnected to the world of work.* Everything else hinges on that. If the people who reside in cities remain separated *from* work, then central cities as social structures cannot be made *to* work. Real reconnection can only come from an acquisition of new skills, physical access to workplaces, and a cultural recommitment to work as a way of life.

Overcome Mental Isolation and Obstacles to Effective Education

To overcome the pervasive pathology of inner-city decay, the people living there must adapt to **future** *labor markets. The jobs will* **not** *adapt to the labor force. The adjustment* **must** *come the other way.* High pay for low-skill work is forever gone. Decent wages in coming decades will come primarily from education and skill. This is not a moral prescription. It is not an issue of fairness. It is a recognition of what is and what can succeed. It may not have been "fair" for so much of the labor force to have been "forced" out of agriculture in the mid-nineteenth century but it was inevitable. It may not have been "fair" for workers to have to have learned to work according to factory practices, but if they had not, they would not have worked at all. It may not be "fair" that workers will have to adapt to the changing skill and educational needs of future jobs, but if they do not, they will not have decent jobs.

First and foremost, effective education must be a top, long-term priority. We *must* find ways to provide viable educational opportunities for children born into these inner-city communities and we *must* find ways to make sure that they can and will take advantage of those opportunities. The forces that now act cumulatively to drag inner-city poor children down must be made instead cumulatively to pull them up.

Changing Schools

To make education more effective two things must change: the schools to which children go and the surrounding culture from which they come. Neither one alone will make much difference. There are two separate but equally essential aspects to producing meaningful change *within* schools. First, resources for schools must be spread more equitably across the whole metropolitan web. To be sure, there is little empirical evidence of a strong past connection between more resources and improved performance, perhaps because they do not matter or perhaps because much of the funding is absorbed by noninstructional expenses. While increased resources will not make better schools inevitable, without more resources, the most poorly funded inner-city schools will be hard-pressed to improve. To move toward equalized expenditures for schools, either the states or the federal government will have to take on more responsibility for funding. That is not a popular position today, but the inequalities in wealth that exist between the fragmented local districts are too great to be overcome in any other way.

Some have suggested equalizing expenditures through a pairing of cities and suburbs via annexation and merger, but that stands little chance of ever being widely adopted and even less chance of resolving long-term inequalities since neither residents nor jobs are tied to any location.[2] Given the current disparities in wealth between suburb and city, new pairings of existing inner with outer communities can only serve as one way income transfers toward the core. Suburban residents will inevitably get fewer services for more taxes. Logic tells us that they can avoid that redistribution by relocating further out. History teaches us that they will. Whether that is "right" or not is really irrelevant. It is the likely outcome. Outer neighborhoods are more likely to attempt secession from central cities, as the San Fernando Valley attempted to do from Los Angeles, than they are willingly to agree to annexation. State legislatures can technically, if not politically, force suburbs to merge with central cities, but they have no power to force residents and jobs and resources to stay in the joined communities. That much history has made clear. There needs to be a shift in education funding at least to state levels if the inevitable pressure to relocate in order to avoid taxation is to be limited at all.

Achieving that will not be easy. There is a widespread suspicion in America that increased levels of funding will simply be absorbed by growing educational bureaucracies. As student enrollment has fallen in many districts the number of administrators has nevertheless steadily risen. If there is to be new funding, improvements in substantive education must be a result. That is the second element of the change needed within schools. It is almost a cliché today that schools must be made more accountable for results; they must achieve more in terms of educational outcomes. There are extraordinary success stories of inner-city schools that work.[3] They have no more privileged students than other schools. They have no more resources. They simply have exceptional people who give much more to, and demand much more of, all their students. They understand the tradeoffs that come with high expectations. To ask much of students is to risk having some of them fail at school. To ask little of students is to risk have most of them fail at life. There must be ways to make these exceptions less exceptional.

One possibility often mentioned these days would be to expand school choice programs or the option to attend "charter schools" to all students. I say "expand" because America has had a pervasive policy of public school choice for most students for most of this century. Fragmentation of the political jurisdictions that make up metropolitan areas means that families with sufficient means to choose among residential locations have always been able to choose from among a variety of schools and school districts, all paid for at public expense. Only those students whose families cannot escape central-city housing markets are confined to a single, inner-city district. The more modern experiments calling for vouchers and charters merely extend to *all* the privileges of choice currently available only to children from middle- and upper-class families. The controversy over vouchers has raged for many years now during which time public schools, especially in central cities, have deteriorated even as funds per pupil have risen.

Choice is not the only option. It is not a cure-all, but it could hardly make matters worse for the children. A recent letter to the *Wall Street Journal* challenged an editorial that had urged acceptance of a proposal from New York's Catholic schools to provide education for 1,000 of the most disadvantaged students in the public system. The author noted that conditions had been horrible when he had attended New York's public schools a decade and a half ago and he argued that, instead of allowing children to abandon them, the time had finally come to fix the public schools.[4] He is correct, of course, but one wonders why, if nothing *has been done* over the past decades, something *will be done* now. Clearly there is something in the school system that is resistant to change. Individual parents may well be reluctant to stake their children's futures on that hope given the history. If the actual options are school choice or more of the same for still more generations of children, school choice looks like the better option. At least then poor children would have the same privilege that fragmentation of jurisdictions gives to middle-class children. Given the history of so many inner-city districts wholly unresponsive to student needs, those opposed to choice carry a strong burden of demonstrating that the existing system can be and *will be* fixed, promptly and effectively.

Changing the Culture

Improved access to better schools can be accomplished through public policy. If only there is the political will, that much government can do. If the evidence of peer group influence is correct, and there is every reason to believe that it is, then something in the youth culture of America must also change if students are to benefit from the better schools. That government cannot do. It must come from a commitment by leaders within poor communities and leaders from without who can credibly speak to those who live there. That is particularly true in the case of poverty communities made up of racial and ethnic minorities.

Those who are poor in America's inner cities today are not responsible for most of the forces that over the years have concentrated them there in poverty, but fixing blame and bestowing innocence is of little use in promoting future change. Those most connected to communities of poverty are going to *have* to take on the responsibility for undoing much of the damage done to children there whether or not it is their "fault"—not as an issue of ethics but as one of real politics. No one else is going to care enough to take it on. No one from the outside can have sufficient credibility on the inside. Children in inner cities, indeed in all of America, *must* be made to see that their futures *do* depend on their education. If better policies do finally succeed in improving the opportunities offered in schools, only the larger culture can make students see the wisdom of taking advantage of those opportunities.

What tragic irony there is in the current belief among so many minority youth, especially African-American youth, that seeking academic success is somehow traitorous to the race, that to be "authentic," one must be ignorant. How have things come to this? Frederick Douglass, who rose from chattel slavery to international renown, credited education, "stolen" from his slave masters because it was forbidden to him by law, as the ultimate key to his freedom. Slavery he characterized not so much as physical bondage but as a "graveyard of the mind."[5] He risked horrible beatings when he learned to read and when he secretly taught other slaves to do so. Their masters knew that enforcing ignorance on the oppressed was the greatest defense of their own privilege.

> Every moment they spent in that school they were liable to be taken up, and given thirty-nine lashes. They came because they wished to learn. Their minds had been starved by their cruel masters. They had been shut up in mental darkness.[6]

Today in America's schools academic success by African-American and Latino youth is ridiculed not by "masters" but by peers. To do well is derided as trying to "act white," to buy into the "wrong" values, to disrespect the culture of the streets. If Laurence Steinberg is right and young people are truly "forced to choose between doing well in school and having friends" they will continue, far too often, to choose having friends. Black youth will continue to do to each other what white slave masters could not do to past generations of their ancestors.[7]

If the larger society cannot find ways to provide educational opportunity to the children of our central cities, especially those in the Concentrated Poverty Areas, *and* if those children cannot be made to see the value of those opportunities, they will remain on the margins of that society. Their poor neighborhoods will become ever more powerful engines of decline, reproducing poverty and dysfunction, generation after generation. Discrimination is still a formidable barrier in American society, but it is not enough simply to attack discriminatory practices. It is imperative that all youth will be ready and willing to move ahead effectively wherever those obstacles are reduced or removed. Not because they broke it, but because only they are in a position to fix it, the leadership of minority communities has to address the attitudes of young people in our cities. There is much talk of seeking a level playing field. That *is* essential. It is also essential that once on that field, all of the players must be willing and able to play. There is little to be gained by leveling the field if we neglect to prepare the players. It is perhaps more important to make them believe that they are the hope for the future than it is to teach them that they are the victims of the past. Changing the "end" facing America's cities must begin by overcoming *all* of the current obstacles to effective education.

Overcoming Physical Isolation and Obstacles of Space

The intense concentrations of poverty that characterize so many central-city neighborhoods are an obstacle both to effective education for the children growing up there and to effective participation in work for the adults living there. The spatial isolation of the nation's poor must be reduced. As long as so many people live in communities of such intensely concentrated poverty their children will continue to grow up *mentally* unprepared for the world of work. They will grow up *physically and socially* isolated from growing job opportunities in the developing edge communities. *A different path to the future for our cities will require coordinated efforts to disperse urban poverty populations. It will not be enough simply to move the concentrations outward from the old core. They must be dispersed and joined to the larger community.*

Redistribution, Not Relocation

It is the interaction of housing markets and housing policies that concentrate the poor in the very places where jobs are on the decline. Employment of all types is increasingly scattered throughout the whole metropolitan web. Low-income housing, decidedly, is not. To avoid the first of the futures visited we *must* make it possible for the poor also to have access to that dispersed employment. They must be able to follow the jobs. That will not be easy but it is not impossible. To succeed, housing for the poor will have to be truly dispersed, truly affordable, and consistently profitable. Failure in any of these aspects will result in failure of the whole.

The resistance of suburban communities to proposals for low-income housing is neither surprising nor irrational. If decentralization of the poor means physically transplanting the ghetto with its drab, deteriorated, high-density housing into new, low-density communities one need not be "racist" or "elitist" to feel uncomfortable about the changes likely to result. Most of those who live in poverty neighborhoods do not really want housing like that in *their* neighborhood either.

Derrick Bell notes that the resistance of the black middle class to low-income housing projects in their neighborhoods has often been as intense as that of the white middle class.[8] Many of the families of all races now living in suburban communities have left central cities precisely to avoid gang violence, crime, and social decay. If that is what is now being offered to edge communities, it is hard to blame them for resisting. If "dispersion" means transplanting slums and all of their problems to the suburbs, no suburb is likely to welcome them. The concentrations of the poor must be broken up and absorbed, not merely moved. This is not only a precondition for political acceptance, it is a precondition for breaking through the conditions that reinforce poverty. Poor people interspersed into large, diverse communities are more likely to become a part of them rather than to replace them with ghettos. Dispersion reintroduces poor people into stable communities that are well connected to work and that still have the established and functioning social institutions that are so often decayed or absent in central-city poverty neighborhoods.

Real dispersion can change how people live as well as where they live. A peculiar combination of events created a natural experiment on the effects of dispersion in the Greater Chicago area. In 1976 the Chicago Housing Authority was found to have used race as the basis for assignment of house-holds to public housing, promoting, rather than reducing, racial segregation within the city.[9] In the remedy phase of the case the judge ordered several thousand Section 8 rent vouchers to be set aside for black residents of public housing to allow them to move out of segregated public housing and into the larger metropolitan housing market.

The court also ordered the city to hire full-time real-estate counselors whose job it was to locate suitable units throughout the greater metropolitan area. As units were found, they were offered in strict order to a waiting list of black households living in the poverty-concentrated public housing. Ninety-five percent accepted the first unit offered. Thus residents were distributed between central-city and edge locations largely at random. Susan Popkin, James Rosenbaum, and Patricia Meaden studied the work behavior of a sample drawn from more than 4,000 poor families dispersed in this manner.[10] In terms of age, education, family size, and work experience, there were no discernible differences between those moving to other cen-tral-city locations and those moving to the suburbs. There was, however, a discernible, indeed statistically significant, difference in work behavior. Women who relocated to suburban housing, closer to employment opportu-nities and surrounded by institutions more supportive of work, were more than 25 percent more likely to be working after their move than were their inner-city counterparts.[11] There is also evidence that their children were more likely to stay in school and attend college, and were less likely to be involved in criminal activity. Relocation did not solve all problems; even after moving, many in both locations remained unattached to work. Still, dispersal into the larger metropolitan web had a significant favorable impact on those moving outward without materially altering the communities into which they came.

Helping Poor Families Out

Any dispersal of poverty concentrations must begin with a strong dose of political reality. Housing regulations, past and present low-income housing subsidy programs, the political fragmentation of metropolitan areas, and pervasive income inequality all combine to promote concentration. All must play a role in promoting dispersal, but they must do so in a way that does not generate crippling political opposition. First, housing codes and con-struction standards will always be needed. There should be no Americans squatting on vacant land, living in shanties that lack running water, sewers, and electricity. We can and must do better than Third World solutions to our low-income housing needs. Housing regulations must be maintained, but modified.

When the New Jersey Supreme Court in its Mount Laurel II decision created an affirmative duty for *all* communities to provide for their "fair share" of *regional* growth, they redefined the purpose of zoning and land-use regulation. Communities in New Jersey were, from that point on, expected to balance protection of the interests of those who live there with the needs of those who might wish to move there. As with all "fair share" plans they are really only fair if *all* communities do, in fact, share. If only one community responds to the challenge it will quickly become overwhelmed while its neighbors watch from the sidelines. Too often conflict is over which community will end up accommodating all, or most, of "them." Then the battle becomes fierce and the outcome ineffective. *Real dispersal of the poor will require that Mount Laurel II type "fair share" principles become the effective **national** norm for local housing regulation and control. Low-income households need not be made a part of each and every building and block in America, but they must have realistic access to **all** of the frag-mented jurisdictions that make up the modern metropolitan web.*

Making Dispersal Profitable

New regulatory standards alone will not, of course, be enough to effect real dispersal. Having established an affirmative "fair share" duty, in the end the New Jersey decision resulted in very little real change in housing. The court had no power to compel private developers to *do* anything in New Jersey or Mount Laurel. While local jurisdictions can enact regulations that *encour-age* mixed-income housing, if it is not profitable to build, it will not be built. As the sponsors of Methunion Manor in Boston discovered, not even well-meaning nonprofit sponsors can continue to provide "affordable" housing that continually loses money. That is an inescapable truism in capitalist America. Dispersal requires more mixed-income housing in the suburbs, and that will come about only if the revenues from that housing cover the full costs of constructing and maintaining it. That in turn means that there must be explicit housing subsidies for the poor if mixed-income projects are to generate sufficient rent without creating unsustainable rent burdens. As always, significant redistribution is only viable on a very large jurisdictional scale.

Local governments can never achieve it. "Affordable" unit set-asides as a precondition for approving building permits are not an answer. The costs to developers are not reduced by such measures; the rent-paying ability of the poor is not increased. Project viability thus depends on either investors being willing and able permanently to subsidize tenants out of their own pockets or higher income residents being willing to pay extra rent to subsidize their lower income co-tenants via direct cross transfers. In practice there is probably a limited future for projects that depend on developers paying for the privilege of doing business or on higher income people being willing to pay a premium for the privilege of living with lower income people. There are some and they are surely to be commended for their commitment to social justice and responsibility. There are not enough of them, however, to make this the answer to the frightful future for all of America's cities visited in the previous chapter.

The Need for a National Program

If increased suburban, mixed-income housing is to affect the organization of space, the subsidies will have to come from government rather than from private developers or co-tenants, and the subsidies will have to come from the highest levels of government possible. They will have to be widely available and generously funded. To subsidize a few at a time will make little difference. Clearly, we are not now in an era when the federal government is seeking new social programs to enact. It seems instead to be seeking ways to abandon obligations it took on in the past. However, significant housing reform and a better future for America's cities will require that it take on this responsibility. A meaningful reorganization of housing for the poor cannot come about without substantial funding on a national scale.

Effective dispersal of the poor, then, must come from national-level programs that both promote *and* subsidize new affordable units, spread across *all* communities, mixed in with market units and externally indistinguishable from them. Subsidized dispersal, however, is a highly charged program that must be designed and implemented with great care. There is a political, and even moral, balance that must be drawn in such programs. If they involve relocating poor people into housing that is measurably better than that occupied by those higher up the income scale whose taxes fund the programs, they will be politically unsustainable. If the units are of a quality that is too low, they will alter the character of suburban communities and will be politically unsustainable. The subsidized units must be of reasonable quality but not luxurious. They must fit in with the surrounding community but be modest in scope. That will not be an easy balance to achieve. *Construction of dispersed, mixed-income housing, encouraged by affirmative fair share regulations, will only come about if there are appro-*

priate **national** *subsidy programs to assure their profitability and sustainability.*

Making Dispersion Possible—The Role of Existing Homes

Materially changing the character of the national housing stock will take a long time, even with substantial subsidies for new mixed-income housing. Most people, no matter what their income level, will always live in older, existing housing. The stock of houses already built is so vast and so long-lived that any new construction can affect it only incrementally. The Department of Housing and Urban Development (HUD) points with pride to the 40,000 new and rehabilitated "affordable" units that are added to the urban housing stock each year under the auspices of the nation's 2,000 Community Development Corporations. For individual households and neighborhoods these new projects can make a real difference; for the nation as a whole they are far too few to matter. At that rate it would take nearly 200 years to add enough units for all of this year's poor families. By then, of course, most of the "new" units will have become quite "old."

New construction of mixed-income housing in nonpoor communities, no matter how heavily subsidized and widely expanded, will not suffice. There must also be an expansion of subsidies that permit low-income residents to participate more widely in the market for existing housing. Some program like Section 8 "Existing" vouchers will have to be widely funded, though the form of the subsidy will have to be structured to overcome some of the "perverse" effects uncovered by the federal housing allowance experiment discussed in Chapter 8.[12] *Dispersal of the poor will also require programs to make existing structures affordable to low-income tenants. Improving web access cannot come from new construction alone.*

Restructuring the Core

Successful dispersal of the poor throughout the whole urban web will, of course, accelerate the current trend toward depopulation of the core, but central cities will not become vacuums. Their structures will not simply disappear. They will not become empty space. What plausible role can old central cities play if the current concentrations of the poor are successfully dispersed? Central cities will still be able to play an important role in their regional economies, but not as the unique and powerful hubs toward which all activity gravitates. That was the form of the past. In the future older central cities can, at best, be one among many nodes in large metropolitan webs. Their revitalization, combined with a program of effective dispersal of the poor, will depend on two things—maintaining an employment base and replacing poverty concentrations with households representing the full range of incomes.

The Employment Base

Even today, there is an abundance of jobs in central cities. The bad news is that the skills of the current central-city residents do not match the skill requirements of those jobs. The current population and the needed work force are not in balance. Although no longer exclusively there, government, law, medicine, education, finance, and central administrative jobs still abound in central cities today. Some service jobs offering high wages for high skills will continue to make economic sense in central cities. Some important transportation nodes will continue to exist there. Museums, cultural activities, and historical tourist districts will still be there. Central cities will have a role to play and an ample supply of some kinds of jobs even as web development spreads growing employment more evenly across the whole of metropolitan space. It is the lower skill jobs, not all jobs, that economic change will reduce and that the logic of location will continue to expel from central cities.

The current spatial problem is that the residents of the city do not have the skills to participate in the jobs that do and will exist there while the employees that do have the requisite skills do not wish to live within the city. *If* national programs promoting dispersal of the poor are at all successful, then half of the spatial problem is solved. Many of the poor will have literally been "helped out." All that remains is to discover policies that can attract more of the nonpoor, potential employees back in.

Residential Replacement

When professional families return to, and invest in, urban neighborhoods today it is a mixed blessing. Called "gentrification" when the characteristics of the entrants are examined, it becomes "displacement" when the impact on the previous neighborhood residents is the focus. As the latter, it is often resisted. However, programs that encourage gentrification, *when joined with effective dispersal of the poor,* should result in *re*placement rather than *dis*placement. If the poor do disperse there will be room for more middle- and upper-income households to move back in and revitalize both neighborhoods and the tax base, *if* they see reasons to do so. First among those will have to be coordinated urban redevelopment projects that improve urban housing conditions for those at all income levels.

Urban residential revitalization projects have only been successful when they have had both sufficient scale and substantial standards.[13] Neighborhood pressures for decay are so strong that a single unit cannot be restructured, but several contiguous blocks can be. Those moving into the redevelopment area have to meet appropriate behavioral and financial standards. They have to take on responsibility for maintaining the quality of life for the neighborhood. In short, urban neighborhood revitalization projects work best when returning residents *and their neighbors* acquire real "ownership"—both financial and emotional.

The role of existing public housing in revitalization must also be addressed. In many cities the stock of existing public housing has become an obstacle to revitalization of the core. Constructed decades ago and heavily deteriorated, it now constitutes a large share of the total stock in many central cities. In far too many cases units have become uninhabitable and irreparable and will have to follow the example of the Pruitt-Igoe project and fall to the wrecker's ball or explosive destruction. In others, rehabilitation is possible, but is desirable only if the purpose of the projects is rethought. When public housing was begun back in the 1930s it welcomed working families and excluded or evicted dangerous and disruptive tenants. In more recent decades it has become refocused on providing housing *only* to the poorest of the poor. Since 1981 Congress has required an implicit policy of "expulsionary zoning," eliminating all but the most distressed residents. All screening and standards have been abandoned. As a result, in many cities public housing has become a repulsing force driving stabilizing, working-class households out of central-city neighborhoods rather than an attractive force holding them in. That policy will have to be reversed. Public housing will have to be rehabilitated and housing authorities will then have to actively seek stable working-class families and provide strict security and careful screening of tenants for behavioral or legal problems.

Community Protections

Finally, all of this—mixed-income housing scattered throughout the web, fair-share standards for all suburban communities, vastly expanded vouchers for the existing market, central-city revitalization projects, and restructured public housing—will be effective and will be politically viable only so long as there are adequate protections for tenants and for landlords as well. Someone once characterized Democrats as people who love jobs but hate employers, unaware, perhaps, of the fundamental inconsistency. Likewise, housing activists often seem to want expanded housing options for low-income households but want to get rid of all landlords. There is a fundamental inconsistency there as well. Potential investors and owners of real property will accept and participate in dispersal and reorganization *only* when it is in their interest to do so. That occurs only when they have adequate protection against the real and perceived risks they face. Landlords must be held responsible for the quality of housing but so, too, must tenants. Easier eviction of those who fail to meet their obligations or who engage in crimes, or intimidation, or destruction of property must be part of the package. If eviction is effectively impossible or prohibitively expensive, landlords will not invest and participate.

If mixed-income housing is to remain mixed it must remain safe, clean, and desirable to a range of households, especially those who can afford to live elsewhere. The poor must be expected to live up to the standards of the communities into which they go, or else those with the resources to leave will do so to be replaced by those with no other options and the worst of slums will reappear. The vast majority of the poor who sincerely want clean and safe housing will lose their opportunity to attain it if they are compelled to live with those who do not. Then we will merely have moved the poor and the inner-city pathologies that now surround them from one geographic concentration to another. Dispersal will fail, and, as usual, the real losers will be the poor themselves.

The Transportation Solution

Make no mistake about it. The reorganization of space necessary for effective dispersal of the poor is vast and the obstacles to success great. If only there were an easier way to overcome the geographic divide between growing employment centers and stagnating poverty neighborhoods. Could not reconnection come from an efficient urban transportation system joining concentrated, inner-city poverty neighborhoods with dispersed suburban labor markets? Could not urban transportation systems be redesigned to function across sprawling, auto-induced spatial webs? In a word, no. There is no system of *public* transit that is well suited to that kind of spatial distribution.

As cities expand outward the area to be covered by transportation networks increases with the *square* of the increase in the radius of development. A web whose radius grows from eight to ten miles increases the area needing transit access by over 56 percent. Collection and distribution problems quickly become immense. In a hub-centered city surrounded by bedroom suburbs, each new suburban community requires only one new line-haul commuting route. In a web arrangement, each new node adds many new potential cross-commuting routes. A tenth node where there had been nine increases the cross-web commuter routes from thirty-six to forty-five, and as the routes multiply the proportion of commuters using any one route correspondingly falls.[14] Moreover, each edge node is itself a subcenter surrounded by dispersed development. Each subcenter must be served by its own collection and distribution system.

America's cities, for better or for worse, are now organized for, and around, private cars and personal transportation. Multinode webs are the cities of the future. That logic is unavoidable, and no form of mass transit can provide the majority of transportation around such structures. Future cities will continue to depend on personalized transit. That reorganization of space is already done, and it is far too late to change that history. To reconnect the poor to the metropolitan economy they, too, will have to be able to participate in that reorganization of space. That means genuine dispersal throughout the whole web.

Which End Will Be Ours?

The force and direction of the currents moving the United States into the future are now clear. That much this expedition has uncovered. We are already in the grasp of two powerful trends that will continue to redefine the logic of location and the organization of space. First, there will be a continued reformation of cities into multicentered webs—large, integrated metropolitan regions marked by what Joel Garreau has called "edge cities." The era of single-focused cities is over. There will never again be a single "downtown" at the center of it all. Second, the character of employment and the composition of America's industrial structure are forever changed. High-wage, low-skill manufacturing jobs are, and will be, on the decline. There will always be some, but there will never again be enough to provide a path to the middle class for large numbers of low-skilled or uneducated workers. Those days are forever gone. Service employment, with wages reflecting education and skill, are the future. Those two fundamental elements of the future we cannot change. They are our future. What is left for us is not to decide whether we will go with this flow, but only *how*.

There are apparently two different channels open to us. The first is much easier to follow, requiring only that we continue to drift as we currently are, heading inexorably toward the first of the futures shown to us by the Spirit of Cities Yet to Be. In this chapter we have found a second possible channel, harder to get to from here but still within our reach. That alternate future can come only from the full application of policy power to reconnect the currently isolated urban poor to the larger society.

The two main policy elements, education and dispersal, are of course linked. Successful implementation of one increases the prospects for success of the other. Failure to implement both diminishes the prospects for success of either. If educational outcomes are improved a larger share of those growing up in poor households will become employable and thus need less housing assistance. If housing assistance effectively connects more poor households to the world of work, children from those households will likely achieve better educational outcomes.

Today educational disadvantages and spatial isolation combine to condemn too many of the children of the urban poor to lives of adult poverty. Educational and physical reconnection of those who are currently poor to the economies of these future cities can combine to reduce the incidence of poverty and the ways in which urban space perpetuate it, generation after generation. There is no third path open to us. We cannot go back upstream. History and development move only one way. We cannot go half way between the channels. It is an all-or-nothing choice and it must be made soon, either purposefully or by default.

15

Epilogue

As dusk was falling across the northern Virginia landscape on the evening of May 2, 1863, Union troops were deployed across a wide swathe in what had been, until just hours before, uncontested Confederate territory. They had executed a masterful movement, slipping in force across the Rappahannock River, and were massing behind the entrenched Southern forces, threatening General Lee's lines of supply and communication. After months of stalemate, the Confederates would be forced to move, either to retreat or to come out from behind their fortifications and do battle on ground chosen by the Army of the Potomac. Everything had changed. There had been a major shift in advantage. General "Fighting Joe" Hooker, in his first action in command of the Union forces, was confident that his much larger force and his new position of advantage would bring clear victory to the North, something sorely lacking in the previous two years.

Still there were inevitable dangers to face. All armies, indeed all collective human efforts, risk disaster from three things: an insufficiency of resources relative to their tasks, a failure of those in charge to understand and respond effectively to the peril around them, or a failure of faith on the part of soldiers in the steadfastness of their comrades. Any of these, or any combination of them, can quickly turn advantage to loss, sure success into certain failure.

For the Union forces that night there was little danger of harm from a resource imbalance. Much greater in number, better fed and better equipped, their supply lines were intact. It was the Southern Army that had been forced to scatter its forces over the winter months because of a shortage of food for the troops and silage for the stock. It was the Southern forces whose supply lines were now in jeopardy. There was no danger of Northern defeat from insufficient resources.

There was no sure safety from the other two dangers, however. Indeed there never is. No matter how overwhelming the resource advantage, it is nevertheless *always* possible to fail because of a failure of vision or a failure of faith. That day Lee, as often before, broke the rules and did the unpredictable, leaving Hooker unable to comprehend what was happening. Lee divided his much smaller force in the face of a vastly superior enemy and then divided it again. He left barely a fifth of his men behind to defend Fredericksburg, and then sent two thirds of the remainder on a wide flanking movement of his own under "Stonewall" Jackson, seeking to outflank the forces that had outflanked him. While Lee stood before Hooker's 70,000 men with a scant 14,000 of his own, Jackson marched south and west from the main body of the army. His movement was observed by Union scouts, but they *expected* Lee to retreat, and so a retreat is what they "saw." Accepting expectation over evidence, the Union forces were wholly unprepared for the flanking attack that came. The soldiers on the right end of the Northern line were dug in, but they had stacked their arms and were preparing dinner when Confederate battle lines suddenly appeared in full fire. The Union Army was placed in mortal peril because of a failure of those in charge to understand what was going on around them.

Still, they might yet have prevailed despite the surprise and difficult terrain, given their overwhelming superiority in numbers, but they also faced a fundamental "social dilemma" common to all such efforts.[1] As the first Confederate assault broke from the trees, the situation facing each Union soldier was clear. If all stood together against the assault they would have been a strong force, the enemy might well have been held until reinforcements could arrive and relatively few of the defenders would likely have perished. However, as seen by each individual soldier, if all around did stand fast while one quietly slipped away, the enemy would still be halted and that one could be assured that he, at least, would not be among the unfortunate few to perish. On the other hand, if all around him lost courage and ran while he did not, then surely many would die in the ensuing panic. Unless he too turned tail and ran and he especially would be unable to affect the outcome but would certainly die. To stand when all others flee is to sacrifice one's life without resulting gain. It is to sell one's life cheaply indeed.

Yet if *all* think that way and run, order is surely lost and many more will be slaughtered in the chaos brought by the unhindered advance of an emboldened enemy. Those lives, too, are lost with little gain. *Whatever* the others do, each soldier is *individually* made better off by running, yet if all respond to that reasoning, the combined effect of those individual decisions will be tragedy for *everyone*. *Only* if they all act in concert and stand fast in the confidence that all others will do likewise can they succeed in the face of such an assault. On that evening in Virginia, trust and confidence failed, panic prevailed, and soldier after soldier made the separate decision that led to their mutual destruction. The decisions that made the most *individual* sense led to *collective* disaster. The vastly superior Union Army, holding a dominating position, ultimately collapsed back across the Rappahannock in ignominious defeat, the victim of miscomprehension, miscoordination, and mutual distrust. The victory that was in their grasp became unattainable.

Cities Under Attack

Surely America's inner cities today face a risk as grave as that facing Hooker's men at Chancellorsville, and it should now be clear that the prospects for withstanding the current assault against them are as dependent on effective coordination of many disparate actions as was the fate of Hooker's soldiers. It should also be clear that our cities risk failure from the same forces that threatened his army, and indeed all armies—insufficient resources, misunderstanding of the situation, or "smart" individual choices yielding collective disaster. For us, the greatest danger comes from the third of these.

For America's cities, there is no question about the sufficiency of resources in any absolute sense. The needs are not overwhelming; this is still a land of real plenty. There are political obstacles to allocating the resources necessary to reach the second path and there are many competing claims on them, but there is no question that sufficient amounts exist to move us to the second channel and the better of our two possible futures, if we so choose.

There remains much misapprehension of the urban situation. Certainly many, like Hooker and his staff, clearly do not fully comprehend what is going on in our cities, but that, too, is a problem that can conceivably be overcome with relative ease. Indeed the whole purpose of this book has been to clarify how cities have come to this juncture and how we can influence their future for the better. This exploration has, hopefully, helped to provide a better understanding of what is before us, what we can do and why, what we cannot do and why not. Improved understanding of the situation is attainable *if* enough people are willing to look at cities with open minds, willing to seek comprehension rather than just confirmation of prior perceptions.

It is the third obstacle, however, that will prove the most daunting. If we are to "depart" from the current "course" and thus change our "ends," as Scrooge was able to change his, we will have to find ways to stimulate cooperation among multiple factions far more accustomed to acting in conflict than in concert. There can be no deserters from, nor passive observers to, this battle. The nonparticipation of even a few threatens failure for all.

The Need to Do It All

The previous chapter outlined all that would be necessary to redirect America's future.

• More resources will have to be put into education and they will have to be available more equitably. Taxpayers will have to see the need for resources and be willing to provide them.

• The resources, once available, will have to be used wisely for the clear benefit of the students. Educational professionals—administrators, bureaucrats, teachers, and union leaders—will have to see improved educational outcomes as the purpose and use the funds wisely and efficaciously.

• Youth culture will have to encourage all students to put forth the effort and make the commitment necessary to take full advantage of the improved opportunities once they occur. Then, ultimately, they will have to be rewarded in labor markets for those efforts.

• *All* communities will have to modify building codes and land-use controls to *encourage,* not just permit, truly mixed-income housing. Separate and isolated districts for the poor in the outer web will simply relocate damaging urban spaces rather than ameliorate them. Genuine neighborhood income integration will have to be affirmed as a *national* norm.

• Real dispersion will be possible only if national subsidization programs become widespread and fully funded for both new and existing housing. Without adequate subsidies, ubiquitous mixed-income housing, even if it is permitted and encouraged, will remain unprofitable to provide and unaffordable by the poor.

• The low-income tenants dispersing into wider web communities will have to meet the behavioral standards of those communities. They, too, will have to take responsibility for the quality of life in mixed-income communities.

Any one of these initiatives would be difficult to implement, even in isolation. To achieve the whole package and do so on a national scale seems a daunting task, yet if we undertake but one of them alone it will have little impact. Indeed it will be unsustainable. It may help some persons but it will not redirect the whole society's urban future.

These elements necessary to change our "ends" are part and parcel of a whole. Unless *all* are undertaken and successfully implemented there will be insufficient power to move us from the current channel to the farther, but better, one where all Americans, in terms of both skills and geography, have ready access to labor markets. These are not items on a menu from which we can select some. They are not separate options. They are a complete package. Failure to undertake any one of them is to court failure for all of them. To do some but not all may be of no more value than doing none.

Can it all be done? I am not optimistic, for success would require getting large numbers of people to make carefully coordinated, interdependent choices against their own short-term self-interest. Stemming the assault on America's cities is every bit as much of a social dilemma as is stemming the attack of an opposing Army. Success for the whole depends on each of us deciding to stand firm when, for each of us individually, it makes more sense to flee. Whenever any one falters in their commitment it creates a breach in the "line" that shifts the logic of individual choices more in favor of others deserting as well, leading cumulatively toward social disaster. Those who are reluctant to stand in the fore need not be evil or immoral. They may just be cautious and prudent. They may rationally lack trust that enough others will stand with them, and, of course, if enough others do not, they *are* fools to stand alone—righteous, just, moral, and wholly ineffective.

If taxpayers burden themselves with new levies to finance improved schools but school systems absorb the funds in bureaucratic bloat and wage increases for employees, there is no gain for the children. Not long ago the school system in Lawrence, Massachusetts, received a massive infusion of state aid to improve education there, yet most of the funds seem to have been wasted. Administrators used the money in seemingly irrational ways—to create a program of bagpipe instruction and to purchase laptop computers for the custodians—while student learning continued to deteriorate.[2] It would be easy for taxpayers to conclude that they have been had, and they would have every reason to resist further funding.

If school systems do reform themselves and provide material changes in the conditions of education but children and youth continue to see school success as a losers' game, all the funds and efforts and sacrifices will have been wasted. If poor children do reject the culture of the streets and work hard in school only to find that the schools they go to are so inferior and the job prospects they face are so limited that there is little payoff to all of their efforts, then their peers were right. They were being conned. It makes sense for each element to meet its obligations *only* if it can be assured that each of the others will likewise meet all of theirs, or else they incur costs with no benefits.

If one community welcomes in-migration of the poor while its neighbors do not, that community is risking becoming the new site for concentrated decay and despair. It is opting for increasing pressure on its public services and for rising taxes. It is risking cumulative capital flight and erosion of its tax base as those able to leave do so. It becomes a small lifeboat coming to the rescue of a much larger sinking ship. It will soon become overwhelmed and flounder itself. Only fully *shared* acceptance of dispersal protects each community, but each community can only decide *individually* what *it* will do, with no means of ascertaining or assuring how neighboring communities will finally respond. If all of the others do step forward, there is little need for us to do so. If they do not, that is a powerful reason for us not to either.

If multiple communities do accept and even welcome their fair share of the poor but the new entrants are all housed in isolated projects, separated from the larger community, then concentrated inner-city poverty and its pathologies just have been relocated to the suburbs. If that is what dispersal offers, it is quite rational for communities to reject the offer. A recent column in the *Wall Street Journal* lamented the destruction of stability and the decline in the quality of life that came about when the Department of Housing and Urban Development (HUD) introduced a large, separated enclave of poor people into a middle-class neighborhood in Phoenix.[3] A rise in crime and a decline in security, a division between "us" and "them," and a decay in neighborhood amenities was what the author saw as the result. HUD used its power to provide housing for a significant number of the poor in that community but in a way that made it clear the poor were not truly a part of it. It created a "reservation" for the poor surrounded by a nonpoor community. Nor did HUD, as ultimate landlord, demand of its tenants the kinds of behavior that make communal life viable in shared structures. If programs of dispersal are not genuine and complete they will end up making a reality out of the worst fears of suburban communities. Political support will quickly unravel and fair-share commitments disappear. True dispersal and strictly enforced behavioral standards are not necessary aspects simply for the benefit of, and to assure support by, the wealthy. They are necessary for the survival of the poor.

The dangerous rocks that lie between the present and the alternative channels are thus these recurring social dilemmas. Successfully altering the future of America's cities will require the commitment and cooperation of *all* segments of society—taxpayers; state, local, and federal governments; school districts; unions; employers; poor people; middle-income people, and upper-income people. Governments at all levels will have to take on responsibilities that they currently compete to avoid. Individuals, of all races and backgrounds, at all income levels, and of all political persuasions will have to recognize that success in this demands things of *each* of us and *each* of us must be willing to take on those responsibilities. We cannot blame it all on those "others." Yet for each actor, for each individual, the choice is clear—if I undertake my part but *all* of the others do not do theirs I am a sucker, taken advantage of by "them." If all others do fulfill their obligations then my participation is unnecessary. As with the troops on the western end of General Hooker's line outside Chancellorsville we can stand only if we all do so together, yet for each of us individually it probably makes more sense to cut and run. Walt Kelly's Pogo Possum indeed said it best, "we have met the enemy and he is us."

Solving Social Dilemmas

True social dilemmas can only be solved by one of two methods. The first is by force. Military officers have long had the authority to shoot their own men if they desert under fire in order to prevent the cumulative collapse their flight may cause. Used early enough and publicly enough coercion on that scale may sometimes be enough to make individuals choose the collectively better option.

Alternatively, social dilemmas can sometimes be overcome by building bonds of trust strong enough to overcome the individualist calculus. Out of loyalty and a sense of duty to their fellows, individual soldiers often do stand in the face of mortal peril. Risks are faced not because of devotion to some abstract political ideal but because of devotion to other persons. "I cannot let my comrades down, and I have faith that they will not let me down." Military units and social organizations work hard to build the personal loyalty and sense of duty essential to solving the "problem." Still that trust is a tenuous thing indeed. Once it begins to erode, the delicate balance that holds the line will quickly fail. At Chancellorsville it collapsed, and all of the potential power of the Union Army was dissipated in chaos and flight. When trust was lost, individual pursuit of self-preservation led to near destruction of the whole Army.

As we approach the future of American cities we are already somewhat late in the game. We are already in chaotic retreat, and it is undoubtedly harder to convince people to stop fleeing when all around them are already in flight than it is to prevent them from fleeing when no one else has yet begun. There is no rigid chain of command to hold the line in place. There is no one to shoot deserters. The only thing that can hold the line together is a pervasive sense of trust that if I turn around and do my part, others will also do theirs. Absent that, it makes little sense for anyone to stand firm, and there is precious little trust in America today.

Social Dilemmas in a Good versus Evil World

At the very beginning of this expedition, as we were first preparing to explore the changing organization of urban space, I warned that a major obstacle to successful understanding would be the pervasive presumption that all social actions and outcomes must be demarcated as either "good" or "evil." That presumption was a barrier to effective understanding of social phenomena. It is even more a barrier to affecting them. The Gordian knot of our social dilemma is pulled tighter yet if all the problems of cities are seen as caused by personal moral failures rather than being an outcome of impersonal evolution in the logic of location. If all we can ever see is *bad* suburbanites who *want to oppress* the innocent poor, or *degenerate* poor who *refuse responsibility* for their own lives, or *wicked* bureaucrats who *seek power for personal aggrandizement,* we will continue to drift down our present path toward the first possible future, pointing accusingly at each other all the way. If what suburbanites, and inner-city poor, and government bureaucrats all do become understandable responses to a shift in the logic of location and a shared social dilemma there is at least some possibility of resolving it.

The two things necessary for an effective solution are first, a willingness on the part of each actor to accept and fulfill his or her responsibility for those elements of the program within his or her control and second, a trust that all others will likewise accept and fulfill theirs. In a world of strict good and evil, any admission of responsibility on my part is confession of having been one of the bad people. Most of us resist admissions like that. In such a world, to trust in those others is to place faith in evil and inherently irresponsible people. Most of us are likewise resistant to that. In perhaps the ultimate irony, our persistent belief that we must always be overcoming evil may in the end lead us to the "bad" future.

In America today we will not even listen to the "others," let alone admit to any wisdom in *their* positions. When liberals argue that the Right's emphasis on personal responsibility is insufficient to bring about effective social solutions to America's urban problems, they are right. It will be insufficient, but they cannot stop there, self-satisfied that they have thus exposed the opposition's "bad" thinking. Even though the issue of personal responsibility has been raised by *them,* it is not wholly without merit. Effective solutions will likely not come about without *including* increased personal responsibility. When conservatives argue that the Left's insistence on government programs at the federal level cannot bring about effective solutions to America's urban problems, they, too, are right. Yet neither can they stop there, equally self-satisfied by the exposure of their opponent's own "bad" thinking. Even though the issue of a national commitment has been raised by *them,* it is not without merit. Effective solutions will have to *include* new federal programs. Neither side is willing to admit that a shift in course will require coordinated changes both in what government can and should undertake *and* in things that government cannot and should not do. Neither side is willing to recognize merit in the opposition's positions because the opposition is not just different—it is evil. We all seek to blame the impending collapse of the line on *their* failings.

Political Leadership and Cities' Social Dilemma

But surely, leaders of extraordinary insight and courage could motivate and coordinate various factions, could orchestrate a solution to the social dilemma, and could promote the necessary shared responsibility and trust. That is indeed conceivable, but that is not where we are today. Leaders on all sides seem more anxious to divide, to accuse, and to blame than to promote change. They sanctimoniously proclaim their own purity and smugly point to the failings of others. They look for failures to exploit rather than successes to duplicate and it is perhaps inevitably so, for that is the easy route to personal political success. In the world of politics the easy answer and the quick allocation of blame, expressible in short and pithy "sound bites," win out over thoughtful analyses every time. Those willing to sacrifice principle for short-term political support almost assuredly prevail. In a world where most of us live in such narrowly defined moral space, we continually elect those who take advantage of those perceptions.

Make no mistake about what would be involved in changing our course. Any shift in channels and reorganizations of urban space will take years to accomplish. It will not occur quickly. The shift from monocentric to web structures has been under way for nearly a century—moving imperceptibly at first, inexorably at last. Successful change in how we adapt to that reorganization of space will not occur instantaneously. Refinancing, restructuring, and reenergizing education will take years. Many of the students already in school will graduate or leave long before meaningful reforms take hold. Most of the adults who are now mismatched with labor markets may never catch up. The changes in education and skills and opportunities will more likely occur across, rather than within, generations. Reshaping housing markets and patterns will take decades. With an existing housing stock approaching 100 million units there is a limit to how much change will come from new construction or rehabilitation in any one year or even one decade. Real change will come from the cumulative impact of incremental changes over lengthy periods, and for decades there will still be places where change is not yet apparent. Redirection of America's urban future can only come from the cumulative effects of incremental changes. That is not a promise or platform likely to attract many political champions.

Even with the best possible combination of strategies there will be multiple short-term failings along the way. There will always be incidents where some player in the social dilemma game opts for the short-term personal gain and where the necessary trust is threatened. There will always be cases of "soldiers" abandoning the line, threatening its stability and the safety of everyone else. No matter what we do, not much perceptible change will *ever* take place in the two years between Congressional elections or the four years between presidential ones. In our political system there will always be an ample supply of claimants who would use that fact to declare failure, to assign blame, and to call for punishing "them," and thus to threaten all of the necessary commitments and to feed fatal mistrust. It will always be possible to gain support and short-term political advantage by urging some of us to cut and run. Once that is begun the whole line will be in grave jeopardy indeed. We will have missed the opportunity to change our course and we will not have changed our ends. We will drift inexorably into the first of the futures shown to us by the Spirit of Cities Yet to Be. That is not yet inevitable but it seems more likely with every passing day. If our course is to be changed we must do so quickly. We must do so comprehensively. We must do so surely and certainly, before it is too late.

Notes

Chapter 1. Cities in America

   1. Alex Kotlowitz, *There Are No Children Here.*
   2. L.A. Fingerhut, D. Ingram, and J. Feldman, "Firearm and Nonfirearm Homicide."
   3. Current Population Reports, Series P60–185, "Poverty in the United States: 1992."
   4. Anthony Downs, *New Visions for Metropolitan American.*
   5. Data from Census Bureau and Mills, *Urban Economics,* p. 84.
   6. Joseph Ganim, *The State of Urban America,* Hearings before the Senate Committee on Banking, Housing and Urban Affairs, April 1993, p. 19.
   7. Carol Moseley Braun, *The State of Urban America,* p. 7.
   8. Carrie Saxon-Perry, *Fiscal, Economic, and Social Crises Confronting American Cities,* Hearings before the Committee on Banking, Housing, and Urban Affairs, United States Senate, May 13, 1992, p. 194.
   9. Henry Cisneros, *The State of Urban America,* p. 72.
  10. Quoted in Charles Glaab and A. Theodore Brown, *A History of Urban America,* p. 11.
  11. Quoted in A.E.J. Morris, *History of the Urban Form,* p. 264.
  12. Quoted in Glaab and Brown, p. 7.
  13. Ibid., pp. 8–9.
  14. Ibid., p. 55
  15. Harold A. Pinkham, Jr. "Plantation to City Charter."
  16. Editors of *Fortune* magazine, *The Exploding Metropolis.*
  17. Glaab and Brown, p. 95.
  18. Ibid., p. 96.

Chapter 2. Unnatural Aggregations and Natural Perceptions

   1. Robert Ricklefs, *Ecology, 3rd ed.,* p. 331.
   2. George Oster and Edward O. Wilson, *Social Insects,* p. 3.
   3. Edward O. Wilson, *The Insect Societies,* or George F. Oster and Edward O. Wilson, *Caste and Ecology in the Social Insects.*
   4. Helen Rountree, *The Powhatan Indians of Virginia: Their Traditional Culture,*

or Rountree, *Pocahontas's People: Indians of Virginia Through Four Centuries.*

5. Ross Hassig, *Trade, Tribute, and Transportation: The Sixteenth-Century Political Economy of the Valley of Mexico,* p. 30.

6. Robert Utley, *The Lance and the Shield: The Life and Times of Sitting Bull,* p. 143.

7. Charles Glaab and A. Theodore Brown, *A History of Urban America.* pp. 25–26.

8. Felipe Fernandez-Armesto, *Columbus,* p. 85.

9. Stephen W. Sears, *George B. McClellan: The Young Napoleon,* p. 287.

10. C.G. Lord, L. Ross, and M. Lepper, "Biased Assimilation and Attitude Polarization: The Effects of Prior Theories on Subsequently Considered Evidenced."

11. D.J. Koehler, "Explanation, Imagination, and Confidence in Judgment," or A. Kariat, S. Lichtenstein, and B. Fischhoff, "Reasons for Confidence."

12. Joel Garreau, *Edge City: Life on the New Frontier,* p. xxi.

13. William Julius Wilson, *The Truly Disadvantaged: The Inner City, The Underclass, and Public Policy.*

Chapter 3. Wind, Wagon, and Water: Cities Before 1830

1. George R. Taylor, *The Transportation Revolution: 1815–1860. Vol. IV, The Economic History of the United States,* p. 15.

2. Curtis Nettles, *The Emergence of a National Economy, 1775–1815, Vol II, The Economic History of the United States,* pp. 251–54.

3. Ibid., pp. 255–57.

4. Howard Chudacoff, *Major Problems in American Urban History.*

5. Taylor, p. 53.

6. Ibid., p. 32.

7. Ronald E. Shaw, *Erie Water West: A History of the Erie Canal 1792–1854,* p. 45.

8. Ibid., Chapter 2.

9. Letter from Jesse Hawley, published in Ontario *Messenger,* January 27, 1841, quoted in Shaw, pp. 24–25.

10. Ibid., Chapter 8.

11. Taylor, p. 137.

12. Quoted in Shaw, pp. 285–86.

13. Ibid., p. 284.

14. Paul E. Johnson, *A Shopkeeper's Millenium: Society and Revivals in Rochester, New York, 1815–1837,* Chapter 1.

15. Shaw, p. 266.

16. Taylor, p. 52.

17. Nettels, pp. 183–84.

18. Constance M. Green, *Eli Whitney and the Birth of American Technology.*

19. Nettels, pp. 183–85.

20. Richard C. Wade. "Urban Life in Western America, 1790–1830," in A.B. Callow, ed., *American Urban History,* p. 103.

Chapter 4. Water, Water, Everywhere: Cities 1830–1870

1. Quoted in J. Mirsky and A. Nevins, *The World of Eli Whitney,* p. 202.

2. Joel Mokyr, *The Lever of Riches: Technological Creativity and Economic Progress,* p. 85.

3. Ibid., p. 85.

4. Cynthia Owen Philip, *Robert Fulton: A Biography,* pp. 120–21.
5. Curtis Nettles, *The Emergence of a National Economy,* pp. 268–69.
6. Philip, pp. 122–23.
7. Ibid., pp. 146–47.
8. Ibid., p. 204.
9. Gary L. Browne, *Baltimore in the Nation, 1789–1861,* p. 84.
10. George Taylor, *The Transportation Revolution,* pp. 77–78.
11. Ibid., p. 80.
12. Ibid., p. 81.
13. Ibid., p. 82.
14. Quoted in Mirsky, p. 190.
15. Quoted in Mirsky, p. 201.
16. Taylor, p. 280.
17. Ibid., p. 281.
18. Wayne Broehl, Jr., *John Deere's Company.*
19. Asa Greene, quoted in C. Glaab and A.T. Brown, *A History of Urban America,* p. 84.
20. Howard Chudacoff, *The Evolution of American Urban Society, 2nd ed.,* p. 76.
21. Ibid., p.78.
22. Ibid., pp. 79–80.
23. Taylor, p. 390.
24. Quoted in Taylor, pp. 390–91.
25. Tracy Kidder, *House,* pp. 133–34.
26. Quoted in Glaab and Brown, p.143.
27. Solomon Robinson, quoted in Glaab and Brown, p. 143.
28. Kidder, pp. 133–34.
29. Glaab and Brown, pp. 143–44.
30. Ibid., p. 84.
31. David H. Donald, *Lincoln,* 1995, p. 336.
32. Glaab and Brown. pp. 86–87.
33. Ibid., p. 96.
34. Chudacoff, p. 121.
35. Glaab and Brown, p. 110.
36. Daniel J. Boorstin, *The Americans: The National Experience,* pp. 115–23.

Chapter 5. Electricity and Steel: 1870 Through the First World War

1. David H. Donald, *Lincoln,* pp. 277–79.
2. Albro Martin, *Railroads Triumphant,* pp. 48–49, 110.
3. Ibid., p. 198.
4. Ibid., p. 122.
5. Ibid., pp. 326–27.
6. Barry Poulson, *Economic History of the United States,* pp. 280–84.
7. William T. Hogan, *Economic History of the Iron and Steel Industry in the United States, Volume 1,* p. 11.
8. Jeanne McHugh, *Alexander Holley and the Makers of Steel,* pp. 78–81.
9. Hogan, pp. 218, 224.
10. Ibid., pp. 305–7.
11. Abram J. Foster, *The Coming of the Electrical Age to the United States,* pp. 238–45.
12. Ibid., pp. 238–39.

13. Ibid., pp. 248–57.

14. Harold Faulkner, *The Decline of Laissez Faire, 1897–1917,* p. 124.

15. Richard DuBoff, *Electric Power in American Manufacturing, 1889–1958,* pp. 43, 48.

16. Ibid., p. 17.

17. Fred Shannon, *The Farmer's Last Frontier, Agriculture 1860–1897,* p. 135.

18. Ibid., p. 138.

19. Faulkner, pp. 332, 417.

20. Shannon, pp. 141–43.

21. Ibid., pp. 145–46.

22. Charles Glaab and A. Theodore Brown, *A History of Urban America,* p. 110.

23. Donald D. Jackson, "Elevating Thoughts from Elisha Otis and Fellow Uplifters," pp. 210–12.

24. Theodore Turak, *William Le Baron Jenney: A Pioneer of Modern Architecture,* pp. 236–45.

25. Howard Chudacoff, *The Evolution of American Urban Society,* p. 81.

26. Ibid., p. 82.

27. Ibid., p. 85.

28. Ibid., p. 96.

29. Ibid., p. 114–17.

30. Quoted in David Ward, *Poverty, Ethnicity, and the American City, 1840–1925,* pp. 76–77.

31. Glaab and Brown, *A History of Urban America,* p. 180.

Chapter 6. From the Great War to the Great Society

1. Robert Lacey, *Ford: The Men and the Machine,* pp. 39–44.

2. Ibid., p. 42.

3. George S. May, *A Most Unique Machine: The Michigan Origins of the American Automobile Industry,* p. 136.

4. Ibid., p. 135.

5. Lacey, p. 105.

6. Ibid., pp. 108–9.

7. Lawrence White, "The Automobile Industry," p. 139.

8. Kenneth T. Jackson, *Crabgrass Frontier, The Suburbanization of the United States,* p. 161.

9. Daniel Boorstin, *The Americans: The Democratic Experience,* pp. 422–43.

10. George Soule, *Prosperity Decade, From War to Depression 1917–1929,* p. 165.

11. *Statistical Abstract of the United States, 1994,* U.S. Census Bureau, Table 1006.

12. Ibid., Table 998.

13. *Statistical Abstract of the United States, 1958,* U.S. Census Bureau, Tables 716, 717 and *Statistical Abstract of the United States, 1994,* U.S. Census Bureau, Table 994.

14. Harold Faulkner, *The Decline of Laissez Faire, 1897–1917,* p. 232.

15. Soule, p. 164.

16. White, p. 136.

17. R.E.G. Davies, *A History of the World's Airlines,* p. 41.

18. Ibid., p. 134.

19. Ibid., p. 479.

20. Nicholas Lemann, *The Promised Land, The Great Black Migration and How It Changed America,* p. 5.

21. Ibid., pp. 3–5.

22. Mark Kramer, *Three Farms, Making Milk, Meat and Money from the American Soil,* pp. 91–101.

23. Daniel B. Suits, "Agriculture," p. 25.

24. Gary Tobin, "Suburbanization and the Development of Motor Transportation," p. 103.

25. Charles Glaab and A. Theodore Brown, *A History of Urban America,* pp. 292–95.

26. The ruling in the case, *Shelley v. Kraemer* [334 U.S. 1] did not explicitly ban such restrictive covenants. It merely decreed that any enforcement of them in court would involve the state in a discriminatory act, and *state* discrimination on account of race would be in violation of the 14th Amendment.

27. Tobin, pp. 105–6.

28. Jackson, pp. 163–64.

29. Ibid., p. 166.

30. Lemann, p. 70.

31. Douglas Massey and Nancy Denton, "Suburbanization and Segregation in U.S. Metropolitan Areas."

32. The term was first used by Joel Garreau in his book of the same name.

33. Data from 1990 Census.

34. Calculated from data in James Heilbrun and Patrick McGuire, *Urban Economics and Public Policy, 3rd ed,* Table 3-4, pp. 42–43.

35. Jackson, p. 268.

36. Ibid., p. 269.

37. Wilfred Owen, *The Accessible City,* p. 1.

38. William Julius Wilson, *The Truly Disadvantaged.*

39. S.C. Gilfillan, *The Sociology of Invention.*

Chapter 7. Urban Housing: Markets, Rules, and Regulations

1. Nicholas Lemann, *The Promised Land: The Great Black Migration and How It Changed America,* pp. 52–53.

2. J. Anthony Lukas, *Common Ground, A Turbulent Decade in the Lives of Three American Families,* p. 161.

3. Ibid., pp. 163–65.

4. Ibid., p. 170.

5. Irving Welfeld, "Poor Tenants, Poor Landlords, Poor Policy."

6. Robert H. Nelson, *Zoning and Property Rights, An Analysis of the American System of Land Use Regulation.*

7. Ibid., p. 9.

8. *Village of Euclid, Ohio v. Ambler Realty Co.,* 272 US 365 (1926), p. 387.

9. Ibid., pp. 386–87.

10. Ibid., pp. 394–95.

11. *Buchanan v. Warley,* 245 U.S. 60 (1917).

12. Bernard J. Frieden, "The Exclusionary Effect of Growth Controls."

13. Ibid., p. 127.

14. George Sternlieb, "*Mount Laurel,* Economics, Morality and the Law," p. 295.

15. *Southern Burlington County NAACP v. Mount Laurel,* 65 NJ 151.

16. Frederick W. Hall, "A Review of the Mount Laurel Decision."

17. *Southern Burlington County N.A.A.C.P. v. Township of Mount Laurel,* 92 N.J. 158 (1983), p. 217.

18. Sternlieb, p. 295.
19. John Stahura, "Rapid Black Suburbanization of the 1970s," p. 282.

Chapter 8. Housing Policies and Prices

1. The Twymons are one of the three families whose stories are told by J. Anthony Lukas, *Common Ground, A Turbulent Decade in the Lives of Three American Families.*
2. Ibid., p. 184
3. Ibid., p. 190.
4. Ibid., pp. 180–94.
5. George Sternlieb, *Patterns of Development,* p. 12.
6. Irving Welfeld, *Where We Live, A Social History of American Housing,* pp. 59–60.
7. Robert Hall and Alvin Rabushka, *Low Tax, Simple Tax, Flat Tax.*
8. Welfeld, p. 169.
9. Derrick A. Bell, Jr., *Race, Racism and American Law,* pp. 562–65.
10. *Buchanan v. Warley,* 245 U.S. 60 (1917).
11. *Shelley v. Kraemer,* 334 U.S. 1 (1948). The Court held that while the 14th Amendment to the Constitution only prohibited states, not private individuals, from discriminating, when a court enforced a private covenant, the *state* was then acting illegally.
12. *Hills v. Gautreaux,* 425 U.S. 284 (1976).
13. Robert Ferber and Warner Hirsch, *Social Experimentation and Economic Policy* and Bernard Friedan, "Housing Allowances: An Experiment that Worked."

Chapter 9. Getting Around: Urban Transportation Policy

1. Anthony Downs, *Stuck in Traffic, Coping With Peak-Hour Traffic Congestion,* p. 114.
2. Ibid., p. 90.
3. James Heilbrun, *Urban Economics and Public Policy, 3rd ed.,* p. 233.
4. This quote is taken from the Metro System's Web page, www.westworld.com/ elson/ larail/blue.html as of 04/29/96, p. 2.
5. Melvin Weber, "The BART Experience: What Have We Learned?" p. 80.
6. The quote is from the original proposal and is quoted in Weber, p. 101.
7. Ibid., p. 101.
8. Ibid., p. 86.
9. Ibid., p. 87.
10. Heilbrun, pp. 320–21.
11. Weber, p. 93.
12. MARTA, "A Year of Motion: Fiscal Year 1995 Financial Report."
13. Eliza Newlin Carney, "A Desire Named Streetcar."

Chapter 10. Governing Sprawl

1. William J. Baumol, "Macroeconomics of Unbalanced Growth: The Anatomy of Urban Crisis."
2. 1987 Census of Governments, Vol. 2., *Taxable Property Values,* Table 1.
3. James Heilbrun, *Urban Economics and Public Policy, 3rd ed.,* p. 432.

4. Clarence Y.H. Lo, *Small Property versus Big Government: Social Origins of the Property Tax Revolt*, pp. 1–5.

5. William Schneider, "Punching Through the Jarvis Myth."

Chapter 11. Mapping Explored Space

1. Stephen E. Ambrose, *Undaunted Courage, Meriwether Lewis, Thomas Jefferson, and the Opening of the American West*, p. 397.

2. Ibid., p. 457.

3. Joel Mokyr, *The Lever of Riches, Technological Creativity and Economic Progres*, p. 179.

4. Ibid., p. 256.

5. Lewis Mumford, *The City in History*, p. 510.

6. Joel Garreau, *Edge Cities*, p. xxi.

Chapter 12. Looking Ahead

1. Quoted *Wall Street Journal*, June 19, 1996, supplement, p. 6.

2. William Wiggenhorn, "Motorola U: When Training Becomes an Education," p. 71.

3. Ibid., p. 78.

4. Dave Walter, ed., *Today Then: America's Best Minds Look 100 Years into the Future on the Occasion of the 1893 World's Columbian Exposition*.

5. Eli Whitney, quoted in J. Mirsky and A. Nevins, *The World of Eli Whitney*, p. 201.

6. Frederick Winslow Taylor, *The Principles of Scientific Management*, p. 28.

7. Ibid., p. 38.

8. Ibid., pp. 83–84.

9. Wiggenhorn, p. 77.

10. Masahiko Aoki, "Toward an Economic Model of the Japanese Firm," pp. 4–5.

11. Wiggenhorn, pp. 71–72.

12. Ibid., p. 77.

13. United States Department of Labor, *Occupational Outlook Handbook, 1996–7*, p. 1.

14. Ibid., pp. 1–6.

15. Daniel H. Weinberg, "A Brief Look at Postwar U.S. Income Inequality," pp. 2–3.

16. Karl Sabbagh, *Twenty-First Century Jet, The Making and Marketing of the Boeing 777*, p. 40.

17. Ibid., p. 68.

18. Ibid., p. 69.

19. Joel Garreau, *Edge City, Life of the New Frontier*.

20. Ibid., p. 439.

21. Ibid., p. 6.

22. Ibid., pp. 315–16.

Chapter 13. Two Tales of a City: The Current Destination

1. Charles Dickens, *A Christmas Carol*, p. 122.

2. City and County Data Book, 1994, U.S. Bureau of the Census, table 3, p. xxxii,

and Statistical Abstract of the United States, 1995, U.S. Bureau of the Census, p. 328.

3. Statistical Abstract of the United States, 1995, U.S. Bureau of the Census, p. 328.

4. William Julius Wilson, *When Work Disappears, The World of the New Urban Poor.*

5. Laurence Steinberg, *Beyond the Classroom, Why School Reform Has Failed and What Parents Need to Do,* pp. 50–52, and Eric A. Hanushek, "The Economics of Schooling."

6. Jonathan Kozol, *Savage Inequalities, Children in America's Schools,* pp. 122, 149, 198, 236–37.

7. Steinberg, p. 22.

8. Ibid., p. 152.

9. Ibid., p. 25.

10. Ibid., p. 19.

11. Ibid., p. 156.

12. Ibid., pp. 159–60.

Chapter 14. Two Tales of a City: The Way to a Different End

1. Charles Dickens, *A Christmas Carol,* pp. 149–50.

2. William Julius Wilson, *When Work Disappears, The World of the New Urban Poor,* Chapter 8.

3. Albert R. Hunt, "The General and the Teacher Trying to Save D.C. School Kids."

4. Phil Hall, "Catholic Plan Can't Help Schools Facing Chaos."

5. Frederick Douglass, *Narrative of the Life of Frederick Douglass, An American Slave,* p. 18.

6. Ibid., pp. 120–21.

7. Laurence Steinberg, *Beyond the Classroom, Why School Reform Has Failed and What Parents Need to Do,* pp. 159–60.

8. Derrick Bell, *Race, Racism and American Law,* pp. 562–65.

9. *Gautreaux v. Chicago Housing Authority,* 296 F. Supp. 907, 304 F. Supp. 736, 436 F. Supp. 306.

10. Susan Popkin, James Rosenbaum, and Patricia Meaden, "Labor Market Experiences of Low-Income Black Women in Middle-Class Suburbs: Evidence from a Survey of Gautreaux Program Participants."

11. Ibid., p. 563.

12. See, for example, the suggestions made in Irving Welfeld, "Improving Housing Allowances."

13. See, for example, the three-part PBS series titled "The New Urban Renewal: Reclaiming Our Neighborhoods," especially episode #1 "Rebuilding Neighborhoods From the Ground Up."

14. In general the nth node adds n-1 new potential connecting routes to the transportation network as it must be connected to each of the previous n-1 subcenters.

Chapter 15. Epilogue

1. The term social dilemma comes from Gary J. Miller, *Managerial Dilemmas, The Political Economy of Hierarchy.*

2. Dave Denison, "A Steep Learning Curve."

3. Marianne M. Jennings, "My Neighborhood Ruined, Thanks to HUD."

Bibliography

Adams, Walter, ed. *The Structure of American Industry,* 6th ed. New York: Macmillan, 1982.

Ambrose, Stephen E. *Undaunted Courage: Meriwether Lewis, Thomas Jefferson, and the Opening of the American West.* New York: Simon and Schuster, 1996.

Aoki, Masahiko. "Toward an Economic Model of the Japanese Firm." *Journal of Economic Literature* 28, no. 1 (March 1990): 1–27.

Baumol, William J. "Macroeconomics of Unbalanced Growth: The Anatomy of Urban Crisis." *American Economic Review* 57, no. 3 (June 1967): 415–426.

Bell, Derrick A., Jr. *Race, Racism and American Law.* 2d ed. Boston: Little, Brown, 1980.

Boorstin, Daniel J. *The Americans: The National Experience.* New York: Random House, 1965.

———. *The Americans: The Democratic Experience.* New York: Random House, 1973.

Broehl, Wayne, Jr. *John Deere's Company.* New York: Doubleday, 1984.

Browne, Gary L. *Baltimore in the Nation, 1789–1861.* Chapel Hill: University of North Carolina Press, 1980.

Callow, A.B., ed. *American Urban History.* Oxford: Oxford University Press, 1969.

Carney, Eliza Newlin. "A Desire Named Streetcar." *Governing* (February 1994): 36–39.

Chudacoff, Howard. *The Evolution of American Urban Society,* 2d ed. Englewood Cliffs, NJ: Prentice Hall, 1981.

———. *Major Problems in American Urban History.* Lexington, MA: D.C. Heath, 1994.

Davies, R.E.G. *A History of the World's Airlines.* London: Oxford University Press, 1964.

Denison, Dave. "A Steep Learning Curve." *The Boston Globe,* June 29, 1997, D1, 3.

Dickens, Charles. *A Christmas Carol.* Boston: Charles E. Lauriat, 1924.

Donald, David H. *Lincoln.* New York: Simon and Schuster, 1995.

Douglass, Frederick. *Narrative of the Life of Frederick Douglass, An American Slave.* New York: Penquin Books, 1982. Originally Published, 1845.

Downs, Anthony. *New Visions for Metropolitan American.* Washington, DC: Brookings Institution, 1994.

———. *Stuck in Traffic, Coping With Peak-Hour Traffic Congestion.* Washington, DC: Brookings Institution, 1992.

DuBoff, Richard. *Electric Power in American Manufacturing, 1889–1958.* New York: Arno Press, 1979.

Faulkner, Harold. *The Decline of Laissez Faire, 1897–1917.* White Plains, NY: M.E. Sharpe, 1951, p. 124.

Ferber, Robert, and Warner Hirsch. *Social Experimentation and Economic Policy.* Cambridge: Cambridge University Press, 1982.

Fernandez-Armesto, Felipe. *Columbus.* Oxford: Oxford University Press, 1991.

Fingerhut, L.A., D. Ingram, and J. Feldman. "Firearm and Nonfirearm Homicide Among Persons 15 Through 19 Years of Age." *Journal of the American Medical Association* 267 (June 10, 1992): 3048–53.

Fortune magazine, editors of. *The Exploding Metropolis.* Garden City, NY: Doubleday, 1958.

Foster, Abram J. *The Coming of the Electrical Age to the United States.* New York: Arno Press. 1979.

Frieden, Bernard J. "Housing Allowances: An Experiment that Worked." *The Public Interest* no. 59 (Spring 1980): 15–35.

———. "The Exclusionary Effect of Growth Controls." *The Annals of the American Academy of Political and Social Science* 465 (January 1983): 123–35.

Garreau, Joel. *Edge City: Life on the New Frontier.* New York: Doubleday, 1991.

Gilfillan, S.C. *The Sociology of Invention.* Chicago: Follet, 1935.

Glaab, Charles, and A. Theodore Brown. *A History of Urban America.* New York: Macmillan, 1967.

Green, Constance M. *Eli Whitney and the Birth of American Technology.* Boston: Little, Brown, 1956.

Hall, Frederick W. "A Review of the Mount Laurel Decision." In *After Mount Laurel: The New Suburban Zoning,* J. Rose and R. Rothman, eds. New Brunswick, NJ: Center for Urban Policy Research, 1977: pp. 39–45.

Hall, Phil. "Catholic Plan Can't Help Schools Facing Chaos." *Wall Street Journal,* October 1, 1996, A23.

Hall, Robert, and Alvin Rabushka. *Low Tax, Simple Tax, Flat Tax.* New York: McGraw-Hill, 1983.

Hanushek, Eric A. "The Economics of Schooling." *The Journal of Economic Literature* 24 (September 1986): 1141–77.

Hassig, Ross. *Trade, Tribute, and Transportation: The Sixteenth-Century Political Economy of the Valley of Mexico.* Norman: University of Oklahoma Press, 1985.

Heilbrun, James, and Patrick McGuire. *Urban Economics and Public Policy,* 3d ed. New York: St. Martin's Press, 1987.

Hogan, William T. *Economic History of the Iron and Steel Industry in the United States, Volume 1.* Lexington, MA: D.C. Heath, 1971.

Hunt, Albert R. "The General and the Teacher Trying to Save D.C. School Kids." *Wall Street Journal,* June 5, 1997, A23.

Jackson, Donald D. "Elevating Thoughts from Elisha Otis and Fellow Uplifters." *Smithsonian* 20 (November 1989): 210–12.

Jackson, Kenneth T. *Crabgrass Frontier, The Suburbanization of the United States.* New York: Oxford University Press, 1985.

Jennings, Marianne M. "My Neighborhood Ruined, Thanks to HUD." *Wall Street Journal,* June 19, 1997, A20.

Johnson, Paul E. *A Shopkeeper's Millenium: Society and Revivals in Rochester, New York, 1815–1837.* New York: Hill and Wang, 1978.

Kariat, A., S. Lichtenstein, and B. Fischhoff. "Reasons for Confidence." *Journal of Experimental Social Psychology: Human Learning and Memory* 6 (1980): 107–18.

Kidder, Tracy. *House.* Boston: Houghton, Mifflin, 1985.

Koehler, D.J. "Explanation, Imagination, and Confidence in Judgment." *Psychological Bulletin* 110 (1991): 499–519.

Kotlowitz, Alex. *There are No Children Here:The Story of Two Boys Growing up in the Other America.* New York: Doubleday, 1991.

Kozol, Jonathan. *Savage Inequalities, Children in America's Schools.* New York: Crown, 1991.

Kramer, Mark. *Three Farms, Making Milk, Meat and Money from the American Soil.* Cambridge: Harvard University Press, 1987.

Lacey, Robert. *Ford: The Men and the Machine.* Boston: Little, Brown, 1986.

Laffer, Arthur B., and Jan P. Seymour. *The Economics of the Tax Revolt.* New York: Harcourt Brace Jovanovich, 1979.

Lemann, Nicholas. *The Promised Land, The Great Black Migration and How It Changed America.* New York: Alfred Knopf, 1991.

Lo, Clarence Y.H. *Small Property versus Big Government: Social Origins of the Property Tax Revolt.* Berkeley: University of California Press, 1990.

Lord, C.G., L. Ross, and M. Lepper. "Biased Assimilation and Attitude Polarization: The Effects of Prior Theories on Subsequently Considered Evidenced." *Journal of Personality and Social Psychology* 37 (1979): 2098–109.

Lukas, J. Anthony. *Common Ground, A Turbulent Decade in the Lives of Three American Families.* New York: Alfred Knopf, 1985.

Martin, Albro. *Railroads Triumphant.* New York: Oxford University Press, 1992.

Massey, Douglas, and Nancy Denton. "Suburbanization and Segregation in U.S. Metropolitan Areas." *American Journal of Sociology* 94 (November 1988): 592–626.

May, George S. *A Most Unique Machine: The Michigan Origins of the American Automobile Industry.* Grand Rapids, MI: William Erdmans, 1975.

McHugh, Jeanne. *Alexander Holley and the Makers of Steel.* Baltimore: Johns Hopkins University Press, 1980.

Miller, Gary J. *Managerial Dilemmas, The Political Economy of Hierarchy.* Cambridge: Cambridge University Press, 1992.

Mills, Edwin, and Bruce Hamilton. *Urban Economics,* 5th ed. New York: HarperCollins, 1994.

Mirsky, J., and A. Nevins. *The World of Eli Whitney.* New York: Macmillan, 1952.

Mokyr, Joel. *The Lever of Riches: Technological Creativity and Economic Progress.* Oxford: Oxford University Press, 1990.

Morris, A.E.J. *History of the Urban Form.* London: George Godwin, 1979.

Mumford, Lewis. *The City in History.* New York: Harcourt, Brace and World, 1961.

Nettles, Curtis. *The Emergence of a National Economy, 1775–1815, Vol II, The Economic History of the United States.* White Plains, NY: M.E. Sharpe, 1962.

Oster, George, and Edward O. Wilson. *Social Insects.* Princeton, NJ: Princeton University Press, 1978.

———. *Caste and Ecology in the Social Insects.* Princeton, NJ: Princeton University Press, 1978.

Owen, Wilfred. *The Accessible City.* Washington, DC: Brookings Institution, 1972.

Philip, Cynthia Owen. *Robert Fulton: A Biography.* New York: Franklin Watts, 1985.

Pinkham, Harold A., Jr. "Plantation to City Charter: The Rise of Urban New England, 1630–1873." In *American Cities and Towns: Historical Perspectives,* J.F. Rishel, ed. Pittburgh, PA: Duquesne University Press, 1992.

Popkin, Susan, James Rosenbaum, and Patricia Meaden. "Labor Market Experiences of Low-Income Black Women in Middle-Class Suburbs: Evidence from a Survey of Gautreaux Program Participants." *Journal of Policy Analysis and Management* 12 (1993): 556–73.

Poulson, Barry. *Economic History of the United States.* New York: Macmillan, 1981.

Ricklefs, Robert. *Ecology,* 3d ed. New York: W.H. Freeman, 1990.

Rishel, Joseph F., ed. *American Cities and Towns: Historical Perspectives.* Pittsburgh: Duquesne University Press, 1992.

Rose, Jerome and Robert Rothman, eds. *After Mount Laurel: The New Suburban Zoning.* New Brunswick, NJ: Center for Urban Policy Research, 1977.

Rountree, Helen. *The Powhatan Indians of Virginia: Their Traditional Culture.* Norman: University of Oklahoma Press, 1989.

———. *Pocahontas's People: Indians of Virginia Through Four Centuries.* Norman: University of Oklahoma Press, 1990.

Sabbagh, Karl. *Twenty-First Century Jet, The Making and Marketing of the Boeing 777.* New York: Scribner, 1996.

Schneider, William. "Punching Through the Jarvis Myth." In *The Economics of the Tax Revolt,* A.B. Laffer and J.P. Seymour, eds. New York: Harcourt Brace Jovanovich, 1979.

Schwartz, Barry, ed. *The Changing Face of the Suburbs.* Chicago: University of Chicago Press, 1976.

Sears, Stephen W. *George B. McClellan: The Young Napoleon.* New York: Ticknor and Fields, 1988.

Shannon, Fred. *The Farmer's Last Frontier, Agriculture 1860–1897.* White Plains, NY: M.E. Sharpe, 1945.

Shaw, Ronald E. *Erie Water West: A History of the Erie Canal 1792–1854.* Lexington: University of Kentucky Press, 1966.

Soule, George. *Prosperity Decade, From War to Depression 1917–1929.* White Plains, NY: M.E. Sharpe, 1947.

Stahura, John. "Rapid Black Suburbanization of the 1970s." *Policy Studies Journal* 18 (Winter 1989–90): 279–91.

Steinberg, Laurence. *Beyond the Classroom, Why School Reform has Failed and What Parents Need to Do.* New York: Simon and Shuster, 1996.

Sternlieb, George. "*Mount Laurel,* Economics, Morality and the Law." In *After Mount Laurel: The New Suburban Zoning,* J. Rose and R. Rothman, eds. New Brunswick, NJ: Center for Urban Policy Research, 1977: pp. 291–98.

———. *Patterns of Development.* New Brunswick, NJ: Center for Urban Policy Research, 1986.

Suits, Daniel B. "Agriculture." In *The Structure of American Industry,* 6th Ed. W. Adams, ed. New York: Macmillan, 1982: pp. 1–35.

Taylor, Frederick Winslow. *The Principles of Scientific Management.* New York: W.W. Norton, 1911, 1967.

Taylor, George R. *The Transportation Revolution: 1815–1860. Vol. IV, The Economic History of the United States.* White Plains, NY: M.E. Sharpe, 1951.

Tobin, Gary. "Suburbanization and the Development of Motor Transportation." In *The Changing Face of the Suburbs,* B. Schwartz, ed. Chicago: University of Chicago Press, 1976: pp. 95–112.

Turak, Theodore. *William Le Baron Jenny: A Pioneer of Modern Architecture.* Ann Arbor: University of Michigan Research Press, 1986.

Utley, Robert. *The Lance and the Shield: The Life and Times of Sitting Bull.* New York: Henry Holt, 1993.

Wade, Richard C. "Urban Life in Western America, 1790–1830." In *American Urban History,* A.B. Callow, ed. Oxford: Oxford University Press, 1969.

Walter, Dave, ed. *Today Then: America's Best Minds Look 100 Years into the Future on the Occasion of the 1893 World's Columbian Exposition.* Helena, MT: American and World Geographic, 1992.

Ward, David. *Poverty, Ethnicity, and the American City, 1840–1925.* Cambridge: Cambridge University Press, 1989.

Weber, Melvin. "The BART Experience: What Have We Learned?" *The Public Interest* (Fall 1976): 79–108.

Weinberg, Daniel H. "A Brief Look at Postwar U.S. Income Inequality." Report P60–191. Washington, DC: United States Bureau of the Census.

Welfeld, Irving. "Improving Housing Allowances." *The Public Interest* (Winter 1982): 110–18.

———. "Poor Tenants, Poor Landlords, Poor Policy." *The Public Interest* (Summer 1988): 110–20.

———. *Where We Live, A Social History of American Housing.* New York: Simon and Schuster, 1988.

White, Lawrence. "The Automobile Industry." In *The Structure of American Industry,* 6th ed., W. Adams, ed. New York: Macmillan: pp. 136–90.

Wiggenhorn, William. "Motorola U: When Training Becomes an Education." *Harvard Business Review* (July-August 1990): 71–83.

Wilson, Edward O. *The Insect Societies.* Cambridge, MA: Harvard University Press, 1971.

Wilson, William Julius. *The Truly Disadvantaged: The Inner City, The Underclass, and Public Policy.* Chicago: University of Chicago Press, 1987.

———. *When Work Disappears, The World of the New Urban Poor.* New York: Alfred A. Knopf, 1996.

Fiscal, Economic, and Social Crises Confronting American Cities. Hearings before the Committee on Banking, Housing, and Urban Affairs, United States Senate, May 13, 1992.

The State of Urban America. Hearings before the Senate Committee on Banking, Housing and Urban Affairs, April 1993.

Index

About the Author

Randall Bartlett is currently Professor of Economics and the Director of the Urban Studies Program at Smith College. He is the author of *Economic Foundations of Political Power* and *Economics and Power: An Inquiry into Markets and Human Relations*. He lives in Northampton, Massachusetts, with his wife and three children.